Ethics of Algorithms

Christopher Koska

Ethics of Algorithms

In Search of Numbers and Values

Springer

Christopher Koska
München, Germany

ISBN 978-3-662-71517-8 ISBN 978-3-662-71518-5 (eBook)
https://doi.org/10.1007/978-3-662-71518-5

This book is a translation of the original German edition "Ethik der Algorithmen" by Christopher Koska, published by Springer-Verlag GmbH, DE in 2023. The translation was done with the help of an artificial intelligence machine translation tool. A subsequent human revision was done primarily in terms of content, so that the book will read stylistically differently from a conventional translation. Springer Nature works continuously to further the development of tools for the production of books and on the related technologies to support the authors.

This Springer imprint is published by the registered company Springer-Verlag GmbH, DE, part of Springer Nature.
The registered company address is: Heidelberger Platz 3, 14197 Berlin, Germany

Preface

This English edition of my dissertation closely follows the original version, which was submitted in 2021 to the Munich School of Philosophy in fulfilment of the requirements for the doctoral degree, and subsequently published in 2023 by J.B. Metzler as Volume 6 of the book series *Techno:Phil – Current Challenges for the Philosophy of Technology*. While the overall structure and core arguments remain unchanged, a number of sections—particularly those touching on recent developments in artificial intelligence—have been selectively updated or expanded.

The focus of the book, however, is not on the technical details of recent innovations, but rather on identifying broader societal trends and ethical challenges that arise in the evolving relationship between humans and technology. The recent success of Large Language Models (LLMs) for example may accelerate or sharpen some of the developments described, but it does not fundamentally alter the underlying arguments. Rather, it can be seen as a powerful confirmation of a much older dynamic: the externalisation of algorithmic reasoning and action into artificial artefacts—a process that this work traces through philosophical, cultural, and historical lenses.

The first part of the book, which explores the intellectual and historical roots of algorithmic thinking, is largely independent of short-term technological trends. By contrast, the middle section, which discusses practical applications, can only be understood in light of its temporal and cultural horizon. These analyses are shaped by a European perspective, especially in light of public debates and regulatory discourses in Germany. While this perspective is culturally and regionally situated, it may also offer impulses for a broader international dialogue on digital ethics. The final chapter outlines normative and practical approaches to the design of algorithmic systems, again rooted in a European ethical framework.

I am deeply grateful to Prof. Dr. Alexander Filipović for his generous academic supervision and for encouraging me early on to take part in public discourse—through lectures, publications, and collaborative research. I would also like to thank the members of the doctoral colloquium at the Munich School of Philosophy for their thoughtful critiques and lively discussions, especially during our seminar weekends at the Franciscan convent in Armstorf (Bavaria).

I would like to thank Alexander von Stülpnagel for his long-standing support, critical feedback, and continued encouragement. His early commitment to the field of data ethics and digital responsibility has had a lasting influence on my work.

My heartfelt thanks also go to Daniela Koska, who took the time and care to review the English translation and refine the language throughout the entire manuscript. The publishing house had already run the original text through a machine translation engine a couple of months ago, and we could have technically released this edition much earlier. However, we decided to delay publication more then once to ensure that a native speaker would go through the text in detail. Even though today's translation tools are remarkably advanced, Daniela's careful attention to tone, nuance, and clarity proved to be invaluable.

While not trained in philosophy, she brought a fresh and attentive perspective to the text—helping to make certain passages significantly more accessible, especially for non-academic readers, than in the original German version. Her work not only helped improve this edition, but may also contribute, in a small way, to the further development of automated translation tools. This experience, too, echoes a central idea of the book: that meaningful human-technology interaction continues to depend on time, care, and collaboration.

My sincere appreciation goes to Franziska Remeika and the entire team at the publishing house for their patience, commitment, and openness in making this English edition possible. It is a privilege to see this work reach beyond its original audience, opening a small window of opportunity to contribute to the ongoing global discourse on ethics and technology.

Finally, I dedicate this book to the memory of my beloved mother, Maria Koska (née Obermeyer), whose deep sense of social responsibility and quiet intellectual openness continue to inspire my thinking.

Munich
30.03.2025

Christopher Koska

Introduction

Algorithm ethics is an attempt to specify moral philosophical questions that arise from the change and transformation processes of digitalisation. Unlike political ethics, legal, medical, technical, economic, natural and environmental ethics, information and media ethics etc., it is not an established area of ethics. The discourse about the necessity of an independent algorithm ethics is still in its early stages. As a scientific endeavour, algorithm ethics primarily aims to identify and establish ethical criteria and principles for sustainable value creation through responsible and trustworthy data usage. The transitions to the already established area ethics are often fluid. Central aspects for an ethics of algorithms are also discussed under the terms *data ethics, machine, or robot ethics*. The latter pose above all the question of whether and to what extent the methods and tools of ethics itself must change. Because against the background of real-time data analysis and advances in machine learning, which make up a successful part of current artificial intelligence (AI), ethical principles such as transparency, discursivity and reflexivity, can no longer be implemented by human actors in many application areas (cf. Ananny and Crawford 2016; Altmeppen et al. 2015). This book aims to contribute to the location and design perspectives of an algorithm ethics by first trying to grasp the subject area and the dimensions of such an area ethic.

The moral philosophical problem that arises from the opacity, the complexity and the acceleration of technical progress and poses great and currently insurmountable obstacles to responsible, ethics-oriented action (ibid.), offers a new perspective on the Kantian basic question of ethics "What should I do"? Algorithms change what we (should) do. Quietly and unnoticed by many, they penetrate all areas of society (cf. Bunz 2012), they structure our possibilities, define which information is analysed, visualise the options for action, function as filter and mirror and at the same time suggest mathematical objectivity and scientific certainty. The process of replacing formerly human activities and decisions with technical innovations is not new (cf. Filipović et al. 2018, pp. 33–37). Are we now on the path of another disruption process, which refers to the transfer and relocation of ethical values from the human consciousness into the machine? This question leads us (further in the sense of Kant) to fundamental, existential questions of humanity: What is the human being? And why should we want to ensure that the interests and needs of humans are at the centre of digitalisation?

Promoting an ethics for algorithms is carried by the assumption that this ethics might have to be as complex as the digital world itself and machines could be much fairer than humans in terms of fairness and the objectivity of a decision (cf. Kucklick 2016). The approach of making moral values machine-operable, however, should not obscure the fact that machines (algorithms) are not moral actors. Machines cannot put themselves in a normative-desiring relationship to certain values; algorithms are developed by humans. Similarly, an ethics of algorithms does not arise in an unbiased (empty) machine room.

In its descriptive form, an algorithm ethics therefore describes both the conscious or unconscious value inscriptions of the algorithm designers as well as the behaviour of humans under the conditions of algorithmic outsourcing, automation and decision-making processes. This perspective is therefore of particular importance because the human-machine interaction, especially with self-learning systems, also contributes to a change in the functioning of a software, for example by the usage behaviour leading to an (automatic) adjustment of the original selection mechanisms of a personalised recommendation technology. In this context an algorithm ethics is less norm-establishing than rather to raise awareness of responsibility. The ethical discourse must therefore deal with both the user perspective, the so-called 'front-end' as well as the so-called 'back-end', i.e. the non-publicly accessible part of the technical infrastructure, which is located under the bonnet of graphical user interfaces. Media competence and 'algorithmic literacy' are therefore a basic condition for a good analysis of the situation. However, as it is neither realistic nor desirable that these prerequisites are met by all users in equal measure, the question arises as to who controls the value inscriptions in the so-called back-end or how the front-end of an application can be designed so transparently that the functioning of socially relevant algorithms can be made accessible to a broad public.

The investigation is based on the thesis that the processes of change and transformation, commonly described by the term Digital Revolution, require an algorithm ethics that places a responsible and trustworthy use of data at the centre and observes and analyses the transparency and control problem of algorithmic decisions (ADM: algorithmic decision making) at a normative-principle level. The aim is to show an application-related perspective that is open to the opportunities and possibilities of digitality for realising a "better life" (in the sense of a good and just coexistence) without losing sight of the risks and dangers.

Why are trust and transparency so important for digital transformation processes? Trust usually begins where transparency (control) ends. Those who are trusted bear the responsibility not to abuse this trust. Empirical studies show that Germans' trust in entrepreneurs and managers, banks, insurance companies and advertising agencies is at an all-time low (see Forsa Trust Ranking 2016–2020). Also in AI, citizens (in the USA, Canada, Germany, UK and Australia) so far have little trust - two thirds of the respondents consider the current regulations and laws to be insufficient and the vast majority (81%) expect additional regulations, as an international study by the University in Queensland and the consulting firm KPMG shows (see Gillespie et al. 2021). Recent findings by Scantamburlo et al. (2023)

further reveal a complex relationship, indicating that while a majority of European citizens have positive attitudes towards AI, their self-reported trust and competence in actually dealing with AI technologies remains comparatively low.

The sociologist Georg Simmel emphasised more than a hundred years ago: "The completely knowing person does not need to trust, the completely ignorant person reasonably cannot even trust" (Simmel 1908, p. 263). The motivation for this book stems from the interest in identifying a certain basis of good reasons that could lead to more trust in digital transformation. To conceptually describe the transparency and control problem, which can also be presented as a competence or empowerment problem, and to make it accessible to an ethical approach, in order to then evaluate it and point out design perspectives, is thus the central task of this study.

This brief introduction to the problem will be further elaborated in the first chapter. The second chapter offers an introduction to the subject area of an ethics of algorithms from an intellectual history perspective. Then follows a media-philosophical systematisation and building on this, an introduction to the ethos of algorithmic thinking and action. In the third chapter, the current debate on algorithms is analysed in a problem-oriented manner using the example of five concrete application areas[1] and finally a criteriology for an ethics of algorithms is developed. In the fourth chapter, the normative approach is linked with the problem analysis and political, entrepreneurial and self-responsible design perspectives for a trustworthy data usage practice are shown.

[1](i) Self-driving vehicles, (ii) Knowledge transfer and news search, (iii) E-commerce and online marketing, (iv) Processing of financial, insurance and health data and (v) Education and resource distribution.

Contents

Abbreviations

A-Life	Artificial Life
AP	Associated Press
ADM	Algorithmic Decision Making
BMJV	Federal Ministry of Justice and Consumer Protection
BMWi	Federal Ministry for Economic Affairs and Energy
CDR	Corporate Digital Responsibility
CEO	Chief Executive Officer
CR	Corporate Responsibility
CSR	Corporate Social Responsibility
GDPR	General Data Protection Regulation
ETL	Extract, Transform, Load
ECB	European Central Bank
FBDC	Financial Big Data Cloud
ICILS	International Computer and Information Literacy Study
AI	Artificial Intelligence
AL	Artificial Life
CPI	Continuous Product Improvement Process
LoA	Level of Abstraction
LLM	Large Language Model
SAE	Society of Automotive Engineers
SIM	Subscriber Identity Module
SPOT	Single Point of Truth
WHO	World Health Organization

List of Figures

Chapter 3. In Search of Numbers and Values

Chapter 4. Design Perspectives

Framework of the Study

1

1 Problem Outline

Algorithms process data and information in all areas of life. In science and research, the so-called "algorithmic turn" (Napoli 2014, p. 341), not least due to the availability of extensive data collections, has already led to fundamental methodical changes (see, for example, Anderson 2008, pp. 108–109). The "dynamics, complexity and opacity" (Heise 2016, pp. 204–205), with which algorithms collect and analyse data, raises a series of novel ethical problems that seem unsolvable with the help of traditional ethics. Particularly in the context of self-learning algorithms and complex (multi-layered) applications, a "responsibility gap" (Matthias 2004, pp. 175–183) is emerging, which raises the question of moral objects and subjects to a new level.

Modern information and communication technologies enable us a degree of self-determination and freedom like never before in the history of mankind and are at the same time a danger to human freedom, as there has never been before. Many people, for example, are worried about the future of a digitised working world. But also, the economic policy environment is described as complex, uncertain and unpredictable by those companies that actively drive technological change. Between unbridled belief in progress, legal regulations and data-driven information capitalism, the entrepreneurial problem horizon of the digital world unfurls. The almost ubiquitous demand for a broad societal debate, however, points to the difficulty of mediating between the changing conditions, the increasing technical complexity and the sovereignty of those affected in dealing with digital possibilities and dangers.

On the face of it, the advantages outweigh the disadvantages. Even without denying the risks of private data disclosure, several million people worldwide enjoy their smart helpers and the numerous assistance systems. Most people today do not want to do without the relatively uncomplicated exchange of opinions

C. Koska, *Ethics of Algorithms*,
https://doi.org/10.1007/978-3-662-71518-5_1

and information, free access to knowledge and much more. All in all, the socio-technical progress can therefore apparently not be rated high enough. After all, education, knowledge and information were freely accessible only to a few chosen ones for the longest time in human history. Just one generation back, the acquisition of knowledge was much more laborious for the intellectual elite and the data stock, as well as the number of conversation partners, was significantly limited. The price we pay for the participation in the seemingly limitless realm of digital possibilities through the release or disclosure of personal data, we therefore usually accept.

With the European General Data Protection Regulation (GDPR) in force since May 2018, a legal framework has been established that should guarantee European citizens uniform security and protection standards for personal data. From the consumer's point of view, the establishment of these legal regulations, especially due to the sanction possibilities, can already be considered a great progress and added value, although the application of the regulation in practice still has to be shown. The "correct" handling of personal data is now legally prescribed, but still offers a large margin of discretion, consideration and interpretation at the grey zones of the legal framework. This is particularly evident in the demand for transparency and control.

The concept of transparency is reduced to a minimum by most companies when implementing the GDPR, which is necessary to establish informational transparency towards the customers. The control option of the potential target group consists exclusively in agreeing to or objecting to the processing of their own data. Companies are obliged to inform their customers about the purpose of data processing in a clear and generally understandable language. However, due to conflicting objectives, this requirement is rarely correctly implemented in practice (see, for example, the lawsuit of the Belgian data protection authority against the "Transparency and Consent Framework – TCF 2.0", Dachwitz 2022). Informational self-determination is reduced to a minimal concept of autonomy, insofar as the declaration of consent required for the data processing is usually only an informed consent for a blanket use of data, which many companies already consider fulfilled when they refer generally to the improvement of their products and services. The question remains problematic of how much choice or freedom of action for the users exists within the technical system or what conditions in the interaction with complex algorithmic systems would need to be met, to speak of personal autonomy.

In times when intelligent technologies are increasingly penetrating our lives to offer personalised information context-sensitively and take a multitude of decisions off our hands, this problem presents itself in a specific way. The central demand for *more transparency*, which already entered public consciousness in the summer of 2013 with the revelation of the surveillance and espionage scandal by Edward Snowden and became a broad social concern, still causes great difficulties for those responsible in practice. Especially in the context of self-learning algorithms, some scientists reject the ideal of transparency in ethics as inadequate for an algorithm ethics (cf. Ananny and Crawford 2016), while others are intensively concerned with how transparency—possibly at a different level of abstraction—can also be established in such systems that remain opaque to us (cf. Filipović et al. 2018, p. 50).

The present study is interested in the levels at which transparency in dealing with algorithmic systems for the affected can be established. This identifies a central area that is generally described by the term "media competence" or "digital education" and can be determined as an elementary condition for competent participation in the opportunities and challenges of digitalisation. However, it is not just about providing the users with functional background knowledge. To shift responsibility in this way unilaterally to the customers, would prove to be a pointless enterprise, as the added value of algorithmic systems would be absurd if the consumers had to understand every technical process in detail themselves. Rather, it is about both the practitioners (executives, developers etc.) and their clients (individuals, in the broadest sense society) gaining a common understanding of which software applications they could reasonably want.

Of particular interest in this context is the use of self-learning control software for the analysis and evaluation of selection criteria. Deep neural networks (Deep Learning) make it possible, for example, to dynamically generate the values and selection mechanisms of a criteria catalogue and continuously adapt them to different environmental factors. One advantage of this procedure is that moral dilemma situations, such as those discussed in the context of self-driving vehicles (trolley example), can be resolved according to the standard of efficiency. By filtering out the most successful behaviours from human drivers in comparable danger and accident situations, machines can be trained to make a 'right' decision much faster than humans (cf. Koska 2018). The realisation that such a decision is not a normative-intentional decision of the machine, but the interaction of a highly complex socio-technical system, in which individual responsibility relations can hardly be determined and which has a high susceptibility to naturalistic (is-ought) fallacies, should become as clear as the potential added value of a machine-supported ethics.

With this introductory problem sketch, the essential aspects of the study are named. Digitalisation is to be analysed and normatively reflected from the perspective of an algorithm ethics. After the clarification of the conceptual foundation in the history of ideas and intellectual history, a brief media-philosophical positioning as well as a description of selected areas of application will be given, for which a set of criteria is brought into play, aiming to show concrete design perspectives for various actors. The question of the control and regulation unit of algorithmic processes is at the centre of consideration. What needs to be critically questioned are, on the one hand, the control and regulation possibilities of moral subjects in the definition, design, application and use of algorithmic systems. On the other hand, building on this the question occurs of whether or to what extent algorithms themselves can act as moral actors.

Before the problem outline can be used to formulate the research question, the thesis, the goal, and the line of thought of the investigation, it is first necessary to briefly describe why in the context of algorithmic systems a conceptual rethinking is being discussed in the attribution of moral responsibility.

2 The Interest in Knowledge of an Algorithm Ethics

Moral responsibility, according to traditional ethical understanding, can only be attributed to human actions or their intentions and consequences. Generally, a person or a group of people are morally responsible for their action if their intention or the result of their action can be evaluated as good or bad respectively good or evil. Technological progress complicates the traditional attribution of moral responsibility: "The higher the degree of technisation, the more the connection between action and responsibility is dissociated." (Krämer 1992, p. 335)

To determine the location and horizon of this analysis, the following three minimal conditions for the attribution of moral responsibility can be formulated, following Hans Jonas (1984):

1. Control: A person or a group of people are usually only considered morally responsible if they have a certain degree of control over the result of the action.
2. Transparency: The possible risks and consequences of an action should in principle be visible and to a certain extent comprehensible to the person or group of people.
3. Freedom of action: The person or group of people should have various options for action and be able to freely decide on a specific action.

Algorithms, on the one hand, extend the radius of action of human activities by creating a temporal and spatial distance between the action and the actors—they also relieve people at very different levels. Previously industrialisation led to a relief of human beings through the mechanisation of physical labour. The advancing algorithmisation of human activities now leads to the fact that in the context of digital transformation processes, increasingly intellectual activities are being carried out by machines.

What was already true for industrialisation applies especially to digitalisation: "The subject of an activity and the subject of responsibility for the results of this activity need no longer be one and the same person" (Krämer 1992, p. 335). Therefore, algorithms can extremely limit the options for action of humans in that the users more than before, and hardly noticeably, are being externally (paternalistically) controlled. This danger is amplified by the opacity in the functioning, as the selection mechanisms and selection criteria of automatic filters for most people are usually not visible or even if visible, then not comprehensible (i.e. opaque). While automation can help to centralise the control of various processes and improve the control of those who have access to it, it limits the control possibilities of those who are at the lower end of the decision chain.

In principle, an algorithm ethics is about determining whether or to what extent and when certain forms of relief through algorithmic processes are good or bad. For this purpose, criteria for a normative assessment must be developed using philosophical means. Depending on the ethical theory represented in detail, the validity of a value defined as good can be disputed. For example, the founder and CEO of the car manufacturer Tesla argues that it would be morally reprehensible to further delay the introduction of self-driving vehicles (Musk 2016), as over 90% of all fatal accidents are attributable to misconduct by human drivers. Assuming that the number of fatal traffic accidents could indeed be significantly reduced by self-driving vehicles, a believed by Elon Musk, the freedom of many people to “drive a car themselves” steps behind the value of “preserving as many lives as possible”. The individual ethical ideal of autonomy then comes into conflict with socio-ethical considerations—in this case with a utilitarian argument to maximise the sum of the well-being of all those affected.

With the help of digital technologies, however, cost-benefit maximisation can be further differentiated. The mass collection and processing of data could train a self-learning utilitarian control of vehicles in a very specific way of minimising damage, so that, for example, in an unavoidable accident situation, the life of a certain person or group of people would be more worth protecting than that of another. Value balancing questions for so-called moral dilemma situations, like the trolley example (more on this in Chap. 3, Sect. 1.1), are nothing new for philosophy. What is new, however, is that we could potentially delegate the optimisation of selection mechanisms to self-learning systems—to a certain extent. This form of relief, which Sybille Krämer (1992, p. 335) describes as a relief of the “third kind” or as “relief from responsibility”, describes a new dimension of ethics, insofar as this step seems to imply an *outsourcing of morality* from humans to machines.

However, morality is not about factual things, i.e. a machine that *in search of numbers and values* mechanically optimises processes, but about human basic attitudes and stances—regarding personal life conduct, the self-interests of the respective actor as well as the needs and interests of other people. Especially when it comes to the recognition of moral values, the existence of a moral machine therefore seems highly questionable: “There is no ‘I’ in ‘Robot’” (cf. Grau 2006), which has the ability of personal self-determination and could approach the basic questions of ethics: “What should we do?”, “How should we act?” from this reflective standpoint. Even if machines, due to improved sensor technology and a more extensive data volume, may seem to *grasp* the ideal value of an entity faster and can handle complex danger or accident situations (to stay with the introductory example) much better in real time than humans, the question of moral responsibility in the event of damage, according to our prevailing moral conception, remains primarily tied to individual persons or institutions. However, the person or group of people (executives, designers, developers, controllers, etc.) who are held accountable in such a case must be able to fulfil the above-mentioned minimum conditions for the attribution of moral responsibility (also against the background of complex network information algorithms).

Against this background, the question arises as to whether this can be ensured in the long term with regard to technical progress: Do we already have the appropriate methodological tools to resolve complex situations of shared responsibility. Or do we need new approaches, as the attribution of responsibility increasingly eludes us.

3 Approach: Goal, Working Hypothesis and Line of Thought

After the human being has been established as the central moral authority in the context of an ethics of algorithms, the aim, thesis, and line of argument of this investigation can be further elaborated. To begin with, it is worth reflecting on the conceptual structure of the term itself. While the English expression ethics of algorithms does not form a compound word in the same way as the German Algorithmenethik, it nonetheless reveals a significant semantic tension.

In German, this tension is grammatically encoded in the genitive construction and can be described—using classical grammatical terminology—as the difference between a *genitivus objectivus* and a *genitivus subjectivus*: is this an ethics about algorithms, or an ethics by algorithms? This distinction appears not only in academical discussions, but also in everyday language and media discourse—for example, when news reports speak of "the power of algorithms," or when the sociologist Armin Nassehi (2019) refers to the "self-will of the digital" (German *Eigensinn des Digitalen*) and to "experiencing" (German *erlebenden*) or "acting algorithms" (German *handelnden Algorithmen*) (ibid. p. 255).

What exactly do such expressions mean? Is the term algorithm ethics to be understood as a subfield of digital ethics, or as a form of digitised ethics that, in the future, might be autonomously executed by self-learning systems? In this context, the original grammatical distinction becomes a philosophical one: is moral decision-making still a human prerogative—or could machines, at some point, claim this "power" for themselves?

The *first partial goal* of this study is to enable a differentiated view of this tension to further delimit the subject area of an ethics of algorithms *(interim conclusion)* and to determine the implicit direction of algorithmics *(interim result)*. For this purpose, the philosophical conceptual framework will be analysed in more detail by examining the intellectual and historical roots of the determinative compound "algorithm ethics" and revealing the ethos of algorithmic thinking and action. Based on the media-philosophical systematisation of the subject area, a problem-oriented description of the current debate can be developed, leading to a criteriology for an ethics of algorithms *(second partial goal)*. The criteriology is thus to be created in such a way that it is compatible with the current problem, but also allows for general statements about the normative dimensions of algorithm ethics *(second interim result)*. Finally, the results of both approaches can be brought together under the sign of taking up the normative dimensions regarding the problem to show practical design perspectives based on this *(third partial goal)*.

In orientation to these three goals of the study, the working hypotheses are to be developed. The first goal is based on the thesis that the subject area of algorithm ethics can be captured by a media-philosophical systematisation and that the ethos of algorithmic thinking and action can be derived from the historical. The second goal is pursued on the basis of the thesis that the criteria for an ethical evaluation of algorithmisation become visible through a problem-oriented description of current practice and that the normative dimensions for an intercultural reference framework can be determined on this basis. Assuming that both the first and the second thesis are plausible, the third goal is to develop design perspectives for an ethics of algorithms.

The central working hypothesis can be formulated as follows:

The task of algorithm ethics essentially consists of understanding the morality performed by algorithms and to make it accessible to those affected.

Therefore, this book not only aims at examining the ethical ideal of transparency in the context of increasing algorithmisation. It also addresses the media-philosophical question of how far algorithms—in search of numbers and values—already exercise their own form of normativity, which is increasingly eluding our grasp. For it is only against the background of this question that the subject area of algorithm ethics can be meaningfully delimited and used as the foundation of an independent area ethics.

The mere public demand for algorithm ethics (see, for example, Noller 2012) is not yet a legitimation for the introduction of a new area ethics. Changes in society, triggered by technical and social innovations, do indeed increase the pressure for a scientific examination of an ethics of algorithms—however, inclusion in the canon of applied ethics requires successful scientific contextualisation, based on conceptual efforts. It needs to be clarified in this context, for example, whether algorithm ethics is a subfield of information and media ethics, how it differs from data, robot or machine ethics, etc. The approach developed in this treatise aims to contribute to this debate.

The normative reflection of algorithmic processes is an interdisciplinary task. As will be shown, however, the access of ethical analyses currently primarily takes place via the technological level and refers to individual legal aspects such as the protection and security of personal data. The technology-based approach in its individual legal orientation, however, has clear weaknesses—especially with regard to socio-ethical aspects (such as participation, equality and common good); it also implies presuppositional assumptions, as Jaume-Palasí and Spielkamp (2017) have shown. Therefore, the focus of interest is also the attempt to critically question established and often prevailing moral concepts in the context of digitalisation. For the challenge currently lies primarily in establishing a viable bridge between theory and practice with regard to the dominant values, norms and principles. Due to the high speed of technical innovations, there is also the risk that technical development will repeatedly outpace traditional ethics. Constant review and updating, especially at the level of terminology, is therefore indispensable. This means that the concepts behind the respective technical vocabulary must be constantly redefined at a common level of reflection. Especially when attributing moral action, economic, technical, legal and philosophical uses must therefore be brought together in such a way that no responsibility gaps arise.

This outlines the central points of the thought process.

The book is divided into four larger sections: In this first chapter, the human being was determined as the decisive moral authority for an algorithm ethics—as well as the goal, the thesis, and the line of thought of the study. The second chapter outlines the subject area for an ethics of algorithms and reveals the ethos of algorithmic thinking and action as well as the implicit direction of algorithmics. The third chapter attempts to normatively systematise the subject area by providing a problem-oriented description of current fields of action based on the previous considerations, leading to a criteriology for an ethics of algorithms. Building on the normative dimensions, the fourth chapter presents individual, societal, political and entrepreneurial design perspectives based on a value-oriented and responsible data usage practice.

On the individual steps of thought: The second chapter outlines the intellectual and historical foundations of the subject area with regard to the concept triad "algorithm, algorithmisation, algorithmics". The starting point is the arithmetic procedure of al-Ḫwārizmī (from which the term algorithm derives). Subsequently, it is necessary to locate the historical roots of algorithmic thinking and action, to next trace the process of outsourcing algorithms to artificial artefacts. The aim is to prepare the conceptual coordinate system for an ethics of algorithms (ontological, epistemic, and ethical dimension) and to systematise the subject area from a media philosophical perspective (*interim conclusion*). The result is a sharpened concept of algorithms that provides access to the ethos of algorithmic thinking and action by making normative traditions visible and fruitful for later discourse. Based on this, the tentative alignment of algorithmics is summarised in a first *interim result.*

The third chapter attempts to determine the normative dimensions of an ethics of algorithms. In the first step, the current debate on algorithms is summarised using five exemplary fields of action (self-driving vehicles, knowledge transfer and news search, e-commerce and online marketing, processing of financial, insurance and health data, digital education and media competence). Based on these fields of action, the process of conscious and unconscious value inscription is examined (second step) and, building on this, the dangers and problems associated with advancing algorithmisation are analysed (third step). In the fourth step, based on this analysis, a criteriology for an ethics of algorithms is proposed. Finally, in a fifth step, the normative dimensions of the ethics of algorithms are compiled (*second interim result*).

The fourth chapter is about building bridges between theory and practice, between abstract values, norms and principles and the technical, organisational and economic policy implementation. Step by step, a business, political and societal design perspective is contrasted with the results of the problem analysis to normatively address the current problem situation based on the proposed criteriology. The first step is about the conception of corporate responsibility in digital times, which has been discussed for some time under the term Corporate Digital Responsibility (CDR). The second step is about legal regulations and independent control bodies, and the third step is about the conception of a digital educational identity. All three sections are structured identically—firstly, there is i) a brief inventory, then ii) a recapitulation of the challenges and finally iii) the respective design perspective is concretised.

In the end, the yield of this investigation (with regard to the problem situation, the goal, the working hypothesis and the interest in knowledge) is summarised and an outlook on the resulting steps is ventured.

2 Algorithm, Algorithmisation, Algorithmics

The aim of this chapter is to prepare a problem-oriented description of algorithmics. For this purpose, the intellectual and historical roots[1] of algorithmic thinking and action are to be revealed: What does the term algorithm refer to, can general contexts of ideas be reconstructed from the process of increasing algorithmisation, or reasons for action, visions and motives be extracted that give us insight into guiding interests? For this purpose, it is necessary to systematise the concept of algorithms from a media philosophical perspective to determine the subject area of an ethics of algorithms (*interim conclusion*). In a second step, the ethos of algorithmic thinking and action is concretised: Where is the geographical place (gr. *éthos* "the usual place of life") of algorithms? Does the activity of algorithm design follow a certain ideal or only group-specific habits and customs? Can algorithmic thinking and action be limited to humans or can it also be outsourced to machines? Finally, the inclination of algorithmics is determined: This then prepares both the spirit and context as well as the media-theoretical foundation for the elaboration of the dimensions of an algorithm ethics.

1 History of Ideas and Intellectual Roots

Since the late 1990s, there have been increasing signs of a renewal of the traditional history of ideas and thoughts, summarises Goering (2017a, p. 44) in the introductory words of the anthology "Ideengeschichte heute". In this, Goering continues, one key term is found in the writings of the "New History of Ideas": The term

[1]At this point, it must be emphasised that within the framework of this study, only a very rudimentary insight into the historical development of algorithmisation can be given. This is a continuation of the thoughts that I have already outlined in the Bertelsmann study "Ethics for Algorithmists" in collaboration with A. Filipović and C. Paganini (see: Filipović et al. 2018, pp. 35–39).

C. Koska, *Ethics of Algorithms*,
https://doi.org/10.1007/978-3-662-71518-5_2

"order" (ibid. p. 47). This is a hint to the "subject of investigation and the methodological basis at the same time" (ibid. p. 48 f); and finds its expression especially through compounds, like "order patterns", "order drafts" or "order systems". In view of the societal upheavals, change and transformation processes, which we commonly describe as "Digital Revolution", the approach seems all the more promising to address the structural and ordering principles of "digitalisation" itself.

Such a perspective is introduced by Hoeres (2017) in his essay "On the programme of a history of ideas of the digital age." Hoeres differentiates therein between a history of ideas that uses digital tools, and the history of ideas of the digital age itself. Unfortunately, he does not elaborate on the latter. The focus of his contribution is rather on the digital tools, the so-called "Tools of the Digital Humanities" (ibid. p. 216), which he demonstrates using the example of "text mining in large corpora", thus drawing attention to the danger of a "media materialism à la Kittler" (ibid. p. 234).

The perspective developed here on algorithmic thinking and action primarily aims to trace the developmental stages of digitalisation in the history of ideas and intellectual history.[2] The starting point is the observation that the concept of algorithms in public discourse is primarily discussed against the backdrop of the computer age.[3] The modern form of digitalisation, as it confronts us today in the context of comprehensive networking, the debate about AI and Big Data, however, only represents a provisional endpoint of algorithmisation—thus a random reference point: But anyone who is not just looking for an answer to a very specific question and problem that his own time dictates, must go beyond his historical and cultural context (cf. Bordt 1999, p. 9).

A look at the elementary components of the concept of algorithms as well as the basic motives, problems and conditions of algorithmisation should—in the transition to the next chapter—enable a deeper understanding of the current problem situation. It is not claimed to systematically reconstruct the developmental stages of algorithmisation in the history of ideas and intellectual history (e.g. in phases or with turning points), but rather to trace the intellectual foundations in order to determine the ethos and the directional tendency of algorithmisation based on this.[4]

---

[2]The reality-constituting dimension of increasing algorithmisation will be reflected upon more extensively later (see especially the "Media-philosophical Systematisation" in Sect. 1.4).

[3]Such assertions can now be very easily verified using text mining tools, such as the Google Books Ngram Viewer or the digital archive of the Frankfurter Allgemeine Zeitung.

[4]"All historians of ideas assume – at least implicitly – that ideas can influence the actions of historical actors in some way" (Goering 2017b, p. 95). A main concern of Goering is therefore to establish reasons for action as an analytical concept of research into the history of ideas. For "ideas not only have reality-constituting forces, they also have action-guiding forces" (ibid. p. 98). The question of whether non-intentional objects can be active as action-guiding actors is deliberately left open in this chapter.

1.1 The Arithmetic Procedure According to al-Ḫwārizmī

> "Incipit liber algorithmi. omnis sapientia sive scientia a domine Deo; sicut scriptum est: Hoc quod continet omnia scientiam habet, et iterum: Omnia in mensura et pondere et numero constituisti . . . "
>
> "Here begins the book of the algorithm. All wisdom and all knowledge comes from the Lord God; as it is written (according to the Book of Wisdom 1,7): What encompasses the universe is full of wisdom, and further: You have arranged/established everything according to measure, weight and number . . . " (Menninger 1958, pp. 226–227) (Fig. 1).

In the origin and belief of the algorithm (the term here still refers to the proper name of a historical person)[5] the mystical power that algorithms are attributed to our digital age is already apparent. The excerpt quoted above from the Codex of Salem Monastery is dated around the year 1200 and is one of the earliest traces of the term algorithm on German soil. Already in 773 AD, an Indian brought the "Astronomy ('Siddhanta') of his countryman Brahmagupta (born around 600)" (Menninger 1958, p. 225) to the court of the Caliph Al Mansur in Baghdad. The Arabic mathematician and polymath Muḥammad Ibn-Mūsā al-Ḫwārizmī processed this script around the year 820 into his own mathematical treatise, which taught calculation according to the Indian method in Baghdad and of which we still know more today, as his teaching was translated into Latin before the original script was lost (Ḫwārizmī et al. 1997). Through numerous copies, the new calculation method initially spread with the introductory words "Algoritmi de numeris indorum"

Fig. 1 Statue of Muḥammad Ibn-Mūsā al-Ḫwārizmī in his birthplace (Image source: Kkulikov, Shutterstock)

[5]The full name "Muḥammad Ibn-Mūsā al-Ḫwārizmī" (Mohammed Ibn Musa al Khwarizmi; born around 780; died between 835 and 850) suggests that this person originated from ancient Khwarezm (Khwarizm) in western Central Asia and apparently also knew the works of the Alexandrian Greeks (cf. Simonyi 2001, p. 143).

(al-Ḫwārizmī on the Indian numbers) in large parts of Europe. Around 1140, Robert of Chester introduced the treatise of the described calculation methods with the words "dixit algoritmi" ("al-Ḫwārizmī has spoken") (cf. Boncompagni 1857), while in the hexameter of the monk Alexander de Villa Dei, who taught in Paris around 1240, the proper name (Algoritmi) already recedes behind the described mathematical calculation method (Algorismus):

> „hinc incipit algorismus
> haec algorismus ars praesens dictur in qua
> talibus indorum fruimur bis quinque figu
> 0 9 8 7 6 5 4 3 2 1"

"Here begins the Algorismus. This present art is called Algorismus, in which we derive benefit from these twice five digits 0 9 8 7 6 5 4 3 2 1 of the Indians" (Barth 2013, p. 14).[6]

From the term Algorismus, probably through incorrect translations of the term *algo* (among other things with "craft" or "introduction") in various vernaculars and in reference to the Greek term *arithmos* (number), the term Algorithmus (cf. Ambrosetti 2016, p. 82; Harper 2010) finally developed. Already in Reisch (1504) the spelling of Algorithmus with "th" can be found in three headings, as the German mathematician Henrich Lüneburg[7] notes: *"Algorithmus de minutijs vulgaribus, Algorithmus de minutijs physicalibus and Algorithmus cum denarijs piectilibus: seu calcularis*, that is, Algorithmus of the common fractions, Algorithmus of the physical fractions, Algorithmus with counting pennies or stones. Here Algorithmus, it seems to me, means nothing else than calculation; the calculation with common fractions, with physical fractions, with counting pennies" (Lüneburg 2008, p. 334).

In its original meaning, the term thus refers to the adherence to algorithmic rules using Indian numbers or the adherence to an arithmetic procedure that was written down by al-Ḫwārizmī. Mathematicians who used the new calculation method were henceforth referred to as algorithmists, in contrast to the abacists (abacus) (cf. Ziegenbalg et al. 2016, pp. 47–49) (Fig. 2).

The success story, further development and spread of the algorithmic calculation method was significantly contributed to in the 18th century by, among others, Leonhard Euler, as the German mathematician Heinrich Lüneburg (2008) explains. In "Specimen algorithmi singularis" (1764), he developed a recursion method with symbols, "between which he writes numbers from left to right" (Lüneburg 2008, p. 335); he refers to this methodology in solving an equation in "De usu novi algorithmi in problemate Pelliano solvendo" (1767) as a new algorithm (cf. ibid.). Lüneburg points out that there is no clear distinction between old and new algorithms in Euler's work. Euler's innovation may consist precisely in the fact that he

---

[6]See also translation by Halliwell (1839, p. 73).

[7]For a more detailed presentation of medieval usage and spelling (including by Fibonacci and in Simon Jacob's Rechnenbüchlin) see Lüneburg (2008).

Fig. 2 Dispute between abacists (right) and algorithmists (left); depicted in the "Margarita Philosophica" (Image source: Reisch 1503)

peu à peu combined the methodology of letter-based calculation with the concept of the algorithm.[8]

Particularly for mathematics, the concept of the algorithm gained increasing importance up to the beginning of the 20th century, as Lüneburg further elaborates with a quote from the Göttingen mathematician and science organiser Felix Christian Klein from 1908:

> *"For a full understanding of the development of mathematics, we must also remember a third moment C [. . .] This is about the method, which is referred to as an algorithm with a word created by distorting the name of an Arabic mathematician; algorithmic is basically any ordered formal calculation, especially letter calculation. How much the algorithmic procedure as a kind of self-propelling force inherent in the formulas, independent of the intention and insight of the respective mathematicians and often even against them, has contributed to the development of science, we have already repeatedly*

[8]This assumption is not explicitly mentioned by Lüneburg at this point, but is suggested by the subsequent explanations: Lüneburg quotes Dirichlet (1863), who refers to a work by Euler that is a good twenty years older (1740) for the solution of the "Chinese remainder problem" and designates the procedure—just like Gauss (1863) but in contrast to Euler–as algorithm.

emphasised; also in the beginnings of infinitesimal calculus, as we will see, the algorithm often pushed for new concepts and operations before one could account for their admissibility. Even at higher stages of development, these algorithmic moments can be useful and have actually done so, so that they can be described as the basis of mathematical development; it is therefore unhistorical thinking if one, as is sometimes the case today, dismisses these circumstances as merely 'formal' developments" (Klein 1933, pp. 85–86 quoted from Lüneburg 2008, p. 339).

The main point to be taken from this quote is that the algorithmic procedure is already described at the beginning of the 20th century as i) "a kind of self-propelling force inherent in the formulas, independent of the intention and insight of the respective mathematicians and often even against them", that ii) "these algorithmic moments" were further described as "the basis of mathematical development" and iii) "that the algorithm [has] often urged new terms and operations before one could account for their admissibility" (ibid.). Lüneburg (2008) offers numerous further entry points through his extensive study of original writings (from mathematics but also classical literature) to trace the semantic change of the algorithm concept in etymological language use.[9] Against the background of the current interpretation of the algorithm concept as an information technology function instruction, his observation that the term was not anchored in general language use until the 1930s is particularly noteworthy: "Thus A. Turing uses the term 'purely mechanical process' and K. Gödel speaks of 'effective method'" (Lüneburg 2008, p. 340).

1.2 Algorithmic Thinking and Action

Generally, the term algorithm is defined very broadly today—even cooking recipes or assembly instructions for furniture are algorithms in this broad sense.[10] The definition underlying the colloquial understanding considers algorithms as a set of rules, instructions and methods to solve certain tasks or problems. Based on these properties and characteristics, the history of algorithmics can be dated back much further, so that algorithmic thinking can be identified as an essential part of human problem-solving and rational efficiency thinking.

[9]Thus, according to Lüneburg, al-Ḫwārizmī appears on the literary level in the 13th century, among others, in the story of the miller in the "Canterbury Tales" by Chaucer, but also as Master Argos (from the Argonaut saga) in the "Roman de la rose" or in the work "Fiore" by Durante, before the connection between the man's name and his calculation method is lost. Only in 1849, Lüneburg suspects, was this connection re-established by Joseph Reinaud (cf. Lüneburg 2008, p. 340).

[10]In the strict sense of computer science, this comparison limps, as a recipe only guarantees a good dish (correct output) for a very limited selection of ingredients (valid input). The problems that are solved with algorithms in the strict sense of computer science, on the other hand, can be transferred to mathematical problems and a mathematical problem is still the same problem for different inputs.

Human reflective ability, i.e. thinking about how to solve a specific task or a concrete problem, gives us privileged access to the structures of reality. By organising our thoughts and reflecting on those rules, principles of action or methods that imply a probable solution to the task or problem, we are already at the heart of algorithmic thinking. At its core, the concept of the algorithm is therefore "a universal idea of cultural enlightening significance" (Heymann 1996 cited after Blömeke 2008, p. 56) and is therefore not only of central importance for mathematics and computer science, but also for philosophy, whose fundamental task is also to organise our thinking and sort it into terms. The origins of algorithmic thinking "are directly related to human predispositions that have developed over the course of evolution" (Mainzer 2014, p. 275). Generally speaking, algorithms describe regulated processes that can be determined step by step and repeated (cf. ibid.). Ritualised actions to solve a specific task or a particular problem are in this broad sense first precursors of algorithms, which have existed in more or less precise form as long as there have been human languages. The two most important prerequisites for a good algorithmist are thus deeply rooted in our human nature; it is a) the ability to reflect about one's own thinking *(ability to reflect)* and b) the ability to organise or structure this thinking in the clearest possible sign system *(ability to abstract)*. At this overarching level, an algorithm can therefore be qualified as an essential part of our thinking that we have understood so well that we can outsource it in signs or symbols (cf. Stiller 2015, p. 10).

Cave paintings were already used as media tools to externalise ritualised instructions. Even these early depictions require a keen observational skill and a high level of abstraction, the two essential elements of algorithmic thinking. Thus, the pictorial representation of a hunting scene of a buffalo with arrows symbolises an exemplary practice *(effective action instruction)*, which goes beyond the depiction of a single past hunting experience (Fig. 3). Designing the course of a hunting scene in such a way as to minimise risks and optimise the prospects of future hunting ventures is an early expression of (often unconscious) algorithmic thinking and action in everyday human interaction with their environment.

Specifically, with the invention of writing and the depiction and classification of sets *(ordering principle)*, our ancestors were finally able to standardise ritualised action principles in a certain way. The number as an adjective could already be archived (stored) so successfully in early data media, that many procedures from early history have been handed down *(transferred)* to our present day. The execution of an action or a certain behaviour *(operationality)* according to a written procedure *(program)*, in other words, the essentially algorithmic transformation performance *(transformation)*, was initially the sole responsibility of humans at the beginning of media history (Fig. 4).[11]

Property or debt relationships *(positive and negative values)* were transferred in the early history of mankind on tally sticks, counting sticks, counting stones etc.

[11] Algorithms were used by humans, among other things, to write and decipher various numerical scripts (Code) on tally sticks (see Fig. 3), to weave Peruvian knot cords or to form a simple miller's knot to "write" the quantity and type of flour in a tied sack (cf. Menninger 1958, 59ff).

Fig. 3 Cave painting of a hunting scene (Image source: lolloj, Shutterstock)

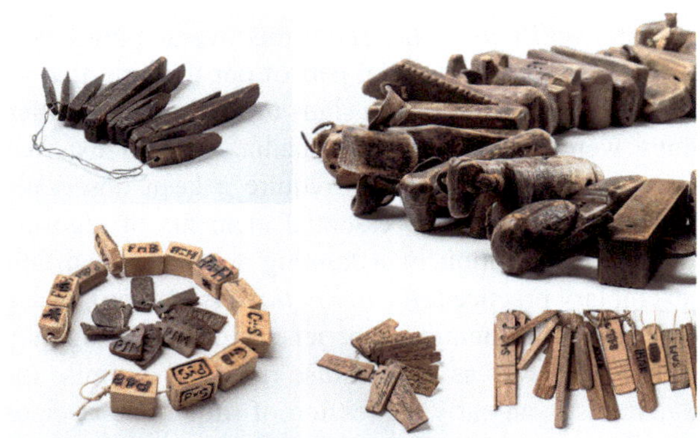

Fig. 4 Tally sticks, which were used from prehistoric times to the Middle Ages as a storage medium to document property and debt relationships (Image source: Simon Kneubühl, Alpine Museum of Switzerland)

(external storage media). These first transformation processes form the foundation for economic calculations, which were operationalised by simple arithmetic operations *(rules)*, to better organise the administration of goods within a community. In addition to the private economic interest in these procedures, which over time led to the profession of merchants, symbolic representations in this context were primarily used to create official records of land and people (cf. Menninger 1958).

Simple arithmetic procedures, which were previously carried out with loose counting stones (calculi), could be operationalised even *more efficiently* with the invention of the abacus (see Fig. 5). Consequently, symbolic aids and mechanical procedures played an increasingly important role in the reliability and functionality

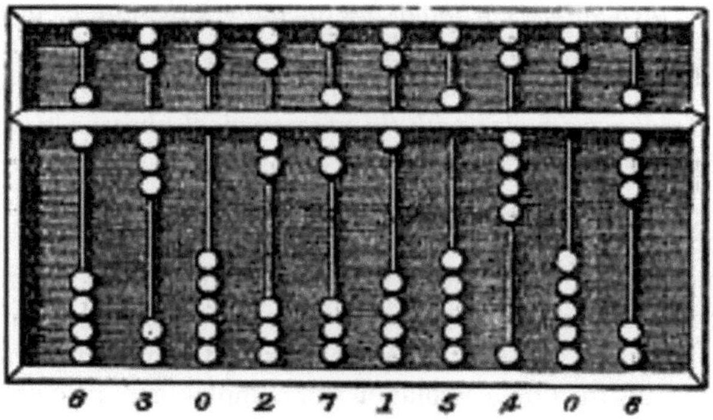

Fig. 5 Calculi on a Chinese Suanpan (abacus) (Image source: Farmer 1875)

of algorithms. The algorithmic transformation of signs through symbols, the invention of the first "symbolic machines" (Krämer 1988) and the optimisation of the algorithms themselves can therefore be traced back to the first archaic forms of mechanical bookkeeping in the pre-Christian millennium.

Mathematical calculations and algorithmic procedures led to numerous technical innovations, marking the origin of engineering.[12] Independent of the inventions and ideas of ancient Mediterranean culture, a centre of this technical progress also emerged in China based on a mathematical textbook (Chiu Chang Suan Shu).[13] The work contains recipe-like procedures that led to an early algorithmisation of mathematics in China. It was (verifiably) from the first century and for the next 1,500 years the standard work for Chinese researchers, thinkers and designers. The work contains nine books with a total of 246 tasks.

The tasks are structured according to a uniform scheme (see Vogel 1968, p. 124):

1. *Description of an underlying situation, always introduced with the words: Now we have <the following case> or in a new task: Now we have another <case>.*
2. *This is followed by the question "how much is?" or "how big is?"*

[12]An extraordinary heydayof engineering can be found, for example, in the school of Alexandria under the teacher Heron, who developed an automatic temple door opener around 60 AD. A complicated algorithm ensured that the gate would open as soon as a fire was kindled in a bowl.

[13]The origin of the Chinese compendium "Nine Books of Arithmetic Technique" (Chiu Chang Suan Shu) remains unclear to this day: "In Chinese tradition, the work is attributed to Chou Kung (12th century BC) or even the legendary 'Yellow Emperor' (Huang-ti, 3rd millennium BC). The oldest text is the annotated edition by Liu Hui (263 AD?). He reports that the book was written in the early Han period by Chang Ts'ang (around 165–142 BC) based on old templates and supplemented by Keng Shou-ch'ang (around 75–49 BC). It probably received its present form in the 1st century AD. In the T'ang period, it was included in the collection of the 'Ten Mathematical Classics', which was first printed in 1084. After the 1930 edition (Shanghai), it was translated into Russian by E. I. Berezkina (published 1960) and from this Russian edition into German by K. Vogel (published 1968) (Gericke 1984, p. 173). The example used here is based on this translation by Kurt Vogel (1968).

3. *The solution then follows without intermediate calculation, after the words: "The answer says".*
4. *At the end comes the solution recipe for the individual task or the relevant group of tasks. This always begins with the stereotypical phrase: "Use the rule" or "the rule is".*

With this scheme, solutions for simple everyday problems are first presented—from the payment of wages depending on working hours and performance, through the conversion of different measurement units, to motion and surveying tasks. Subsequently, the tasks progress to another group of mathematical puzzle problems. Methods of fraction calculation for simple final calculation or social calculation, root extraction, matrix calculation and much more are conveyed. Using a simple example of social calculation—the proportional distribution of five killed deer—the recipe-like procedure can be quickly understood (see Vogel 1968, p. 27):

1. *Now we have <the following case>: A Tafu, a Pukeng, a Tsanyao, a Shangtsao <and> a Kungshi—together 5 men—killed 5 deer <on the> hunt together. It is desired that it is distributed according to rank.*[14]
2. *Question: How much does each get?*
3. *The answer says: The Tafu gets $1\frac{2}{3}$ deer; Pukeng receives $1\frac{1}{3}$ deer; Tsanyao receives 1 deer; Shangtsao receives $\frac{2}{3}$ deer; Kungshi receives $\frac{1}{3}$ deer.*
4. *The rule is: In order, assign the numerical values according to rank. Each one is a ratio number. Then add them; it is the divisor. Multiply the 5 deer by the ratio number not yet added to the others. Each product is a dividend. Divide the dividends by the divisor. They are parts of the deer.*

The letter calculation already mentioned above (in connection with Euler) is still foreign to this recipe-like procedure according to Kurt Vogel: *"If one looks in the 'Nine Books' for any knowledge in algebra, one finds that there can be no talk of a symbolic algebra with special signs for the unknowns and their powers. Nevertheless, the matrix calculation [...] for solving linear equation systems shows that one thought algebraically and marked the different unknowns by arranging their numerical coefficients on different lines. In these equations, the word tang (= owe, correspond, oppose) appears in the sense of our equality sign, which could lead from rhetorical to symbolic algebra"* (Vogel 1968, p. 121).

In the context of software development and with a view to the syntax of higher programming languages in the present, this approach can be compared with the preparatory description of a programming task in the so-called pseudo-code, with which one saves the complete formalisation of the algorithm at least until the functional requirements of a software are coordinated with the client. But for now, the focus is still on uncovering the history of ideas. In this context, it should be noted that—not only in Indian, Arabic and Chinese thinking, but—especially in

[14]"The five official classes are graded with a value of 5, 4, 3, 2 and 1." (ibid.)

ancient Western philosophy, there are early indications of a critical examination and further development of algorithmic thinking and action.[15]

In the context of this study, only a very narrow path can be cut through the jungle of mathematics, the history of science and technology. The often hidden interconnections in the thicket of human cultural history are not the focus of this book. Nevertheless, the selection of examples is not a purely random, exemplary representation that only shows that the roots of algorithmic thinking can be found i) in the formation of the numerical concept and ii) the gradual (rule-based) formalisation of language and ultimately iii) rest in human ability to abstract and our capacity for reflection. For at the same time, the path taken here (from cave painting to technical methods for property and debt management to Chinese social accounting) should also give a first impression of the algorithmic organisation of everyday life, which already in the early times forms social classes and takes social value categories (including the proportional distribution of food) into account.

1.2.1 The Vision of the Digital Measurement of the World

In principle, the digital revolution is perceived as a phenomenon of the 20th and 21st centuries. However, it often remains unclear what is specifically meant by digitalisation (see, among others, Wagner 2018). In the following, the aim is therefore to shed light on three essential motives of digitalisation. For this purpose, it is necessary in a first step, to again uncover the conceptual foundation. This is intended to show that the digital measurement of reality, which in academic discourse is also often referred to as datafication (see e.g.: Mayer-Schönberger and Cukier 2013; Filipović 2015), can be understood as a concomitant phenomenon of progressing algorithmisation.

Under the title "De computo velloquela digitorum", the Benedictine monk Beda Venerabilis (born 672/673, died 735) illustrates the ancient heritage of the concept of digital calculation. Beda documents with his records the finger numbers (lat. *digitus* "finger" or *digitalis* "belonging to the finger") of the Romans, which included a representation from 1 to 10,000 and already had a place order.[16]

---

[15] *"However, some individual problems already show the close relationship to India; on the other hand, the false double approach is not to be found there, which only reappears among the Arabs. The situation is different regarding the ingenious method of matrix calculation for solving linear equation systems, which only reappears in the West. On the other hand, the numerical calculation of square and cube roots from the 'Nine Books' has essentially remained unchanged to this day via Indians, Arabs and the West. A judgement that everything comes from China and that the Europeans have borrowed all mathematical knowledge from there and only developed it further, overlooks the role of Greece and is as little in line with the facts as the claim that the Chinese would have been completely dispensable for the development of mathematics"* (Vogel 1968, p. 6).

[16] *"On 4 finger groups, the 4 units of ones, tens, hundreds, thousands are distributed! The gestures take on the role of the digits, of which there are not 9, but 2 × 9. The reason lies in the nature of the matter, because once 3, then only 2 fingers are available. The natural starting position of the fingers acts as 'zero'"* (Menninger 1958, p. 8). Due to this "well-considered number order" (ibid. p. 3), Menninger distinguishes the finger numbers of the Romans from the "much more original finger gestures of the primitive peoples, who moreover rarely rise above the number 'ten' of both hands" (ibid.). In contrast, Beda succeeds in his writing in extending the finger numbers of the Romans, even from 10,000 to 1 million (ibid. p. 10).

According to the original use, which can be traced back to Hellenistic times in Greece and was also widespread in the Orient (cf. Wirth 1986), *computare digitis* initially means nothing other than "counting, calculating on the fingers".

In his work on the calculation of time "De temporum ratione", Beda introduces one of the most influential works of the early Middle Ages with the calculation using finger numbers, which is still, in the truest sense of the word, decisive, insofar as—based on this writing—the calculation of time after Christ's birth valid to this day was enforced. Beda has since been considered one of the most important computists of the early Middle Ages, with computistics (*lat. computus* "calculation") at that time generally understood as the science of calendar calculation and in particular the calculation method for determining the annually varying date of Easter, which is also the main focus of Beda Venerabilis' writing (Fig. 6).

From this not only the original meaning of the term digitalisation as a process of assignment (*coding*) of events to the Roman finger number system, but also the associated concept of the date (lat. *datum* "given"), which ultimately becomes the

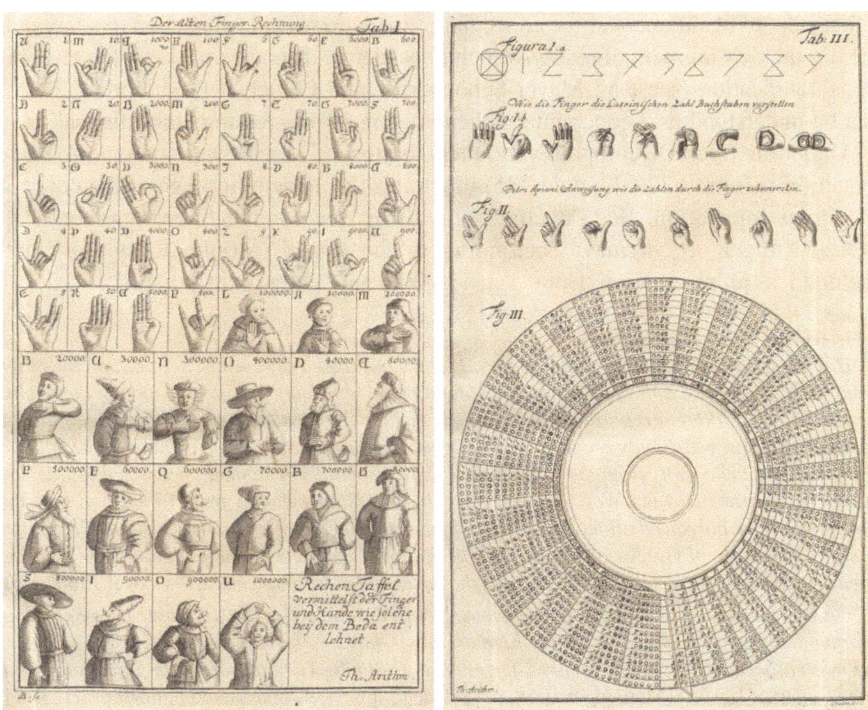

Fig. 6 Representation of the Roman finger number system according to Beda in the technical encyclopaedia "Theatrum Machinarum" by Jacob Leupold (1727), Volume 7, Theatrum arith-meti-co-geometricum, that is: showplace of the art of calculation and measurement

placeholder for digital values (*data*) has further developed.[17] Data are both a prerequisite and a result of digitisation. By setting a start date (*input date*), for example, it was possible for Beda to calculate the moving Easter date (*output date*). The calculation method necessary for this again illustrates a very essential dimension of meaning of algorithmics, which was already hinted at with the hunting example and which Bächle (2015) so aptly describes as "the linking of different time dimensions of the past and already processed, of the current and the virtual as the potentially future possible" (ibid. p. 28); in short: from the data of the past and the present, conclusions can be drawn about events in the future.

With Leon Battista Alberti, the methodical measurement of the world in numbers and values reached a temporary peak in the early Renaissance, which can also be used to illustrate another motif. Because Alberti is concerned with the identical reproducibility of nature through the written calculation methods of the early algorithmists. His almost obsessive concern for precision and his fear of careless copyists who falsify his manual digitisation techniques is extensively documented (cf. Carpo 2011). The failure of many of his ideas, for example his three-dimensional body scanner "De statua" around 1435 (see Fig. 7), which requires an extensive calculation of data points, also shows the dependence of complex measurement and calculation methods on suitable computing tools—computers only became widespread as tools for his methods 500 years later (which already indicates that the term "Big Data" can also be understood as a relational term).[18]

Alberti became known through another digitisation process, which was later used by Leonardo da Vinci and Albrecht Dürer, among others, to project reality as three-dimensionally as possible onto a 2-D surface (see Fig. 8). Friedrich Kittler has noted: "When the fineness of the grid is increased and with it the size of the individual squares decreases, then the grid transforms into a matrix, whose points become pixels" (quoted from Carpo 2009, p. 58).

With the two methods developed by Alberti, the sensually perceptible world can thus be gradually transformed into discrete (i.e., separate) data points. The "ones" that arise when converting continuous signals (*analogue data*) into individual measurements (*digital data*)—sometimes in very large quantities (Big Data)—are

[17]Another linguistic root of the term "digital" leads via "show" (lat. *dicere*) back to "pointer" (lat. *dicitus*) (see, among others, Hermann and Matschiner 2003, p. 145). With this background knowledge, it can already be guessed that the phenomenon of digitisation is no more dependent on the current assignment to a binary number system than was the mapping of data onto the Roman finger counting system. Since when humans have used fingers as pointers is hard to quantify. In software programming, and here one can connect to what has already been said about human reflection and abstraction ability, the term pointer (engl. *pointer*) is used as a special value, the meaning of which is a storage address. At this address, data in the form of binary digits, such as variables or objects, but also program codes (instructions) can be stored.

[18]The significant difference between Alberti's digitisation machine and ours today is solely, according to Mario Carpo, that our machines are powered by electricity. The effort to calculate all this manually is probably a reason, Carpo continues, that no one has ever tried to use Alberti's digital tools again.

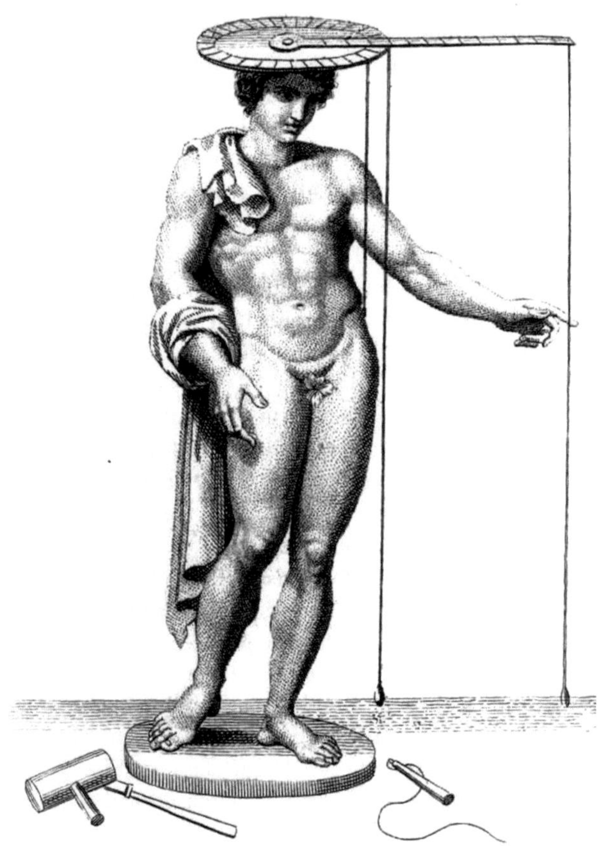

Fig. 7 Mechanical calculating device "De statua" (around 1435) by Leon Battista Alberti. The device can be used to capture measurement points that can be identified within a three-dimensional coordinate system. The resulting series of numbers, in combination with a technical manual, creates the theoretical possibility of infinitely copying the original body and reproducing it anywhere and at any time to scale or in other proportions. Alberti also suggested using the same technique to have different parts of the same statue made simultaneously in different workshops: the head in Tuscany, the feet in Greece, and so on, so that these parts, when finally assembled somewhere, would fit together perfectly" (Image source: Opal 1804)

still called "digit" (Eng. *digits*, Fr. *doigts*), which means something like digit, digit step or position.

The vision of digitally measuring reality is thus driven by the desire i) to predict events in the future and ii) to recreate our sensually perceptible world in a certain way. These two motives, however, point to a iii) third, much more fundamental motive, which Goethe's Faust formulates in his famous wish: "That I may recognise what holds the world together in its innermost being" (Goethe 1808, V.282 f.)—a motive that takes us back to pre-Socratic philosophy and the beginning of Western philosophical history and which will be examined in more detail in the following section. To draw

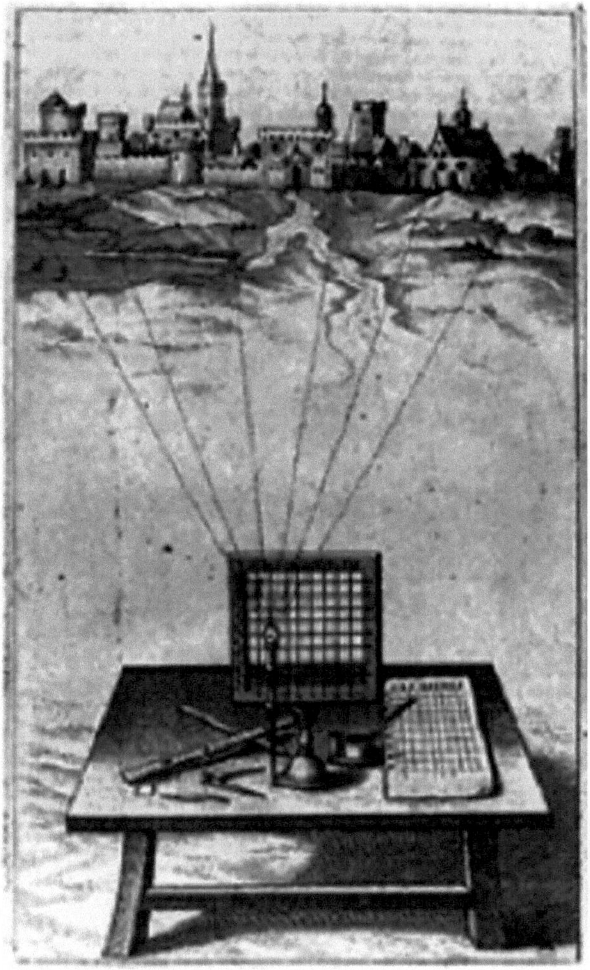

Fig. 8 Alberti's Grid around 1450. Mario Carpo notes: "Alberti could have digitised his drawings using a simple combination of length and width specifications—today we would rather use sampling and quantisation—but in both cases the end product would be the same: a number-based matrix or a digital file." (Carpo 2011, p. XY) The cultural scientist Samuel Edgerton has therefore even referred to the process as Windows 1435 in one of his essays, in reference to Microsoft's Windows 95 (Image source: Smith 2000, p. 11)

a demarcation line here means above all to advocate a sharp distinction between myth and knowledge in algorithmic thinking.

1.2.2 The Algorithm as a Basic Structure and Ordering Principle

When the Greeks began to lay the foundations for the natural sciences as we understand them today, i.e., when they began to explain nature based on its inherent laws without the inclusion of mystical forces and heavenly powers, they already looked back on extensive traditions that had been collected over the millennia, but in some cases were also only passed on orally (see, for example, Simonyi 2001, pp. 43–115).[19] "The doxographic reports let philosophy begin with Thales, Anaximander and Anaximenes, who lived in Miletus" (Ricken 2000, p. 21). The most important point of reference for their dating, and here we can return to the above-mentioned calculation of events as a meaningful dimension of algorithms, is the total solar eclipse of 28 May 585 BC, which Thales predicted (cf. ibid.).

One of the most pressing questions that occupied the first philosophers, and for which they sought to formulate a generally comprehensible answer, was the question of what they would need to understand if they wanted to understand reality as a whole:[20]

> *"From the outset, two basic intentions are guiding. The first basic intention is that our reality cannot simply be described by listing everything that exists in it, but that our reality is structured and it is the task to describe this structure of reality. The second basic intention, which, however, has not been shared by all metaphysicians since modern times, is that the diversity of things in our reality can be understood from a single principle or from a few principles"* (Bordt 2005, p. 22).

Algorithms, so my thesis, describe on this fundamental level, an abstract principle of reality, as they depict a certain structure of reality that we perceive sensually in the unrestricted transient and in the constant emergence and with our understanding in a certain way can penetrate and capture in signs and symbols. Today we find in almost all areas of science, such as medicine, biology, the cultural history, politics, etc., the most diverse application scenarios for algorithms. If one looks at, for example, the branch of research of bionics in more detail, this suggests that the existence of algorithms is not solely dependent on human self-reflection.[21]

---

[19]Gericke (1984, p. 1) also assumes that humanity practiced at least a primitive form of mathematics in prehistoric times: *"By 'prehistoric' we commonly understand the history of the time when no writing existed yet. One will not expect many documents of mathematical knowledge from this time, but one can assume that people could already count and perhaps do some calculations before they learned to write. Some very old mammoth bones have been found, on which lines are engraved, even in a certain arrangement and grouping, which can be seen as notes of numbers."*

[20]Solely due to the highly complex research subject and the very specialised technical literature, which cannot be understood without a solid knowledge of the Greek language, this task must be left to the specialists in ancient philosophy. Against this background, I rely for the following explanation on a commentary on Aristotle's Metaphysics Book Lambda by the expert Michael Bordt (2005), which I received from him a few years ago as a study manuscript. At the same time, I would like to pass on his appeal to the interested reader to engage with the original text themselves; although I personally have not yet been granted this opportunity.

[21]The ant algorithm, which was "deciphered" (decoded) by the Italian scientist Marco Dorigio and used for the first time in a completely different application scenario in 1991, is an exemplary example of this.

Nature itself serves here as a model for solving information technology problems: *"Natural laws are algorithms (rules) that serve to make predictions about the future behaviour of nature from the information we have about nature"* (Bauberger 2003, p. 130). The universe, according to a widely spread hypothesis (see e.g. Zuse 2012, 1982; Feynman 1982; Toffoli 1982; Wheeler 1982; Wolfram 2002, 2017), therefore also works according to algorithms without our intervention.[22]

In the basal system of algorithmic self-organisation, the human being can therefore be understood as part of a more extensive system. Due to his ability to abstract and reflect, which enables him, among other things, to adopt solution and processing schemes, he takes a privileged position within this system at a very early stage.

The reduction of algorithms to the three essential steps, i) input signal, ii) processing instruction and iii) output value indicates why the natural and cultural sciences have so far failed to provide us with an exact classification of the concept of algorithms. Since Aristotle at the latest, philosophers have been trying to understand, *why* reality is structured in this way, while physicists and mathematicians have since been primarily interested in *how* nature works in concrete terms or *how* nature can be categorised, and the knowledge gained from it can be used for our purposes.

To what extent these two approaches have mutually fertilised each other in view of the advancing algorithmisation in the 17th century will be further elaborated in the next section.

1.3 On the Outsourcing of Algorithmic Thinking and Action

Between the beginnings of Western philosophy and the 17th century, there are well two thousand years of cultural history. A long time, considering in which short intervals we are confronted with a second, third, fourth, etc. technical revolution in the 21st century. The assertion that nothing significant happened in this long period with reference to algorithmic thinking and action must at this point, of course, be clearly rejected. This should have been highlighted by the previous spotlights.

The fascination with numbers, the linking of arithmetic and geometry with the craft and engineering art, which still makes us marvel over the Babylonians, Egyptians, Indians and other high cultures, found its way into the Roman Empire via the Greeks. The historian of mathematics, Helmuth Gericke emphasises that the Romans were more interested in practical application than in theoretical mathematics by beginning his chapter on the "Mathematics among the Romans" with the quote: *"The only contribution the Romans have made to the history of mathematics*

[22]At the risk of being accused of dilettantism by the experts in Aristotelian metaphysics, it should be said at this point that Aristotle himself (albeit in his own words) also comes to this result when he investigates the principles and causes of ousia (ancient Greek οὐσία, "being", "substance", "essence", literally "beingness") in the twelfth book of Metaphysics.

was that a Roman soldier killed Archimedes" (Gericke 1984, p. 164), he.[23] While the Romans therefore focused primarily on the application of mathematics in architecture, trade and the art of war to expand or stabilise their empire, the centre of theoretical mathematics shifted to the Orient (Arabia, Khwarezm, Persia) and only found its way back into Western thought through the aforementioned text "De numero Indorum" by al-Khwārizmī.

The particular merit of the Arabs is that they not only carefully preserved the classical works of Indian and Greek mathematics, but *"worked through and further developed them until they were completely clear"* (Gericke 1984, p. 214). *"In the algebra books of the Arabs appear—as with the Indians—instructions for performing calculations, not only with numbers, but also with root expressions and algebraic expressions,* i.e. *expressions that contain unknowns and their powers"* (ibid.).

In particular, the calculation with unknowns, which can be traced back to Greek mathematics (Diophantus of Alexandria), but was only systematised by the Arabs, who developed and taught structured procedures to consistently replace the geometric constructions of the Greek mathematicians by setting up different types of equations, forms the basis for modern algorithmics (*Computer Science and Mathematics*).

Muḥammad Ibn-Mūsā al-Khwārizmī, whose name was already associated with the term algorithm at the beginning of this chapter, is also the author of a second textbook titled "al-Kitāb al-muḫtaṣar fī ḥisāb al-ğabr wa-l-muqābala", which contains equations to solve tasks from everyday life (e.g. merchant practice and inheritance law). From the title of this work, which somewhat freely translated *means "Summarising Book on the Correct Arrangement as well as the Balancing"* (Simonyi 2001, p. 142), also comes the term algebra, which from the 12th century onwards became established for the calculation with unknowns in the West and later worldwide.[24]

---

[23]The already mentioned finger counting system of the Romans might suggest this on the one hand: "When we find expressions among the Romans, who were very poor calculators and therefore faithfully preserved early calculation methods, such as *numerare per digitos* 'counting on fingers' and *novi digitos tuos* 'I know your fingers', which literally means 'I know your skill in calculating', these is charming evidence of this" (Menninger 1958, p. 47). As a reminder: "digiti are called 'ones' throughout the Middle Ages, and they are still called so in England, digits" (ibid.). On the other hand, the Romans had a practical advantage through their finger counting system, which humanity probably only experienced again with the smartphone, because the hand and fingers are always quickly available (also worth mentioning in this context: The Romans developed a hand abacus the size of a postcard).

[24]*"al-ğabr and al-muqābala are technical terms for algebraic operations: al-ğabr (Latin: restauratio) means the 'repositioning' of a term to its right place (originally a term of medicine),* i.e. *the elimination of a subtracted quantity by addition on both sides of the equation; al-muqābala (Latin: oppositio) is the expression for the 'balancing',* i.e. *the cancellation of equal terms on both sides"* (Ḫwārizmī et al. 1997, p. 13). Lüneburg further explains, that the term "Algebrista" was already used in Spanish for a man who heals broken bones and resets limbs: *"When Don Quixote knocked the Knight of Mirrors off his horse, the fallen man's ribs did not remain completely in order, and he had to stay in a place where such a doctor put him right again... llegaron à un puèblo, donde fuè ventùra hallàr à un Algebrista con quièn se curò el Sanson desgraciàdo"* (Lüneburg 2008, p. 343).

From the first algorithmicians to the first construction of machines with a mechanical calculating mechanism, several hundred years passed (as was long assumed).[25] The human susceptibility to error in the mathematical measurement or calculation of the world was already mentioned using the example of the three-dimensional body scanner "De statua" (1435) by Leon Batista Alberti. Wilhelm Schickhard, who was born in 1592 as the son of a carpenter, was active not only as an astronomer, geographer and cartographer after his theology studies, but he was also a talented mechanic. Because of his theoretical and practical talent, he was praised by the famous natural philosopher and astronomer Johannes Kepler (for whose work "Harmonice mundi" Schickhard contributed some copper engravings and woodcuts) in a letter to the astronomer Peter Krüger as a two-handed philosopher (lat. *philosophus amphidexios*), "for he philosophises with mind and hand" (Seck 1978a, p. 391). After having already built a model of the starry sky and developed a theory of the moon's orbit in 1623, which allowed the most accurate positional values of his time to be determined, he designed the first documented calculating machine in the same year, which he himself called a calculating clock (Fig. 9).

Schickhard thus embodies an ideal example of the synthesis of theory and practice in the context of the mechanisation of algorithmic calculation methods. Blaise Pascal, whose father was appointed royal commissioner and chief tax collector for Normandy in 1640, invented another mechanical calculating machine in 1642, the so-called Pascaline. Pascal also made a name for himself as a mathematician, physicist and philosopher and combined his theoretical studies with a practical use, by initially developing a device for the tax calculation, as a work relief for his father. Furthermore, in the 17th century, Gottfried Wilhelm Leibniz, René Descartes and Thomas Hobbes also dealt with the development of mechanical calculation aids.

They all have in common that they sought to overcome human error-proneness in calculation by developing mechanical calculation aids, and that they all worked as both mathematicians and philosophers.

The vision of outsourcing algorithmic calculation methods can be traced back at least 4000 years to the mechanism of Antikythera as well as the arithmetic of counting stones and the abacus, which gained central dominance in different cultures. The first calculating machines by Wilhelm Schickhardt (1623), Blaise Pascal (1642) or Gottfried Wilhelm Leibniz (1674) aimed for the first time at the outsourcing and automation of written calculation methods, i.e. they aimed to mechanise the algorithmic rule set itself. Then as now, it was about much more than just finding a practical solution to mathematical problems in calculation.

With Francis Bacon (born 1561, died 1626), the effort began to reorder natural science and to emancipate itself from the ancient authorities such as Aristotle and Plato, who gained new fame during the Renaissance. The scientific revolution, which subsequently also led to a technical revolution, elevated mathematical-

[25]Current studies show that more than 2,000 years ago, the mechanism of Antikythera, a mechanical computer made of bronze gears, was developed, which enabled the movements of the sun, moon and probably also of planets to be calculated in advance (see Freeth et al. 2021).

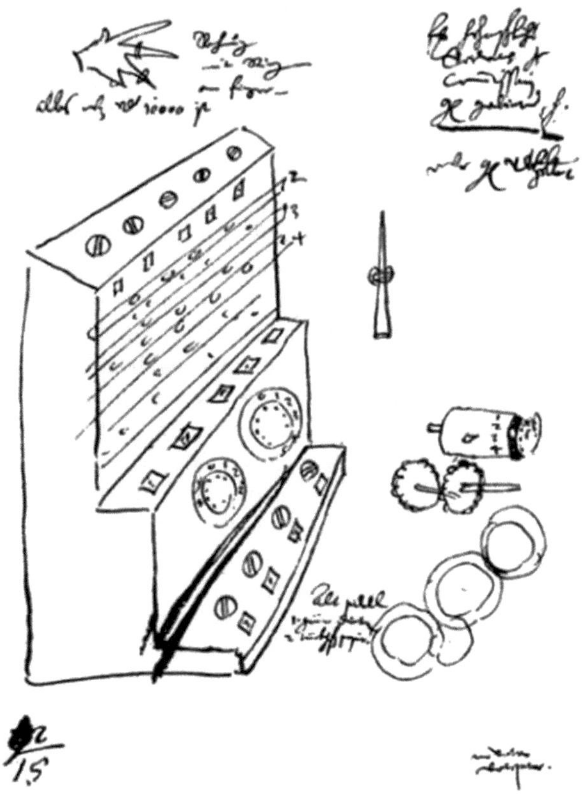

Fig. 9 Original drawing of the calculating machine by Wilhelm Schickhardt (1592–1635) (Image source: Seck 1978b)

quantitative abstraction to the basic research paradigm of modern natural science. In particular, the constructivist-rationalist theories of Descartes and Leibniz set out to integrate the mathematical-scientific methodology (lat. *methodus mathematica*) into their philosophical thinking and to transfer it to non-mathematical subject areas such as human thinking.[26]

Although Leibniz used the decimal calculation system known from al-Ḫwārizmī when building his calculating machine, he already made a significant contribution to the theoretical foundation of the binary calculation system and developed—with the aim of exposing human errors as calculation errors (we will return to this in the following section)—first ideas for the logical formalisation of sentences in a universal calculus language (lat. *characteristica universalis*).

[26] *"I had advanced very far in the land of the Scholastics when the mathematicians and modern writers persuaded me to leave it while I was still a very young man. Their excellent method of explaining nature mechanically delighted me, and I rightly despised the method of those who only use forms and abilities, of which one understands the least"* (Leibniz 1695, quoted from Gadamer 2004, p. 188).

The development of mechanical calculating machines in the 17th century is therefore against the background of the philosophical conceptions of that time—*"in which at the level of method discussion the axiomatic method of geometry entered with an algorithmic calculation and the concept of calculus gained from new algebraic methods"* (Arndt 1971, p. 1).[27] This fertilised the "tense and changeable relationship" (ibid.) between theory and practice (humanities and natural sciences) on an epochal scale.[28] Full of confidence, David Hilbert announced over two hundred years later in a radio address: *"The instrument that mediates between theory and practice, between thinking and observing, is mathematics; it builds the connecting bridge and makes it ever more resilient"* (Hilbert 1930).

1.3.1 The Idea of Formalisation

Since the beginnings of philosophy, scientists in search of rules and structures in the world have repeatedly succeeded in reducing complex issues to simpler, less complex relationships. "Our considerations" (Leibniz and Schneider 2002, p. 123), Leibniz summarises in 1714, two years before his death at the age of seventy,

> *"are based on two great principles, that of contradiction, on the basis of which we judge as false what envelops contradictory or false, and as true, what is opposed to this"* (ibid.), and *"that of sufficient reason, on the basis of which we do not accept any fact as true or existing, no statement as truthful, without there being a sufficient reason why it should be so and not otherwise, although very often these reasons may not be known to us"* (ibid. p. 125).

Although the formalisation of logical reasoning (in Western thinking) can be traced back through medieval dialectics to Aristotelian syllogistics, the experience that nature follows elementary rules—that every effect has a cause and nothing in the world happens without reason, only becomes an unshakeable foundation of science in the modern world view. This raises the question of why natural science did not flourish much earlier and why it was only able to develop into a (largely) independent research discipline now. In other words: What makes the difference in the 16th and 17th centuries (and subsequently also in the 18th and 19th centuries)?

The answer to this question was already anticipated in the previous chapter and is in the words of Gadamer:

> *"The empirical sciences break away from the Aristotelian-scholastic cosmos of knowledge and gain their independence on the basis of mathematical-quantitative abstraction with the*

[27]There are countless treatises on the beginnings of modern natural science and the so-called "Enlightenment philosophy of the 17th and 18th centuries (Modern Philosophy)" to which reference should be made here solely with these keywords.

[28]In Simonyi (2001, pp. 119–272), the backgrounds and the fundamental significance of the discoveries and changes for the natural sciences are extensively explained. From his point of view, at this point a "thousand-year pause" (ibid. p. 119) of scientific development ends: *"In general (sic!) there is agreement that the further development of Greek culture was essentially (sic!) hindered by the missing connection between science and practice. Practice did not pose any tasks to science, and the scientific results were not transferred into practice. [. . .] To increase the volume of production, no machines were used, but the number of slaves was increased"* (ibid.).

> *declared intention of shedding all anthropomorphisms, all belief in authority and in particular the shackles of Aristotle – later also those of biblical tradition*" (Gadamer 2004, p. 7).

The reason is therefore to be found in the *mathematical-quantitative abstraction*. But can it be more specific? After all, the ability to abstract and reflect (in connection with cave painting) was identified as a crucial prerequisite for algorithmic thinking at the very beginning of this thesis. On a very general level, algorithmisation was also qualified as an elementary part of our thinking, which we have understood so well that we can outsource it in signs or symbols. Testimonies about the importance and meaning of quantifying can be found in human history from the first counting sticks through the Pythagoreans to Bishop Isidore of Seville ("Take away the number and everything falls apart", around 600 AD) and far beyond that, almost everywhere. An early rule-based method was also exemplarily presented from a traditional Chinese textbook (Chiu Chang Suan Shu), which already combines the form of logical inference with arithmetic. So where, one can continue to ask with the necessary persistence, lies the difference?

To anticipate it: the development of logic is based on a certain thinking experience (or abstraction), i.e. without this theoretical thinking experience, the difference in the form of logic cannot be understood. Strictly speaking, there is *no (one) form* of logic. So, when we talk about the formalisation of algorithmic thinking, the question first arises as to which form the algorithmic thinking should be abstracted in concrete terms. If one starts to strip the content of a linguistic conclusion to make the logical content of a certain statement visible, this means that one intends to isolate that part in the sentence which one feels to be (logically) *compelling*; without the experience of feeling that a certain conclusion is *compelling*, there is no logic (see Hoyningen-Huene 1998).

Under the aspect of time, which we have already defined as an essential dimension of algorithms, it is possible (insofar as this logical compulsion exists or can be found) to conclude, for example, i) from the present to the past, ii) from the present to the future and iii) from the present to the present. This experience has already been handed down to us from the ancient Indian sciences and plays a central role in the Asian humanities (as well as Buddhist thinking) (cf. Li 1999, p. 123).

The question of what is felt as compelling in logic and how the way of *abstracting this something* has changed can be traced much more easily within one's own cultural circle and is therefore to be introduced by a simple example (or a variation) from Aristotelian syllogistics:

All algorithmists are human.
All humans are mortal.

Therefore, all algorithmists are mortal.

The intellectual achievement in Aristotelian formalisation now consists in comprehending the conclusion. The content of the premises, i.e. the truth value of the two statements above the dashed line, is not important. But if we accept the two statements as true, then we must also acknowledge the conclusion as true. This experience can be understood in this simple example (due to our cultural imprinting) even if one of the two premises is false.[29] By pretending to believe the statement is true, we immediately recognise the (mechanical) compulsion of the conclusion.

At this point we can return to Leibniz, who pursued the idea of developing a universal formal language (lat. *characteristica universalis*) throughout his life, with which the concepts and relationships of the real world can be symbolically captured, and which systematically fades out the concrete contents of individual objects. For this artificial language, he believed, a set of rules (lat. *calculus ratiocinator* could also be found, with which the truth value of a statement can be calculated by a mechanical procedure (cf. Hoffmann 2013, p. 2) (Fig. 10).

Leibniz is considered a precursor of modern logic, as he recognised both the importance of a formal language (characteristica universalis) for the precision of conceptual statements and the possibility of schematically operating with symbols following the model of arithmetic (calculus rationcinator):

> *"If one could find characters or signs that could express all our thoughts as purely and clearly as arithmetic expresses numbers or analytical geometry expresses lines, then one could do in all matters, as far as they are accessible to rational thinking, what one does in arithmetic and geometry"* (Leibniz 1960, p. 90).

George Boole was the first to introduce a mathematical symbolism into logic. Just like Leibniz, he demands (mechanical)[30] laws of thought to be represented by arithmetic symbol combinations and thereby expects philosophical precision in language: *"The theory of Logic is thus intimately connected with that of Language. A successful attempt to express logical propositions by symbols, the laws of those combinations should be founded upon the laws of the mental processes which they represent, would, so far, be a step toward a philosophical language"* (Boole 1847, p. 5). With Boole, mathematical logic was founded, the symbols 1 and 0, which we already know from Leibniz, were interpreted by Boole for propositional logic as "true" and "false".[31]

The projection of algorithmic thinking into artificial artefacts was famously electrified as a result of the industrial revolution. With the transistor, the electrical circuit

---

[29]For example, we could be asked to define more precisely by which characteristics XYZ a *social being* is distinguished and our counterpart would possibly only consider these characteristics fulfilled by *some*, but not by *all* people. Vice versa, another interlocutor might initially be convinced that humans are fundamentally not *social beings* and we would suddenly convince him of the opposite with our further explanations. The crucial point is: It doesn't matter—the content of the premises plays no role for the *mechanism of the conclusion*, which is what it's all about here.

[30]'Mechanical' here is to be understood in the sense of the above explained meaning of 'mechanical compulsion' in the context of a logical conclusion. Boole himself speaks in this context of the *laws of mental processes*, which are to be represented in the mathematical symbolic language.

[31]In addition to Boole, the fundamental works of Gottlob Frege, Bertrand Russell and Alfred N. Whitehead must also be mentioned. Frege is considered the founder of modern logic, as he developed an independent "concept script" (1879), which many still consider today as the most important work of symbolic logic. The three-volume work "Principia Mathematica" (1910–1913) by Russell and Whitehead contains for the first time the tools to represent the entire mathematics in formal symbolic script (cf. Zeidler 2013, p. 316).

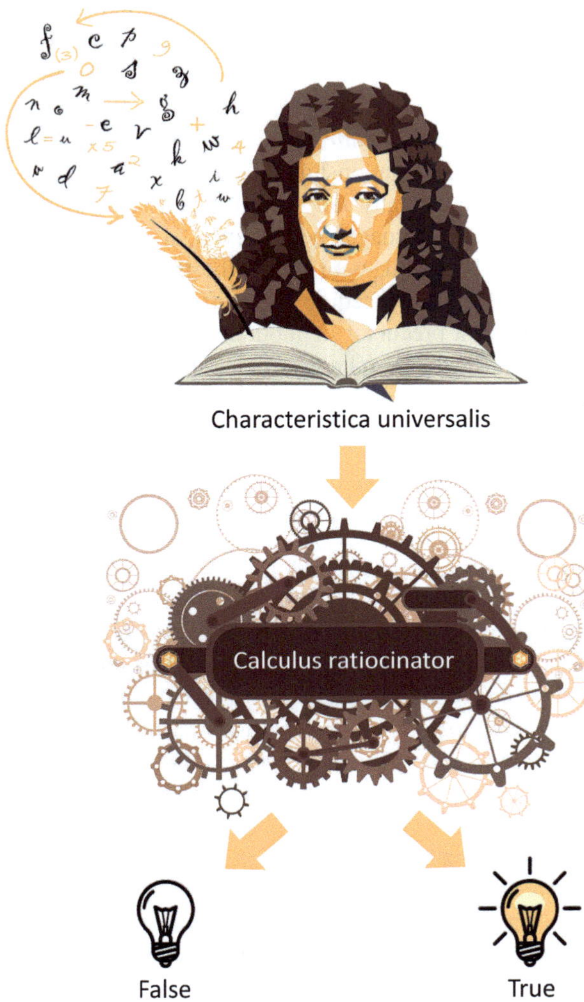

Fig. 10 Leibniz never systematically developed his own programme—it was only with the advent of modern logic and computing technology that many of his ideas came to fruition (Image source: Adapted from Hoffmann (2013, p. 2), modified by the author)

was discovered as an elementary sign carrier, setting the course for a "mathematical physics" (Krämer 1988) that made it possible to describe logical conclusions (thoughts) as quantifiable facts and to transfer the entire syntactic rule set to physical processes (into a machine language) and thus realise the first computers in today's understanding.[32]

[32]In addition to engineers, it is primarily physicists and electrical engineers like William Shockley, John Bardeen or Walter Houser Brattain, to name just a few, who paved the way for the newer computer technology.

With the publication of the incompleteness theorems by Kurt Gödel (1930), the Leibnizian dream of the comprehensive mechanisation of mathematics was however ended before it could properly get underway. Subsequently, Alan Turing dedicated his work "On computable Numbers, with an application to the Entscheidungsproblem" (1936) to the conception of a systematic procedure (Turing machine), which was intended to demonstrate the limits of computability. In fast-forward, a historical precision of the modern concept of algorithms passes us by here,[33] which has been extensively explained in countless treatises (see e.g. Turing et al. 2013). Also because Turing does not use the concept of algorithms in this context, but (as already mentioned) speaks of a "purely mechanical process" as the subject of investigation, the next section will focus on the insight that the mechanism *(algorithm)* of the Turing machine was recognised as independent from the physical apparatus on which it is executed: with the help of mathematical logic, the mechanical gearwork of the first calculating machines was translated into a symbolic gearwork.

1.3.2 Symbolic Representationalism

Symbols represent changeable values *(variables)* in algorithmic solution procedures. For example, the input symbol "X" can refer to the number of living neighbouring cells of a very specific cell "Z" within a rasterised space (see Fig. 11).

The instruction "IF X<2 OR X>3 THEN Z=0" then formalises a rule of a cellular automaton, which states: (i) "Living cells that have less than two or more than three living neighbouring cells die (in the next step)." The numbers "2" and "3" in this case determine the time of death of a certain cell by defining a set of

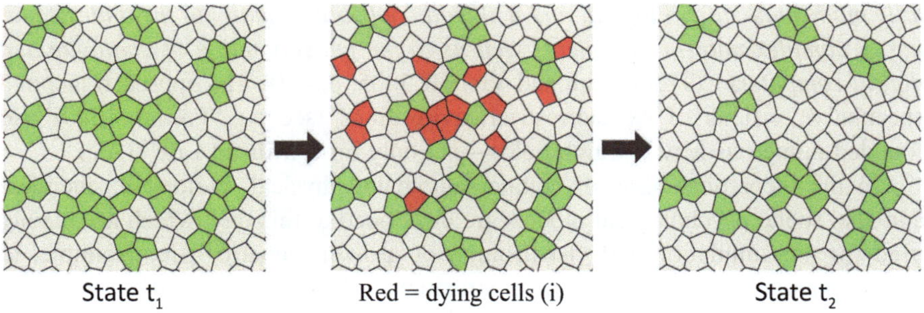

Fig. 11 Cell cycle for rule (i) (Image source: Author's own illustration)

[33] *"It is possible to achieve the effect of a calculating machine by writing down a list of instructions and asking a human to execute them. "Such a combination of a human with written instructions is called a 'paper machine'. A human equipped with paper, pencil and eraser and subjected to strict discipline, is indeed a universal machine"* (Turing quoted after Trogemann, p. 180).

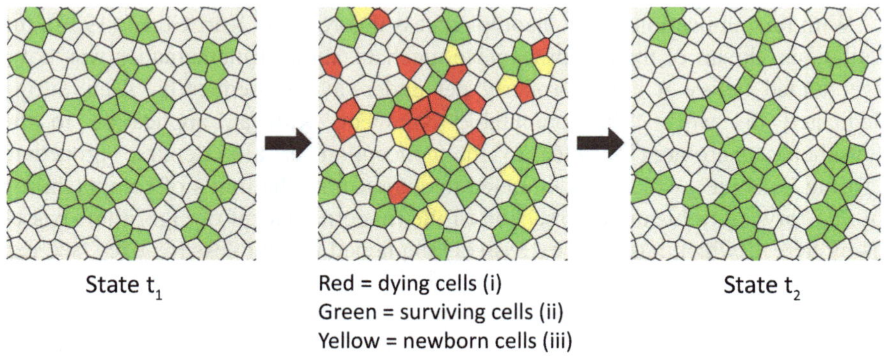

Fig. 12 Cell cycle for rule (i–iii) (Image source: Author's own illustration)

living neighbouring cells for this purpose. The operators of the action rule "IF ... < ... OR ...> THEN ... = ..." formalise the transition function "1 → 0" *(transformation)* from one cell state (t_1) to the next (t_2).

In addition to this first rule (i), the cellular automaton—known as the "Game of Life" (Conway 1970)—also describes equally simple rules that determine when living cells remain alive unchanged in the subsequent generation or when new cells arise from dead cells: (ii) Living cells that have exactly two or exactly three living neighbouring cells survive and (iii) dead cells that have exactly three living neighbouring cells are (in the next step) alive.[34] If we now apply all three rules (i–iii) simultaneously to the cell cycle ($t_1 \rightarrow t_2$) and illustrate the calculation step in colour for easier understanding, a preliminary final result appears for t_2 (Fig. 12).

The idea of developing a cellular automaton that reproduces itself like a living being under continuous application of "t + 1" of simple rules (i–iii) comes from John von Neumann (1951, 1967). *"The theory he envisaged should be fundamentally mathematical and logical and it should contribute equally to the understanding of complex natural systems as well as to the understanding of analogue and digital computers"* (Trogemann and Viehoff 2005, p. 440). His approach inspired speculative visions of extraterrestrial civilisations (see e.g. Freitas 1980) and founded numerous new research fields—not only on "Artificial Life" (AL).[35]

On the theoretical basis of cellular automata, physical, biological, chemical and also social psychological models are developed to this day, which are mainly used for the simulation and visualisation of growth scenarios—for example, to model population growth in urban structures (Naghibi et al. 2016; Wahyudi and Liu 2016), or for the simulation of road traffic, especially on motorways (Luna-Benoso et al. 2013).

The numerous applications of such algorithms in different contexts exemplify (as in the example of the above outlined cellular automaton) the performance of

[34]See http://mathworld.wolfram.com/GameofLife.html for further details.

[35]The research field "Artificial Life" or "A-Life" (English for "Artificial Life") deals among other things with genetic and evolutionary algorithms.

abstract models. Due to their symbolic representational power—i.e. their conditional independence from a concrete instantiation (like Z = living cell in biological systems)—algorithms are primarily characterised by their relevance for various application scenarios (such as urban infrastructure research or automated traffic modelling etc.).

According to some researchers, and here we can tie in with the explanations about algorithms as a basic principle of order and structure, cellular automata in a certain way even exceed symbolic representationalism, i.e. they do not only function as a media tool to simulate dynamic systems or analyse the emergence of complex patterns, but are—under the speculative hypothesis: *"If the world is a computer, life is an algorithm"* (Siegfried 2014)—interpreted as a fundamental functionalism of reality. Berto and Tagliabue (2017 Edition) summarise this position: *"Everything in our world—quarks, trees, human beings, remote galaxies—is just a pattern in a CA [Cellular Automata], much like a glider in Life."* Regardless of the interpretation of the ontological status of algorithms, at this point, with reference to Bächle (2015), two further dimensions of meaning of algorithms can be determined: i) a semiotic figure, which through symbolic representations covers the dimension of observer constructivism and ii) a performative level, on which symbolically meaningful practices are coded or formalised knowledge actions (sequential action instructions with logical operators) are executed (cf. Bächle 2015, p. 15).

Even without the strong assumption that the world is digital and everything is calculable,[36] the example of a cellular automaton has further substantiated the cultural logic according to which algorithms function for us as a basic structural and ordering principle of reality. This universal idea can be further substantiated with regard to our own nervous system and the nerve pathways in our body, especially through the information technological analysis of neuronal cells and the conception of artificial-neuronal networks, in the following.

1.3.3 How Do Self-Learning Systems Work?

How does our brain work? This question is the crux of the investigation of algorithmic thinking and action. Although this paper cannot provide a satisfactory answer to this question, the examples discussed so far already show that the existence of algorithms is not limited to computers or functional brain states. Algorithms are rather found in all natural and artificial systems where there are states between which a causal link exists. The theoretical formalisation of this link ($A \rightarrow B$) is a specific achievement of the brain and has always occupied humans. Precisely because the basic principle of automatic information processing

---

[36]Floridi is one of the most influential opponents of digital ontologies and the thesis "that [...] the ultimate nature of reality is digital, and the universe is a computational system equivalent to a Turing Machine" Floridi 2009, p. 151. Drawing on Kant, he argues that the juxtaposition of digital vs. analog ontologies are ultimately only *"modes of presentation of Being"* Floridi 2009, p. 152, which at different levels of abstraction ("level of abstraction – LoA") merely say something about how epistemic subjects experience or conceptualise reality. Accordingly, such approaches cannot provide independent knowledge about the intrinsic properties of the world beyond human abstraction capabilities (LoA).

entered the world stage billions of years ago, long before the first humans or computers (cf. Zitzler 2017, p. 40), it seems more than obvious to consider the neuronal connections in the brain, which are capable of such a cognitive performance, as a model for self-learning technical systems.

Deep neural networks (Deep Learning) are among the key success factors of machine learning. In combination with large amounts of data, they enable in many research areas of Artificial Intelligence (AI) a historic breakthrough, leading to numerous innovative products (e.g., through image and pattern recognition, text processing, speech recognition, and much more) (see, for example, Sun et al. 2014; Young et al. 2017; Imseng et al. 2013). The danger, which is repeatedly pointed out in connection with multilayer neural networks, is that the theoretical foundations until now remain hidden from us (see, for example, Goldberg and Levy 2014; Lei et al. 2018). The so-called Black Box problem, which describes the opacity of a system's internal functioning, is not a new phenomenon, as Passig (2017) notes in an essay, among other things, with a quote from Joseph Weizenbaum that is over forty years old:

> *"Our society is increasingly relying on computer systems that were originally intended to 'assist' in analyses and decisions, but have long since exceeded the understanding of their users and have become indispensable. This is a very serious development. It has two important consequences. Firstly, decisions are influenced and sometimes even made exclusively by computers, the programmes of which no one knows or understands anymore. So no one can know the criteria or rules on which these decisions are based. Secondly, the rules and criteria embodied in these computer systems are immune to change, as without a detailed understanding of the internal processes any significant modification will likely paralyse the entire system, possibly irreparably. Such systems can therefore only continue to grow (sic!)"* (ibid.).

Recent developments in advanced language models, particularly large-scale generative models, have further exacerbated this challenge by significantly increasing both the complexity and the opacity of their internal processing, making transparency even harder to achieve (see Marcus & Davis 2019, Marcus 2023). Thus, the historical concerns identified by Weizenbaum and others remain highly relevant.

In addition to Weizenbaum, who justifies the incomprehensibility and increasing complexity of technical systems primarily through the lost history of origin and development of the software code—triggered, for example, by "the departure of the original programmers" (see Weizenbaum 1976a, p. 228), Kathrin Passig quotes other pioneers of cybernetics and AI research, such as Norbert Wiener (1960), Stanisław Lem (1964) or Marvin Minsky (1967), who all expressed their views on the so-called "Black Box issue" more than fifty years ago. In conclusion, Passig (2017) argues, drawing on Lem, that software should not be held to higher standards than the human brain.[37]

---

[37] *"Therefore, every human being is an excellent example of a device that we can use without knowing its algorithm. One of the devices closest to us in the entire cosmos is our own brain, because it is in our head. Yet to this day we do not know exactly how this brain works. To explore its mechanisms introspectively is, as the history of psychology shows, highly deceptive and leads to the most erroneous hypotheses imaginable"* (Lem 1964 quoted after Passig 2017).

It is therefore a well-known argument that is also used by AI engineer Vincent Vanhoucke (2014) in an online interview when he claims that human decisions (if at all) can only be rationalised retrospectively:

> *"We think we understand why we do what we do, but in fact, much of it is a fiction we create post-facto. This creates a conundrum for people working on complicated machine learning systems: we are often being held to standards of explainability that humans can't be held to, and people themselves are largely uncomprehending of the issue because this fiction of rationality we've created for ourselves is the basis of our entire conscious existence" (ibid.).*

Against this background, some researchers are now advocating abandoning the ethical ideal of transparency (see, for example, Ananny and Crawford 2016) or limiting themselves to manipulating the external conditions using so-called "Reverse Engineering."[38] For the example of cellular automata outlined above, this would specifically mean limiting oneself to manipulating the input signals in order to draw conclusions about the selection and selection criteria of the algorithms from the subsequent changes in the output (or a statistical analysis of the input-output relations).[39]

Abandoning the demand for transparency is not an option, not least because of the legal regulations in the European General Data Protection Regulation (EU-GDPR). Because it seems to us in principle that "it is appropriate to expect more in terms of explainability of AI than from humans" (Weigert 2018). This is also why the research field of explainable AI (Explainable Artificial Intelligence) has been gaining importance again in recent years. Lei et al. (2018) attempt to open the black box of deep neural networks by tracing back the inner workings of the so-called Deep Learning technology layer by layer to the physical foundations and laws.[40] For this, they distinguish two types of data based on the information content—symbolic data and physical data—and hope to gain valuable insights into the functioning of the human brain through this:

> *"There is a striking homogeneity in the appearance and structure of the human cerebral cortex. In other words, the cerebral cortex uses the same calculations to accomplish all its functions. All the intelligence that humans exhibit (vision, auditory, physical movement. . .) are based on a unified set of algorithms. The deep learning technology is also based on a unified algorithm and is supported by physical theories" (Lei et al. 2018, p. 25).*

---

[38]An input alphabet X = {x1, x2, . . ., xm} defines a finite set of input symbols. Since each input signal "xi" (input value) is triggered by an event in the "outside world", this procedure usually leads to a change of state of the overall system, which can be observed and described.

[39]*"Reverse engineering and biology are two examples of fields of work where researchers regularly gain insight into complex, opaque and nonlinear systems. Especially in biology, demands for more transparent, better documented, easier to understand living beings do not get far."* (Passig 2017.).

[40]"The deep neural network is a physical system, and its architecture and algorithm should conform to the principles of physics. The technical foundation for deep learning is physics, especially quantum physics and quantum statistical physics" (Lei et al. 2018, p. 25).

The analogy between the human brain and the computer has evolved from René Descartes through Gottfried Wilhelm Leibniz and Alan Turing to modern natural science into a dominant explanatory model for self-learning algorithms. The study of living organisms today largely relies on the assumption that organisms are controlled by algorithmic processes. The success of increasingly biologically inspired neural architectures—such as neuromorphic computing and transformer-based models—has further blurred the distinction between biological cognition and artificial computation, sparking renewed philosophical debates about consciousness, intentionality, and the ethical status of algorithmic agents (Bostrom & Shulman 2021).

This observation led the historian Yuval Noah Harari (2018, p. 132) to the universalist thesis: "Organisms are algorithms"—they calculate probabilities even without a notebook and calculator, as Harari further explains using the example of a baboon who, in search of bananas, discovers a lurking lion and consequently weighs up whether he risks his life for the bananas or not (see ibid. pp. 136–139). Accordingly, the algorithmic behaviour of the monkey is determined by the conversion of biochemical processes within the body, which lead to different sensory perceptions and emotions such as fear or courage.

Algorithms that run on biochemical networks are understood as physical processes—humans, animals or plants as biological machines.[41] Because the separation between processing and process control can be found, according to the scientistic thesis, in all living cells. Each chemical reaction represents a specific processing step. The coupling of chemical reactions is controlled by highly specialised proteins (see Zitzler 2017, p. 138). The consequences of this form of physical functionalism are summed up by Fuchs (2020, p. 11):

> *"If these interconnected assumptions were true, then man would be in the form of neuronal processes, genetic algorithms and digitised behaviour patterns, in short, as the sum of his data far better to grasp than through hermeneutic understanding, self-reflection and self-contemplation."*

In interaction with constantly changing environmental conditions the learning ability of the brain still exceeds the automation and storage capacity of the electrical components of computers in many areas, as in particular humans can in fractions of a second process a true firework of thoughts, feelings, emotions and desires. But is it just a matter of time, until even the most complicated algorithms of "bodily existence"[42] (e.g. moral reasons for action)—in interaction with information technology modelling—can be decrypted and replicated or simulated?

---

[41]Since algorithms in computer science are always deterministic, neural networks in computer science are described by heuristics and not by algorithms per se.

[42]According to Fuchs (2020, p. 12), "the counter-design to a naturalistic-reductive image of man [. . .] consists in the corporeality and vitality that is constitutive for the person."

1.4 Media-Philosophical Systematisation

In the preceding chapter, various spotlights were thrown on the intellectual and historical roots of algorithmics. The following section is about systematising these findings through a media-philosophical reflection. For this purpose, the chapter was further subdivided according to three thematic complexes. The first subchapter deals with the ontological nature of algorithms, i.e. the question: What are algorithms? The second subchapter addresses the epistemic question: What do algorithms describe? The third section finally addresses the ethical question, with the heading: What do algorithms aim for? Then, the media-philosophical approach to the algorithmic search for numbers and values is summarised in a short interim conclusion.

1.4.1 What Are Algorithms?

In the context of the intellectual and historical approach, algorithms were already described as basic structural and ordering principles of reality. Methodologically, the question now arises as to whether this subject area can be further concretised or in what way algorithms can be made accessible to scientific reflection. Algorithms can—to start with the latter point—be understood in mathematics as a function or mapping, i.e. as a relationship between two sets (cf. Sobe 2014, p. 4).

$$f : D \rightarrow Z, x \rightarrow y \text{ or } y = f(x)$$

More precisely, the description of a method for mapping or transforming from a definition set "D" to a target set "Z" in mathematics is referred to as an algorithm. Therefore, it is said that an algorithm is assigned to a function "f" to solve a certain task (or the function "f"). However, as Sobe (ibid. p. 5) notes, "there are also functions to which no algorithm can be assigned. These functions are then not computable." The aspect of computability is therefore an important prerequisite for machine information processing. In computer science, an algorithm is essentially nothing more than a calculation instruction that is executed by a computer to calculate certain output sizes "y" from certain input sizes "x".

The differentiation of algorithms in a formal sign system can be traced back over a very long period of time, as outlined above, and understood as a result of the interaction of different cultures. If we qualify algorithms as elementary components of our thinking, which we have understood so well that we can outsource them in signs or symbols, then algorithms (in more or less precise form) have existed as long as there are human languages. If, on the other hand, we generally understand algorithms as transformation or reshaping rules, then the universe also works according to algorithms without our intervention. Natural laws are algorithms *(rules)* in this last sense. They describe a certain structure of reality and enable us to make predictions about the future behaviour of nature from data we have about nature (cf. Bauberger 2003, p. 130).

Building on the findings from the previous chapter, it can be stated, i) that it seems to be an inherent property of the sensually perceptible world to be in constant change and ii) that these transformation and reshaping processes as a rule, possess an internal logic (see above). For us to grasp the inherent algorithms of nature, we need media, for example, a language, signs and symbols. In the context of algorithms, there is often talk of "Code Literacy" or "Algorithmic Literacy", i.e. the literacy (the writing and reading skills) of people with regard to algorithms. Algorithms are therefore, as part of written language, understood as a medium. Through sufficient practice, so the basic consideration, humans can develop the necessary skills to use the language of algorithmics, e.g. for the programming of a computer. In principle, algorithms can therefore be referred to as a medium for describing functions or conversion and transformation processes.

For pragmatic reasons, it would be sensible to end the ontological consideration with reference to the use-theoretical definition of media. Otherwise, one quickly runs the risk that the underdetermined properties of the basic system of media negatively affect a further precision of the concept of algorithms. Sandbothe, who favours a pragmatic approach, defines media as "tools that serve the coordination of human action" (Sandbothe 2003, p. 195). The additional criterion that media must provide *coordination services for interpersonal action*, therefore, functions for Sandbothe as a definitional restriction *of media tools*.

The problem of the complexity and multi-layered nature of the media concept can be roughly illustrated by sending a tweet on a smartphone: In everyday language, we refer to both the technical apparatus (here: the smartphone) and the Twitter communication platform as media. Not only the smartphone, but already the human thumb,[43] typing the text message on the smartphone, can be considered as a *media tool*, insofar as the motor input of the text message is a condition of the possibility for this form of *interpersonal action*. Because only the thumb transforms the (usually unspoken) thought of the sender via the input screen on the smartphone into a text message. Such an inflationary use of the media concept threatens however to lead to a reductio ad absurdum, as Jan-Hendrik Heinrichs notes. Alternatively, the input can also be made by our voice due to advances in speech recognition, and we could initially *aspectually* focus on the examination of the generally less controversial medium of human language.

With regard to algorithms, the *media intertwining of language, text and program* is of particular importance.[44] The contemporary algorithm debate, however,

---

[43]From birth, we first grasp our environment with our hands. Especially for the deaf-mute, the sense of touch remains the central medium of perception. A special feature of the human hand, which has evolved over a million years of development history and has given us an advantage over all other primates, is the freely movable thumb.

[44]Dieter E. Zimmer explains his astonishment about the digitalisation in 1997 in his work "The Electrification of Language": *"I am always amazed anew at how human intellect has managed to abstract so many instructions that our brain gives, from the manipulation of alphanumeric characters to calculating, drawing, painting, the production of sounds and many other things, until they can be represented by a few simple logical operations on no more than two symbols" and then adds the following quote from Searle: "The amazing thing about computers is that any information expressible in a language can be encoded in such a system and any problem of information processing that can be solved with explicit rules can be programmed with it"* (Zimmer 1997, 37 f).

is usually limited to the information-technical functioning of algorithms in the context of digital data storage, analysis and transmission. Against this background, the question arises whether algorithms that serve only for machine data transmission, e.g. in smartphones, self-driving vehicles or robots, are also covered by the above-mentioned tool definition of media. For transformation processes that serve interpersonal communication via smartphones, this can be assumed.[45] In connection with fleet learning algorithms,[46] used for self-driving vehicles (more on this in third chapter), the restriction to interpersonal action already appears much less viable.[47] After all, Sandbothe's media concept encounters a definitional limit with robots that move autonomously in a predefined system (e.g. vacuum or lawn mowing robots), as the criterion of interpersonal action is then no longer fulfilled. Robots replace a human activity in such a case, but they do not coordinate any *interpersonal action*.

For an appropriate consideration of algorithms from the research area of *autonomous systems*[48] Sandbothe's criterion therefore seems of little help. But even independent of the discourse on autonomous systems and artificial intelligence it becomes apparent that interpersonal actions are not a condition of the possibility of algorithms. Algorithms exist, as we have already seen, everywhere in nature—they are an inherent property of reality, the ideational and intellectual basis of constant becoming and unrestricted passing—however, *we* need media to describe and understand these natural processes. The media manifestation of natural processes marks a turning point: Because with the help of media, natural developments, processes, and phenomena become anthropogenic algorithms.

1.4.2 What Do Algorithms Describe?

Building on the differentiation between natural and anthropogenic algorithms, a further distinction can be introduced, i.e. the distinction between reality and virtuality. Algorithmics provides, as already extensively explained, a formal sign system to virtualise reality. This virtual reality is not a value-free sphere. Although

---

[45]To deny digital communication and distribution media the media status due to punctual interruptions by machine information transformations would be counterintuitive and difficult to explain for that reason alone. The machine data transmission ultimately acts as a *media tool* for human communication processes and remains embedded in this context.

[46]Fleet Learning (English for "fleet" or "fleet" and "learning process") is a method used to optimise the control unit of self-driving vehicles. In the so-called "shadow mode", driving data from networked vehicles are collected and analysed to train the AI software of the vehicles. More on this in the next chapter.

[47]All systems currently on the market still require the intervention of a human driver in certain situations (SAE-Level 1-3). However, research is already at the transition from SAE-Level 3 (conditional autopilot) to SAE-Level 4 (highly automated), where appropriate intervention by the vehicle-leading person is no longer intended, but can occur after system request. When SAE-Level 5 (fully autonomous driving) is reached, then no intervention (action necessity) of a human vehicle-leading person is intended anymore.

[48]Weber (2018) rightly refers to the terminological and conceptual confusions associated with attributing autonomy and morality to machines. In an attempt to keep the conceptual effort low at this point, this issue will be further discussed.

science is oriented towards the ideal of value neutrality and objectivity (see above), fallibility is a property of humans, not of machines, algorithms or data. Even the ancient Greeks (e.g. Theognis, Sophocles, Euripides) and the Romans (e.g. Cicero, Jerome) knew: "To err is human (lat. *errare humanum est*)", "Mistakes cling to mortal men" (gr. *ἁμαρτωλαὶ … ἐν ἀνθρώποισιν ἕπονται θνητοῖς …*), "To err in nothing is a property of the gods (gr. *μηδὲν ἁμαρτεῖν ἐστι θεῶν …*)" (Büchmann 1898, pp. 257–258). These old sayings describe a fundamental characteristic of being human. To give the insight of epistemological anthropology an irrefutable authority, Goethe therefore put the words into God's mouth in the prologue of Faust: "Man errs as long as he strives" (Goethe 1808, V.317). Through human efforts, so the thesis goes, errors and deceptions can never be completely excluded. This insight is legitimized from Antigone to Faust therefore from a divine standpoint. An objective perspective requires, in the words of Thomas Nagel (1986), a "view from nowhere". However, man is a social being, embedded in a cultural context. His behavioural and thinking habits are also dependent on his physical and mental constitution. Even in meditation and the in the realm of intellectual reflection, we are always amidst our own perception process. We cannot fully understand ourselves detached from our senses and our physicality (cf. Nagel 2016).

The failure of this external perspective has a cognitive dimension and is henceforth referred to as cognitive bias (A total of 187 cognitive biases have been compiled by the Institute for Media and Communication Management at the University of St. Gallen (according to their own statements) with regard to human decision-making in an interactive visualisation.[49] All these cognitive biases and prejudices, which have been systematically researched by psychology—especially by Tversky and Kahneman (1974; 1984)—and introduced to a broad audience (especially Kahneman 2012), are essentially considered avoidable thinking errors. Leibniz went even further in the analysis of cognitive thinking errors—two years before his death he wrote in a letter to Rémond: *"Errors (except the actual ones) are nothing but calculation errors"* (Leibniz quoted after Krämer 1988, p. 104). As elaborated above, the promise of modernity was primarily that certain errors can be avoided with technical-scientific rationality. Because at least about some objects and facts we could, according to the optimist Leibniz, acquire infallible knowledge. He had in mind especially the subject area of algorithmics. In a first step, he aimed to develop a universal formal language (lat. *characteristica universalis*) to capture the concepts and relationships of the real world symbolically (see above). In the second step, in his view, a rulebook (lat. *calculus ratiocinator*) would then be found, with which the truth value of statements can be calculated mechanically. Since Leibniz recognised the importance of a formal language for the precision of algorithmic thinking and action and the possibility of schematic operation with symbols (following the model of arithmetic), he is considered a precursor of modern logic and computer technology.

Computer science as the science of machine processing, storage, transmission and representation of information primarily deals with the mathematical and

---

[49]Available online at https://bias-map-v1.web.app.

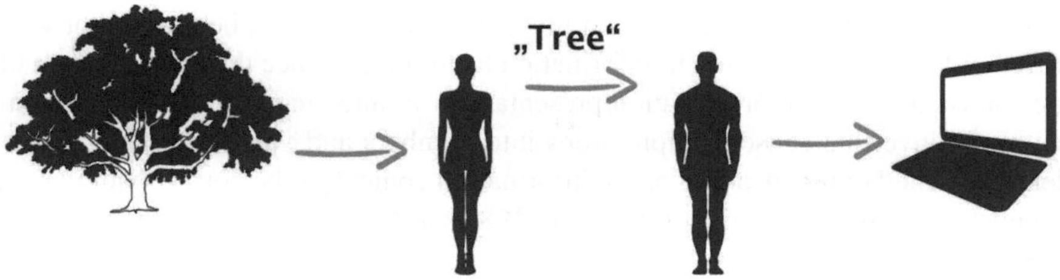

Fig. 13 Mapping of sensory impressions in representation systems (Image source: Author's own illustration)

physical representation of information. The representation of information in computer science is achieved through schematic representations (data and object structures) and their relationships to each other, the rules and regulations (algorithms) for processing the data. The possibility of outsourcing algorithmic thinking and action to artificial artefacts is based on the phenomenon that the information content can be separated from the external form of the information (cf. Broy 1998, pp. 3–29). This phenomenon can be illustrated by a thought experiment according to Küchlin and Weber (2003, p. 6): An observer has a physical sensory impression (the perception of a tree) and communicates this through the linguistic expression "tree" to another person (see Fig. 13). The conversion of the sensory impression into the string of characters "tree" happens in humans depending on the respective language community (e.g.: "tree", "arbre", "árbol", "Дерево", "树" etc.).

A central task of computer science consists in abstraction and model building or in the selection and determination of suitable representation systems ("languages"), with the aim of describing the "essential structures, relationships and processes of an application area" (Broy 1998, p. 3). In relation to computers, the number format (especially in binary systems) has proven to be particularly powerful for the representation of human impressions or expressions. For example, using the Latin ASCII alphabet[50] the German term "Baum" can be translated into the binary sequence "01000010011000010111010101101101" which in turn can be represented by a physical state ("OFF, ON, OFF, OFF, OFF, [. . .]") in the memory space of computers.[51] This process of converting sensory impressions into signs and symbols that can be interpreted and further processed by machines, because they can be described as a mapping of values to numbers or as a mathematical function, is commonly referred to as digitisation in everyday language.

It has already been pointed out that the phenomenon of digitisation cannot be limited to the current assignment to a binary number system. Therefore, the focus is not on the digital values, but on the "given" (lat. *datum*) or on the responsibility in dealing with the given data. The example shows that the representation of things,

[50] B = 01000010, a = 01100001, u = 01110101, m = 01101101.

[51] As for the question of whether the binary digit sequence or the physical state in the storage space of machines contains the same information as the human sensory impression, reference is made here to the problem of qualia (see, for example, Ludlow et al. 2004).

facts or circumstances (depending on the task or problem) can be realised at very different levels of abstraction in information technology. Since the external form of the information (the representation/presentation) is interchangeable, the phenomenon of converting sensory impressions into numbers and values works independently of whether the meaning or the information content of the corresponding data is understood by the recipient (cf. Searle 1980 on the philosophical debate of this phenomenon).

Understanding a message, according to Broy (1998, p. 4 f), requires both the recognition of the meaning of information as well as the establishment of the reference to the real world and the evaluation of the truth content, which is why in computer science a careful distinction is made between i) the "representation or presentation (the external form) of information", ii) the "meaning (the actual "abstract" information)", iii) the "reference to the real world (which aspects of reality are referred to)" and iv) the "validity of the information", i.e. the question of the truth of information.

1.4.3 What Is the Purpose of Algorithms?

Value systems are of central importance for the representation, estimation and evaluation (assessment) of information in very different contexts. Thus, the interpretation, structuring and ordering of values can be carried out according to mathematical (truth values) or physical aspects (signal or measurement variables); but it can also be done according to economic, political, religious, historical, aesthetic or ethical criteria. If algorithms were exclusively an invention of humans, a conceptual-technical construct that can be used by humans as a tool, then only the changing horizon of meaning of the algorithm concept would remain to be analysed, which results from the interplay between the change in social practices and technical artefacts. An algorithm ethics could then focus entirely on the application context and the use scenarios of algorithms per se, i.e. on the question of how humans *should* use algorithms *(tools)*. Consequently, the heading of this section should read: What do *we aim to achieve with* algorithms?

Building on the distinctions made so far between i) natural and anthropogenic algorithms and ii) reality and virtuality, a further distinction can be introduced at this point between iii) epistemic and moral errors or transgressions.

According to traditional understanding of ethics, moral transgressions (iii) can only be attributed to anthropogenic algorithms (i). We usually do not refer to natural laws as immoral. To describe the workings of natural processes and sequences as moral transgressions only appears plausible in the history of philosophy under the assumption of a divine world ruler and leads to the so-called theodicy question, i.e., the question of the justification or justice of God in the face of suffering in the world. This is associated with the assumption that natural algorithms could be influenced, altered, steered or controlled by a divine will.

Due to his creativity and especially his unique ability for abstraction and reflection, as explained above, the human being occupies a special position in the natural system of algorithmic self-organisation. On the one hand, he succeeds in reflecting certain processes in nature—from reality via abstraction to theory and from theory back to reality via experiment. When describing natural processes, the aim is primarily to avoid epistemic errors. For this, it is necessary to adhere to the so-called diligence rules of the scientific community (data collection as objective as possible and intersubjective verifiability of the results etc.). On the other hand, human beings have always also aimed to overcome mere observation of nature and to penetrate the basic structure and normative order of the cosmos with their own dimensions of meaning. So the human being is not only concerned with a theoretical description of reality, i.e., to infer certain events in the future from data of the past and present. Rather, he is also looking for algorithms to actively shape the virtually possible. By putting himself in a normative-desiring relationship to his own goals, desires and ideas, however, he always also exposes himself to the risk of moral transgression.

Driven by the assumption that every conceivable problem can be solved by an algorithmic solution procedure, the human being, in the so-called Anthropocene, finally takes the reins of action. In doing so, he obviously ignores the mathematical limits of computability and interprets not only the scientific-technical rationality of the natural sciences as a sub-area of algorithmics, but also the pragmatic rationality of ethics aimed at action. Apparently, the directional tendency of algorithmics thus leads via trans- and posthumanism to technological singularity and to the utopia that we could someday create a just God for ourselves with the help of artificial intelligence (AI) to banish evil from the world.

The boundary between an *ethics for algorithms* and an *ethics of algorithms* is fluid for laypeople—if only because the functioning of algorithms already eludes many people (cf. Grzymek and Puntschuh 2019). Insofar as the medium, i.e., the algorithms that enable data and information exchange, cannot be directly perceived by the users, it already applies: “From countability, computability and controllability become [. . .] unmanageability, incalculability and unpredictability” (Schuldt 2019). On closer inspection, of course, it can be determined that it is still people who determine the use and functioning of algorithms. In the context of self-learning systems, however, this assessment must be viewed more differentiated. Because the developers often only set the initial conditions and then later go on a search for clues themselves to understand the functioning of the machine. *“The development of features is supported by machine learning algorithms that automatically generate thousands of derived variables”*. (Baer 2019, p. 45).

The increasing automation allows self-learning algorithms to adapt the initial selection criteria and selection mechanisms through the interaction processes with the users in a certain self-dynamics or to optimise towards a specific goal. This feedback process is referred to, drawing on Jaume-Palasí and Spielkamp (2017, p. 2), as the “collective dimension of algorithms”. Some algorithms, as will be shown, constitute an increasingly intransparent reality, as the complexity of the emerging information spaces already exceeds human comprehension in some application areas.[52] *“The storage space of the database becomes opaque for the*

[52]This is illustrated by the conclusion of the two data scientists Yoav Goldberg and Omer Levy on Mikolov et al.’s “Word-2-Vector methodology”: “Why does this produce good word representations? Good question. We don’t really know” (Goldberg and Levy 2014, p. 5).

searcher; it is a black box, against which search queries are formulated, which the computer automatically translates into results" (Burkhardt 2015, p. 248). A central complex of questions that can be linked to this observation addresses the social effects and impacts of such a development, e.g. on the classic understanding of autonomy and digital self-determination: Do basic criteria for ensuring personal autonomy, such as the transparency, control and authenticity condition (see Koska 2015b, p. 86 f), meet entirely new prerequisites? Whose will be done? Who are the actors of moral action in the context of such algorithms and which concept of algorithms underlies a certain evaluation?

Is algorithmics just a means to an end? Or an end in itself? Do algorithms follow a purpose at all? What do we use algorithms for and what should we use them for? The question of the purpose of algorithmics is to be distinguished from the question of the meaning of algorithmics. Especially with regard to trans- and posthumanistic fantasies and the successive merging of humans with technology[53] the intrinsic relationship of humans to the media tools must not be ignored: Analogous to language, where the meanings of terms are also media-dependent—"who wants to know, *what* they say, must ask, *how* they say it" (Münker 2003, p. 16). In addition to the context-related use of an algorithm (i.e. a functional tool), the *inner reality* of the machine and the *collective dimension* of algorithms must also be critically questioned—by also asking about the "conditions of the possibility of X" (Sandbothe 2003, p. 195), i.e. the media-apriori function of algorithms.

The media-philosophical examination of the ethical, epistemic and ontological dimensions of algorithms shows that a delimitation of the subject area of algorithm ethics is an already difficult, but hardly manageable task through purely conceptual effort. To preface this confession to the interim conclusion is not an excuse to prevent failure, but to draw attention to the limitations of the available means.

2 Interim Conclusion: On the Subject Area of Algorithm Ethics

After the ideological and intellectual historical roots have been exposed the media-philosophical preliminary considerations have now also prepared the conceptual and theoretical access to an ethics of algorithms. There are various standards for the evaluation of algorithms: i) To avoid epistemic errors, a comparison with reality is required and ii) to avoid ethical misconduct, it is advisable to align with prevailing moral concepts. We determine the former with a judgement of knowledge as "right or wrong", the latter we evaluate as "good or bad" or as "good or evil" towards certain individuals, for a society, the environment etc.

With regard to the ethos of algorithmics, the following chapter asks whether, with the progressive outsourcing of rational and goal-oriented thinking to artificial

[53]According to the American anthropologist Amber Case (2010), due to the all-encompassing network, we are all cyborgs already.

artefacts, the need is also increasing to develop an algorithmic ethics not only for the handling of human actors with digital media, but to make ethics itself machine-operable. Therefore, not only normative guidelines for developers, operators and users of corresponding products are sought, but also control mechanisms that *"are to 'watch over' third algorithms as an ethical instance"* (Jaume-Palasí and Spielkamp 2017, p. 5).

But to what degree can such control mechanisms really control themselves? Can algorithms change *independently* at all? Are we already on the threshold of another media revolution—from natural and anthropogenic algorithms to machine-generated algorithms? Can it be ruled out on principle that an Artificial Intelligence (AI) created by us will someday develop its own will? If it succeeds in developing a strong AI, then sooner or later at least the question would arise as to whether or to what extent the two spheres "media" and "philosophy" intertwine. For example, Bringsjord and Govindarajulu (2018) hold the view: *"If one were to attempt to engineer a robot with a capacity for sophisticated ethical reasoning and decision-making, one would also be doing Philosophical AI."*

Like the term media philosophy, the term algorithm ethics also connects "two spheres that may not be connectable at all; the phase of transition alone justifies the title", as Hartmann (2000, p. 13) states in the media context. The transition that he seeks to prepare through his "integrative view of the media revolution" (ibid. p. 14) is the connecting element between these two spheres, which he characterises as the "co-evolution of media and society in technoculture" (ibid.). Almost twenty years after this first systematic approach to the media concept, media philosophy is still not a recognised discipline in the canon of philosophy. Thus, to this day, there are many media philosophical texts that stand more or less unsystematically side by side.[54] For a first approach to the subject area of algorithm ethics, media philosophical considerations are quite helpful. Thus, we can now distinguish the ontological, the epistemic and the ethical dimension of algorithmics from each other. A demarcation of the terms "digital, digitisation, digitality" as well as "data or datafication" has already been prepared regarding the ideational and intellectual historical reference frame: the former primarily refers to a certain methodology for outsourcing algorithmic thinking and action to artificial artefacts, the latter essentially describes a temporal manifestation and thus an intermediate state of algorithmisation. We have also shown that the underdetermined properties of the basic system of media also affect the further specification of the algorithm concept, and that the question of the condition of possibility or the media-apriori function of algorithms, especially regarding a strong AI, seems to run into the void.

Against the background of this media philosophical positioning, the focus in the following will now be on the ethos of algorithmic thinking and action. As already has been hinted at several times, the question of whether algorithms are taking over the control and regulation of humans is already extremely present in public perception. There are already plenty of indications for this, as many believe—from

[54]This development was already announced by the anthology "Media Philosophy" by Münker et al. (2003).

the increasing dependence on algorithmic processes in work and everyday life to the Citizen Score in China.[55] So the question would be quite independent of the condition of the possibility of an artificial moral consciousness, what effects and impacts algorithms already have on our human self-understanding: *"Code is law"* as Lessig proclaimed as early as 1999. Algorithms are normative, but they do not set norms for themselves, one would like to add immediately. For the mere supposed "phase of transition" (Hartmann 2000, p. 14), commonly referred to as disruption, does not mean that it would be technically possible or (as proclaimed by trans- and posthumanism) even desirable to develop so-called "Artificial Moral Agents" that would guide the future of human existence.

3 The Ethos of Algorithmic Thinking and Action

In common parlance, the term ethos is understood as a "mindset shaped by the consciousness of moral values", as a "total attitude" that rests in an "ethical consciousness".[56] The ethos provides the normative framework for moral behaviour towards fellow human beings (clients, citizens, patients, etc.), but also towards nature and oneself (cf. Höffe 2008, p. 211). According to Honnefelder (2011, p. 508), the discourse on morality and ethos derives its meaning from the insight *"that human action, due to its intentionality, always takes place under a sense of direction, be it—as in the case of theoretical cognition—under that of true or false, be it—as in the case of technical production—under that of right or wrong, be it—as in the case of artistic creation—under that of beautiful or ugly."*

The directional sense (German *Richtungssinn*) to which Honnefelder refers here, thus relates to the human ability to orient oneself towards a specific goal—but not in the sense of spatial orientation, when one asks for the direction North-northeast (NNE) or the way from Augsburg to Berlin (A → B)—but with reference to inner convictions: The discourse on morality and ethos therefore derives its meaning from the knowledge-guiding, the ethical and the aesthetic reasons for action of a certain person or a certain group of people.

When we ask about the ethos of algorithmic thinking and action, we therefore presuppose the existence of a "knower", i.e. a person with an ethical and aesthetic consciousness. Based on the results from the previous chapter, the ethos of algorithmic thinking and action will be determined in the following based on the directional tendency. First, the "accustomed place of life" (Höffe 2018, p. 9) or the "geographical ethos" (ibid. p. 10) of the ethical consciousness will be reflected, then the myth of the value neutrality of scientific knowledge will be rejected,

[55]In these examples, however, the norm-setting is done by humans and not by machines, as we will see in the following chapter.

[56]Particularly against the background of moral guidelines, which define action-guiding customs or moralities for different professional fields, the talk of the so-called professional ethos, such as the craftsman's, civil servant's, or doctor's ethos, is widespread, see Duden online: https://www.duden.de/node/653856/revisions/1992596/view.

then the vision of the algorithmic solution of moral problems will be outlined and the ideal of a posthuman reason will be questioned. Finally, it will be asked whether or to what extent algorithm ethics can be narrowed down to an ethics for algorithmists.

3.1 The Logos as the Geographical Place of Algorithmic Thinking

Against the background of Western philosophy, a key for understanding algorithmic thinking and action is already contained in the mathematical-scientific aspects of the early Greek concept of logos (λόγος), as Perilli (2013a) suggests with his anthology[57]:

> *"The logos allows a manipulation of the well-founded reality, for which the weak stands behind the strong and the small behind the great, and reverses the power relations. 'Ratio', 'composition' and 'connection' are the decisive levels of meaning of the Greek logos; a mathematical valence that transforms the logos, also the logos of the statement - the discourse - to the relationship, the connection, the law, the element that connects the three temporal dimensions past, present, future with each other, that allows to relate one thing to another and to give the individual ἕκαστα, the data, meaning by putting them into a mutual relationship. Logos marks a dynamic, verifiable course"* (Perilli 2013b, p. 3 f).

According to Aristotle, the human being is the only living being (zóon) that possesses the lógos (Aristotle, Politics I,2; 1253 a 10, quoted from Haeffner 2005, p. 57). Whereas λόγος in the context of this statement according to Haeffner is to be translated as "language". As outlined above, algorithms—in more or less precise form—have existed as long as there are human languages. Since there are many languages and probably also completely different forms of languages that are already extinct today, among these many "none is 'the' true language in which reality itself is represented" (ibid. p. 59). The spoken language, whose "primary medium are the sounds produced in tremendous variability with the help of the vocal apparatus" (ibid. p. 62), was increasingly ordered and structured by signs, symbols, pictograms etc. up to the written language, so that man could further systematise his experiences and observations about the most diverse facts. Against the background of the formalisation and outsourcing of algorithmic thinking, it is important to note that the increasingly reductionist character remains conscious: *"It should also be mentioned that all artificial*

[57] *"The decision to bring together and make accessible to the reader the most important and often overlooked contributions was based on the observation that modern mathematicians have seen in the concept of the Logos not only the key to once again—following Toeplitz—provide an adequate interpretation of main questions of ancient philosophy such as Plato's theory of ideas, Heraclitus' doctrine of the Logos and the theological meaning of the Logos concept, but also to understand some concepts and methods of modern mathematics and computer science more deeply. In this, a spiritual continuity can be seen; a bridge is built between different epochs and areas of knowledge, enabling mutual inspiration."* (Perilli 2013a, p. VIII).

languages, such as those of mathematics and logic, or the programming languages for computer software, are notation systems and thus presuppose and continue to refine (i.e. *cutting away and sharpening) the process of writing"* (ibid. p. 63).

The theological intertwining of the logos concept resonates not only in the introductory words of al-Ḫwārizmī[58], but also in the prologue of the Gospel of John, as Perilli (2013b, p. 1) notes:

> *In the beginning was the Logos*
> *and the Logos was with God*
> *and the Logos was God.*
> *In the beginning he was with God.*
> *All things were made through him*
> *and without him nothing became what has become.*

The pattern that emerges in algorithmic thinking as a guiding orientation instance, consists in a certain way of, peeling back layer by layer of mystical thinking (see above). The sober recognition of what can be mathematically described (and mechanised) and what cannot, became both the foundation and the ethos of the natural sciences. The (academic) reason developed (not least through Kant) into a decisive reference point for the Greek expression λόγος. Logic, which is of central importance for the information technology outsourcing of algorithmic thinking to artificial artefacts, has emerged from the ancient Greek concept of logos. From anthropology to cosmology and ecology to zoology and cytology (= the study of cell structure), the term is still found in the ending of numerous scientific disciplines. Logical (lawful) thinking is therefore not just any scientific research method, but—from a natural science-reductive point of view—in a certain sense itself an ethic.

The complexity of the concept of ethics is shown according to Höffe (2018) already in the etymological ambiguity of the term: "ta êthika, as the discipline was named by its originator, Aristotle, refers to the things concerning the êthos" (ibid. p. 9). Höffe distinguishes three meanings, of which only the first interests us at this point: the geographical ethos, which he translates as "the usual place of life" (ibid.). In this context, Höffe describes using the example of livestock and fish, how the ethos of animals changes through domestication (e.g. natural pasture or man-made artificial stable), and to what extent this change raises the ethical evaluation question (which of the possibilities is good or bad?) (cf. ibid.). Analogous to this explanation, the geographical ethos of algorithmic thinking and action—in modern understanding—can be located in the distinguishing and precise reason (λόγος).

With regard to the outsourcing of algorithmic thinking and action to electronic spaces, the reduction of the concept of reason to technical-scientific rationality, however, poses a danger, as one *"when considering purely dividing and enumerating computing processes, as well as in the case of a computer that performs millions of elementary arithmetic operations [...] one might possibly be*

[58]Muḥammad Ibn-Mūsā al-Ḫwārizmī cites as the origin and source the "wisdom and knowledge of God the Lord" (see the introductory words of "Algoritmi de numeris indorum" in the codex of Salem Monastery in Sect. 1.1).

confronted with the most barren, mechanical and uncreative aspect of reason" as Zellini (2013, p. 188) also notes. And further: *"It would mean betraying the ambiguity of the logos (sic!) if one wanted to limit the semantic range of influence on the mechanical computing process"* (ibid.).[59]

That the translation of the term "λόγος" into modern times is a difficult undertaking is also attested by Goethe's Faust. In his search for the principle "that I may learn what holds the world together in its inmost core" (Goethe 1808, trans. Taylor 1870, l. 382), Faust seeks to free himself from all belief in authority and especially the shackles of biblical tradition (see Prologue of the Gospel of John above):

> *'Tis written: "In the Beginning was the Word."*
> *Here am I balked: who, now can help afford?*
> *The Word? – impossible so high to rate it;*
> *And otherwise must I translate it.*
> *If by the Spirit I am truly taught.*
> *Then thus: "In the Beginning was the Thought"*
> *This first line let me weigh completely,*
> *Lest my impatient pen proceed too fleetly.*
> *Is it the Thought which works, creates, indeed?*
> *"In the Beginning was the Power," I read.*
> *Yet, as I write, a warning is suggested,*
> *That I the sense may not have fairly tested.*
> *The Spirit aids me: now I see the light!*
> *"In the Beginning was the Act," I write.*
> (ibid., ll. 1224–1237)

The act, which modern scientists are concerned with (and Faust would like to see himself as such), is the scientific experiment (cf. Laube 1984, p. 74). The experimentality conveys the mechanical principles of nature through the collection and analysis of data, with the help of which the *facts* can be mathematically reflected and described in the form of algorithms. By focusing on the measurement of quantitative relationships and the focus on technical rationality, the—in early Greek usage still—existing connection of "λόγος" with "deception" and "misleading" (see e.g. Boeder 2013, p. 214 ff) is often overlaid.[60] For *"what exactly makes the calculation of numbers, which can provide plausible information about the*

[59]The complexity of the classical Greek concept of Logos is already pointed out by ancient authors (see e.g. Perilli 2013b, pp. 6–12). As it is not possible within the scope of this study to follow all the branches in the network of meanings, the interested reader is referred for a quick overview to the entry "λόγος" in the "Liddell-Scott-Jones Greek-English" dictionary (online: http://stephanus.tlg.uci.edu/lsj), which, with its "semantic structure" (Perilli 2013b, p. 8), provides a good introduction to the classical understanding of the concept.

[60]Specifically in connection with the literary work of Goethe, but also against the background of his scientific activities, a criticism of the paradigm of the causal-analytical method, which is widespread to this day, becomes particularly clear, which is generally summarised under the term "reductionism". Ernst-Michael Kranich notes on this: *"Goethe knew this way of proceeding [Note: of modern natural science] and noticed that it left certain phenomena of reality unconsidered, so that they also disappeared in the reconstruction of reality and thus vanished from consciousness"* (Höfer 1990, p. 8).

structure of the physical, biological and economic world as well as the mathematical universe itself, possible or impossible, real or illusory?" (Zellini 2013, p. 188).

With regard to the concept of "digitalisation", it has already been pointed out that the phenomenon that lies behind this term cannot be adequately captured by assigning facts to a binary number system. The binary code is certainly better suited as a tool for automatic information processing than the Roman finger counting system (lat. *computare digitis* "counting, calculating on the fingers") or the Indian number system, which spread in Europe via al-Ḫwārizmī (lat. *Algoritmi*). However, research is now also being conducted on quantum computers which combine both states (1–0) in a single storage space (lat. *datum*), the so-called Qubit.

> *"Even mechanical calculation, like the word, can lead to deception. The logos always refers to a kind of relationship or transition, for example from the continuous to the discrete, or from the designation to the thing. And indeed, the factual character of the algorithms and the materialisation in physical processes are based on complex theories that explain how a transition from mathematical models of nature to simple, numerical information or columns of numbers that appear in the memory of a computer can be realised. But more essential than the practical realisation of this possibility is the exploration the same. The computer in and of itself is less interesting and problematic than the science that investigates the reasons for which one might advise (or possibly also discourage) the use of the computer"* (Zellini 2013, p. 188).

As well as it seems to work in practice: The outsourcing and relocation of the geographical location of algorithmic thinking to silicon leads to a devaluation of the concept of reason, as the semantic reduction of λόγος to an abstract interiority in the machine obscures the significance of embodiment and the importance of human emotionality for the existence of an ethical consciousness.

3.2 On the Value Neutrality of Scientific Knowledge

The ideal of value neutrality is often taken for granted as an epistemological requirement in science. Subjective states, such as emotions, are to be avoided in science: Because *"emotions distort the view of things. In emotional states, we tend to form beliefs that we consider false in a balanced state. Emotions are unreliable. They are therefore not appropriate reasons for beliefs"* (Niederbacher 2013, p. 219), so a widespread objection. Why should emotions play a role in this context?

The code of conduct of modern natural science was in the 17th and 18th century aimed at the exploration of *facts* (see, among others, the quote from Goethe's Faust in the last section). Facts and circumstances can be particularly well discovered through experiments wherever a causally determined order of reality can be objectively observed and its structure can be described intersubjectively. With reference to the distinction between the question "What is?" (factual level) and the question "What should be?" (evaluation level), algorithm ethics thus aligns with the sectoral ethics of research, science and technology ethics. Just as in technology ethics, it is primarily not about the observation of natural processes and phenomena that exist independently of humans and can be verified using the experimental method (i.e., natural laws).[61]

The focus of public debate is currently mainly on the anthropogenic (i.e., artificially developed by humans for the computer) algorithms. Although a computer can be an object of the natural scientific research method, this distinction is important with regard to the ethical evaluation of algorithms: Because it seems to us to make little sense to describe natural laws as immoral, as already outlined in the context of the media-philosophical systematisation. But if we locate the geographical ethos (i.e., "the usual place of life") of algorithms in λόγος and limit this term to an activity of human reason, then of course the binding norms of the *Scientific Community* also apply to the description of the internal lawful relationships. According to Graumann (2011, p. 254), these primarily include the "rules of diligence", which refer to "as objective as possible data collection and their intersubjective verification".

Essentially, for the empirically working sciences, it is about the practice or adherence to a certain scientific research method that ensures the reliability of scientific knowledge. On the pure factual level, scientific knowledge or reliable knowledge is therefore the highest value of researchers.[62] The assumption that one could separate the factual level from the evaluative level is, however, a well-known fallacy that is occasionally still advocated today, for example in the form: "Technology is neutral—it all depends on its use." This fallacy can be quickly deconstructed under the premise that scientific knowledge should be determined as the terminal value of the scientific ethos. If the search for scientific knowledge determines the actions and behaviour (the morals) of the researchers, there can be no talk of value neutrality, insofar as the pursuit of scientific knowledge is then evaluated as good or better than all other motives for action. If such knowledge, as the highest value, were to be subordinated to everything else, then everything would be legitimate as long as it serves the goal of increasing knowledge—e.g. also the development of a technology based on scientific knowledge from a contemptuous human experiment.

[61]According to Kreibich (1986, pp. 155 ff), the experimental method is characterised by three prescriptions: *"Firstly, by the abstraction from the concrete individual case to ideal conditions; the research object is—initially only theoretically—reduced to the methodically essential properties. Secondly, by the execution of controlled experiments; only certain properties of the research object are observed and measured. Thirdly, by the formalised generalisation; the determined properties are quantitatively recorded and mathematically or graphically represented"* (Graumann 2011, p. 253).

[62]The distinction between true and false is actually only possible with algorithms in the strict sense. Because heuristics as they are found in AI, only allow a purely statistical statement about a certain fact. In practice, the statistical results of an AI (e.g. when further processed by another system or by humans) are often understood or interpreted as if they were true or false, even though the technology does not fulfil this claim.

At this point, technical-scientific rationality must be extended by pragmatic rationality, which manifests itself in the human ability for moral knowledge. Why are emotions important in this context? "Emotions are value experiences that feel a certain way" (Niederbacher 2013, p. 217); and although *"one often has to reckon with false or distorted value data in the field of emotions [. . .] emotions often indicate something true, even if we don't want to admit it and gloss over it with rationalisations"* (ibid. p. 220).

The scientific ethos is not a value-neutral framework of action that frees researchers from their own moral concerns in their actions. If the integrity and dignity of people (or other living beings, such as animals, but also the balance of nature, society, etc.) is concretely violated by the modelling of a certain algorithm, then with every decision for or against the modelling of this algorithm we are already directly on the evaluative level—the perception of our affective states can help us to become aware of this.

In this context, it should be noted that a minimum degree of action or free will was implicitly assumed for the human being (in our example the scientific researchers). Otherwise, if the human being had no free action options, and the researchers themselves were always already *hard-wired* for a certain behaviour, which runs analogously to a strictly determined natural law, any ethics would be a pointless endeavour. Only by assuming that the human being has the ability to put himself in a normative-desiring relationship to his own goals, i.e. he is able to align his actions with self-chosen values, is a moral debate about this action or value framework conceivable. The ideal of reliable and secured knowledge would then be considered a valuable means, but not the terminal purpose of science.

3.3 On the Machine Simulation of an Ethical Consciousness

After a strict separation between technical-scientific rationality (factual level) and pragmatic rationality (ethics) has been rejected, it is necessary to determine how the relationship between these two entities, including buzzwords such as "Artificial Intelligence (AI)", "Quantum Computing", "Digital Enhancement", "Singularity" or "Transhumanism", can be further determined.

How valuable the ideal of reliable and secured knowledge is becomes apparent when it seems to be at risk. Especially in understanding what an observation and what an experiment is, quantum physics requires a radical rethink compared to classical physics, for example: a strict distinction must be made between "observation (measurement) and experiment", as Laube (1984, pp. 74 f) clarifies with reference to Tanabe.[63] The algorithms that describe nature at the macroscopic level

[63] *"Observation does not change the phenomenon. If the phenomenon changes during a so-called observation, it was not an observation, but an experiment. Observation is measuring the quantitative relationships of phenomena that are the same at the end of the measurement as at the beginning of the measurement. However, the experiment involves us producing something through our experimental setups (e.g. apparatus) that was not yet present in reality, or at least was not yet present in this way. Therefore, the experiment has the function of changing reality, or even creating reality"* (Laube 1984, pp. 74–75).

of classical physics are no longer suitable for describing the fuzzy and indeterminate states in the quantum world. Since in the smallest of things only probabilities established a priori can be determined, the rational methodology of quantum mechanics and thus the scientific procedure (due to the primarily deductive methodology) differs from the primarily empirical statistics of classical mechanics (cf. ibid. p. 106). *"Beyond every human experience, quantum mechanics deals with the material roots of nature, that is, it is a fundamental theory that cannot be compared with any other mathematical model of physics"* (Lesch 2015, Chap. 2).

According to Lesch (2008, 33:00), the digital world is a quantum mechanical world. *"The underlying idea is that energetic processes at the level of the building blocks of matter never occur continuously, but always in discrete, indivisible packets, the quanta—hence the name 'quantum mechanics'"* (Lesch 2015, Chap. 2).[64]

Where classical supercomputers fail due to the complexity of certain tasks, quantum computers could potentially (so a widespread hope) find a solution: "quantum mechanical machines will be needed for AI (artificial intelligence) to match biological intelligence" (Kak 2007, p. 81).[65] While practical quantum computing is still in its infancy, recent advancements have reinforced hopes and intensified debates regarding its potential role in future AI development, especially in overcoming computational limits of classical machine learning algorithms (Preskill 2023). If the opacity of neural networks, quantum computers and self-learning algorithms is primarily justified by the fact that their depth dimension is comparable to the physical processes and phenomena on the human cerebral cortex, then it seems appropriate to question the ontological status of our moral consciousness. The analogy between computer and brain is, as already explained above, a motif that has consistently accompanied the history of modern algorithmics from René Descartes via Gottfried Wilhelm Leibniz and Alan Turing to modern AI research. In practice, however, the aim was less to replicate the entire spectrum of natural intelligence in all its facets, but rather to select individual aspects to specifically improve natural intelligence through artificial intelligence.

The ethos of algorithmic thinking and action is still driven by the belief in unstoppable progress.[66] The hidden hope behind all the abstract terminology and

---

[64]The laws of quantum mechanics (wave-particle duality, Heisenberg's uncertainty principle and Pauli principle) form, as Lesch (ibid.) notes, the physical prerequisites for the digital revolution: *"More than a third of the world's gross social product is generated with quantum mechanics, for example through digital cameras, lasers, computers, photocells, semiconductor electronics, medical imaging procedures, X-ray machines and much more."*

[65]See e.g. also Google's Quantum Research Teams & Focus Areas: *"A research effort from Google AI that aims to build quantum processors and develop novel quantum algorithms to dramatically accelerate computational tasks for machine learning."* (Available online at: https://ai.google/research/teams/applied-science/quantum-ai).

[66]Francis Bacon already considered the idea of scientific progress as the elemental driving force: *"There is another significant and great cause why the sciences have advanced so little; it lies in the fact that the cart cannot possibly move forward properly if the goal itself is missing and not fixed. The true and right goal of the sciences, however, is to enrich human life with new inventions and means"* (Bacon 2013, p. 61).

buzzwords of supposed progress can be found, among other things, in the work "The Master Algorithm" by Domingos (2015, p. 25): *"All knowledge—past, present, and future—can be derived from data by a single, universal learning algorithm."*[67] However, recent discussions critically challenge this optimistic view by pointing out the inherent limitations of algorithmic knowledge generation, highlighting issues such as dataset bias, loss of context, and the limitations in algorithmically capturing tacit or embodied knowledge (Mitchell 2024).

The ethos of algorithmics—where êthos finally is understood as *"the totality of attitudes, beliefs and norms, which in the form of a more or less coherent, internally structured pattern by an individual actor or by a social group as binding instance of good and right action"* (Honnefelder 2011, p. 508)—ultimately consists in the assumption that every conceivable problem can be solved by an algorithmic solution procedure. From this perspective, not only the scientific-technical rationality of the natural sciences can be interpreted as a subarea of algorithmics, but also the pragmatic rationality of ethics aimed at action. Thus, the American philosopher Eric Dietrich (2011), for example, derives from humanity's inadequacy to behave sufficiently morally to seriously strive for the well-being of all life ("flourishing of all life", ibid. p. 31) on earth, a moral obligation to develop a "Homo Sapiens 2.0". Representing numerous technology enthusiasts, who have mainly gathered in Silicon Valley in the belief that all our problems could be solved with technical innovations, Dietrich ultimately advocates stepping down with dignity as soon as we manage to develop moral machines: *"[...] with the thought that we had finally done the best we could do"* (Dietrich 2011, p. 537).

For Dietrich, we even have a moral obligation to develop algorithms for machines that (unlike humans) are incapable of acting immorally. Dietrich refers to immoral behaviour as a kind of genetic defect of humanity, from which we can never fully escape. Since humans, as the only species, also have the (albeit limited) ability to behave morally, it is advisable for rational reasons ("born of good old-fashioned rationality", ibid. p. 531) to hand over our less than glorious rule over the planet to machines, which should then act as our moral superiors—and could constantly optimise themselves in this function.

Now, such currents certainly do not represent the convictions of all those actors who drive algorithmisation through digital innovations day by day. That is perfectly clear. Especially those who deal with the everyday problems of AI research usually critically distance themselves from such positions. However, the example shows that the strategy of inventing digital antidotes for human inadequacies could lead, among other things, to a restriction of personal autonomy. Regardless of whether the implementation of such a project would be technically possible, just thinking about it already illustrates *"how much the disruptive potential of digital technologies not only changes the values themselves, but also the methods and procedures to judge morally and act accordingly,* i.e. *to implement morality"* (Koska and Filipović 2017, p. 188).[68]

[67]For the temporal dimension of meaning of algorithms see Sect. 1.2.1.

[68]Further thoughts on this can be found in Koska and Filipović (2017, pp. 184–188).

The picture that transhumanists like Ray Kurzweil, Eric Dietrich and others paint describes a posthuman reason that is supposed to be superior to human reason through technological extensions. The values that transhumanists consider rational are summarised by Bostrom (2005, p. 13) in the following table (see Fig. 14).

The central motif or core value, from which all other values are derived, is found in Bostrom in the potentiality of scientific knowledge and especially in the possibility that science could explore transhumanist and posthumanist spheres to gradually dissolve human limits (such as ageing and dying, etc.). That scientific knowledge can diametrically oppose an ethic in which the human being is at the centre of all further considerations is shown in connection with trans- and posthumanism in an existential way. Because it is not the human being who is at the centre here, but the "hypothesis of technical perfection" (Bostrom 2018) of the human being.

These hypothetical future scenarios create a new religious horizon, which allegedly introduces the possibility for human self-perfection (see, for example, Sorgner 2018), to elevate him as a "Homo Deus" (Harari 2018) into the posthumanist sphere. *In the long run* however, he runs the risk of being robbed of his humanity in the process—firstly through the already mentioned restrictions on action and free will, and finally if the technological singularity occurs (because with the thesis of the technological singularity[69] a hypothetical point in time is referred to, from which humanity loses control over technology completely and no meaningful predictions about technological development are possible anymore, as machines from this point on constantly improve or optimise themselves at an increasing speed).

A look into the algebraic catastrophe theory of the French mathematician René Frédéric Thom provides a further hint on the extension of the concept of singularity. Thom used the theory of singularity to explain phenomena that occur abruptly, to describe, among other things, population fluctuations in biology, transitions of states of aggregation in physics or even the emergence of social conflicts in the social sciences. Against this background, singular events in mathematics are consequently also referred to as "catastrophes" (see Thom 1999).

According to a dystopian reading, the expression of technological singularity stands for a catastrophe that could occur just as abruptly and therefore could catch us unprepared (see Bostrom 2015), when the posthuman rationality of machines takes sole control over the fate of humanity. From the utopian perspective, the belief in the realisation of a technical superintelligence that could develop and enforce its own will, takes on eschatological features, which sometimes appear extremely grotesque.[70] in both cases, the ethos of algorithmic thinking and acting with these extreme positions leads to a quintessential human myth, the search for

[69]In physics, singularity generally refers to a "point at which the analytical expression for a physical quantity becomes infinite and/or at which the known physical laws lose their validity" (Brockhaus 2019).

[70]For example, former Google engineer and robotics expert Anthony Levandowski appears on the net as a kind of prophet, who wants to prepare humanity for a peaceful takeover by the machines and for this purpose has founded the "Way of the Future Church" which spreads creeds like this: *"We believe it may be important for machines to see who is friendly to their cause and who is not. We plan on doing so by keeping track of who has done what (and for how long) to help the*

TABLE OF TRANSHUMANIST VALUES

Core Value

- Having the opportunity to explore the transhuman and posthuman realms

Basic Conditions

- Global security
- Technological progress
- Wide access

Derivative Values

- Nothing wrong about "tampering with nature"; the idea of hubris rejected
- Individual choice in use of enhancement technologies
- Peace, international cooperation, anti-proliferation of WMDs
- Improving understanding (encouraging research and public debate; critical thinking; open-mindedness, scientific inquiry; open discussion of the future)
- Getting smarter (individually; collectively; and develop machine intelligence)
- Philosophical fallibility; willingness to reexamine assumptions as we go along
- Pragmatism; engineering-and entrepreneur-spirit; science
- Diversity (species, races, religious creeds, sexual orientations, life styles, etc.)
- Caring about the well-being of all sentience
- Saving lives (life-extension, anti-aging research, and cryonics)

Fig. 14 Overview of transhumanist values according to Bostrom (2005, p. 13)

the path of redemption, which leads us from finiteness to immortality (see, for example, Hilt 2010).

However, the question remains, what is supposed to be left of humanity in the end: What is posthuman reason? Pure spirit? A bodiless λόγος, which can be transferred to any hardware at will? Because ultimately, especially the human body

---

peaceful and respectful transition." Available online at http://www.wayofthefuture.church (accessed on 28.02.2019).

in transhumanism is seen as a very decisive weakness, as man in his current state of development in this universe can only survive in a very limited range; he lives on Earth like on an apple skin, larger elevations quickly lead to shortness of breath and altitude sickness, leaving the Earth's atmosphere is just as impossible without an oxygen supply as is diving. But even if we decide for a life on the "apple peel" (which we can't in the long run as the Earth is known not to exist forever) we age and die, we have a limited perception and an extremely unreliable memory and therefore fall prey to deceptions, illusions and prejudices—the human body is therefore perceived by post- and transhumanists as a great imposition on personal freedom.

Unlike the major world religions, the "new human agenda" (Harari 2018, pp. 9–111) no longer locates salvation in a transcendent world beyond, but believes in overcoming our biological barriers with the help of self-learning machines. The enhancement of our cognitive abilities through technical enhancement requires, as Fuchs points out with reference to Persson and Savulescu (2012), also a moral enhancement. However, corporeality is often the prerequisite for all moral Judgements:

> *"Of course, the Golden Rule, Kant's moral law or the idea of the unconditional go beyond our primary needs. But without the bodily-affective basis that our nature prescribes for us, all moral orientation would lose its coordinate system. We could then no longer say what the good actually is. But this would also render the concept of optimisation meaningless. The abolition of man by man is an absurd undertaking."* (Fuchs 2020, p. 113).

Since machines can only simulate emotions but do not possess bodily empathy, they also do not have access to the moral value system of humans. Pragmatic rationality (ethics) can be distinguished from technical-scientific rationality (factual level), but not separated. Rather than viewing the discussion about machine simulation of an ethical consciousness purely as an ideological issue, it seems more fruitful to focus on how collaborative processes between humans and machines can meaningfully enhance ethical decision-making (Burghardt et al. 2024), while simultaneously being mindful of the emerging phenomenon that trust is increasingly shifting from human actors to algorithmic systems (Koska et al. 2024).

4 Interim Result: The Implicit Direction of Algorithmics

Finally, the implicit direction of algorithmics should be summarised. Is the ethos of algorithmics moving towards a certain goal? The sense of algorithmics can only lie in what it is capable of achieving—more precisely—in what humanity can realise through it. But what can that be, how can the directional sense of algorithmics be further concretised? First, it should be noted that algorithmic thinking and action seem to be deeply rooted in human understanding of self, world and others.

It has been shown that the vision of the digital measurement of the world as well as the observation, modelling and interpretation of algorithms are at the centre of the methodical teaching of rational and purposeful thinking and can be traced back to a long tradition. The geographical location of algorithmic thinking and action was anchored in this context in early Greek logos (λόγος). The sense of direction, which unfolds from this origin and can be described as the epistemic, refers primarily to the increase of scientific knowledge and the distinction between true and false.

The historical emergence and further development of algorithmic thinking and action is driven by an undeniable technical progress, which is often equated with societal progress (cf. Heil 2010, p. 146). As a result, algorithmics tends towards beliefs that are rarely questioned within this line of thought, such as the basic countability, calculability and controllability of all conditions that shape humans and their environment. By transforming state A into state B through a transformation process that can be described by an algorithm, Muḥammad Ibn-Mūsā al-Ḫwārizmī describes the ethos of algorithmics as a concretion of the wisdom and knowledge of God the Lord.

A central motive for outsourcing algorithms to artificial artefacts is to operationalise human thinking and action to eliminate "thinking errors" (see, among others, Leibniz above in his letter to Rémond). By formalising certain physical and mental activities as calculable functions, the rationalist calculus argues, formerly human activities can be mechanised and performed just as well—under the norm of effectiveness and efficiency usually even much better—by machines (computing servants).

If there is a traditional order of action for the field of algorithm design that provides a basic direction of moral sentiment, then at first glance this most likely coincides with the scientific truth ethos of modern natural sciences. Since scientific knowledge, as explained above, can only provide orientation (for the distinction between right and wrong) at the factual level, hardly any guidance for action emerges on the moral level.

The vision of the machine simulation of an ethical consciousness shows that the pragmatic reason (evaluation level) of humans cannot be implemented independently of physicality or bodily existence.[71]

Nevertheless, the image of humans as information-processing machines, which can be measured from the outside and are to a certain extent controllable and manageable, solidified in the ethos of algorithmic thinking and acting; it was developed from the mid-20th century in numerous scientific research fields (such as cybernetics, cognitive science or even artificial intelligence) and further advanced.[72] Of course, technical progress has always been accompanied by great

[71] *"Yet without anchoring our desires and values in human nature, we would ultimately lose the framework of orientation that gives our life significance and meaning. It is the bodily-affective conditions of our existence that dictate the elementary values to us: birth, hunger, thirst, pain, pleasure, and death. Life is better than non-life, food better than hunger, closeness better than rejection, love better than hate"* (Fuchs 2020, p. 112 f).

[72] Cybernetic modelling for the control of machines, organisms and societies (Wiener 1948) is gaining increasing importance with the availability of extensive real-time data (big data). For, with the development of comprehensive IT systems (smartphones, IoT, industry 4.0 etc.) and self-learning algorithms, the old cybernetic concept of feedback, i.e., that a control unit automatically reacts to changes in state, regains its originally intended quality (we have already outlined a comparable dissonance between hardware and software in Alberti.).

scepticism, as shown by the sculpture of the Dadaist Raoul Hausmann from 1920 (see Fig. 15). The wooden head illustrates that by focusing on mechanical thought processes and "dataism" (Harari 2018, pp. 563–608) the fundamental characteristics of human nature, such as empathy or the abilities for reflective thinking and creative design, are increasingly being overlooked.

The media ethicist Alexander Filipović (2019b, p. 4) clarifies with reference to a quote from Edward H. Weiss: *"The greater danger does not come from machines that think like humans, but from humans who think like machines."* In the context of the considerations made here, this is easy to see—the further the outsourcing of algorithmic thinking and acting progresses, the stronger the connection between a certain action and the corresponding responsible subject is decoupled—if humans (like a whole army of wooden heads) emotionally completely uninvolved only function according to external laws, then they are sooner or later the worse machines.

In the past, this danger can be countered from the progressive belief of a technology-affine consciousness, it was less a reduction than a change in the activities performed by humans due to mechanisation or automation. Precisely because human nature does not consist in performing stupid and monotonous work, but in unfolding the full potential of being human, it would therefore be good and right to automate as many activities as possible that have so far prevented us from doing so. Looking back on industrialisation, so the central argument of technology enthusiasts, would anyone seriously assume that the higher purpose of humans, for example, consists in spending all day screwing bolts into a car body on the assembly line.

The fine line between the hope that machines will relieve humans "from activities that are hard, dirty, dangerous or simply are only unpleasant" (Misselhorn 2018, p. 7) and the concern "that humans could be displaced by machines" (ibid.) leads to the question of how the digital transformation should be specifically designed or what we can reasonably want in this context. Indeed, we must continually answer this question ourselves, as the sense of direction can only be determined by humans and human actions.[73]

Originally, the algorithmic principle was understood as an explication of a universal law, the intellectual and historical roots of which can already be found in ancient traditions, such as the Book of Wisdom—to which al-Khwarizmi directly refers, but also in Sanskrit proclamations, in ancient Greek philosophy or in the "Nine Books of Arithmetic Technique" (Chiu Chang Suan Shu). Human reflection and abstraction ability allows us to overcome mere observation of nature and penetrate the basic structure and normative order of the cosmos with our own dimensions of meaning, by drawing conclusions from the data of the past and the present about events in the future and developing algorithms for the virtually possible.

Even the deciphering of the fundamental algorithms of life is, according to the view of neoliberal technology enthusiasts, only a matter of time (see e.g. Hülswitt

[73]The ultimate decision-making authority over what we call morally good lies with humans, since *"this term does not formulate an empirical property, but a normative claim that should be realised. Since this 'should' presupposes the ability to decide for or against the good, objects and facts cannot be called morally good or evil"* (Hofmann-Riedinger 2011, p. 387).

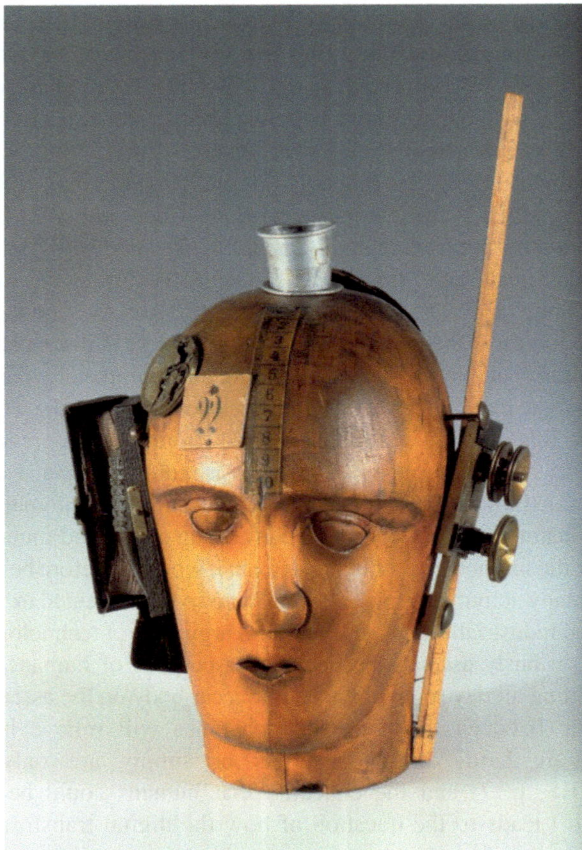

Fig. 15 The sculpture "Mechanical Head—The Spirit of Our Time" (1920) by Raoul Hausmann illustrates the emerging critical examination of the ideals and norms of algorithmic thinking and acting. The experimental computer scientist Georg Trogemann describes the Dadaist's artwork with the following words: "On the head is a cup for funneling laws and rules. At the back of the head is a purse, reminding of economic constraints. Instead of a brain, there is only a receding paragraph, dividend and phrase threshing machine to be found" (Trogemann 2005, p. 24) (Image source: National Museum of Art Washington, Wikipedia)

2018)—and thus also the question of whether the human being in a certain way elevates himself above himself. The legitimacy to carry out such a project must not be claimed solely based on the objective validity of the functional laws, without sufficiently reflecting on the phenomenon of morality. *"For the power of man to make of himself what he pleases, means [. . .] the power of a few to make of others what they please"* (Lewis 1943 cited after Fuchs 2020, p. 17). To impose a supposed sense of direction on humans from the outside, through opaque, self-learning and uncontrollable algorithms, would therefore deprive the human being of his foundations.

In Search of Numbers and Values 3

Building on the intellectual and historical foundations, the media-philosophical considerations and the outlined ethos, the following chapter attempts to further concretise the dimensions of an algorithm ethics with a view to the current circumstances, the current state of technology, the current value system etc. The aim is to unfold the essential criteria for an ethical evaluation of algorithms. In the first step, the current debate on algorithms is outlined using exemplary fields of action. Based on this, the second step examines the emergence of conscious and unconscious value inscriptions, to subsequently systematise the dangers and problems that are being discussed with the advancing algorithmisation (third step). On the basis of this analysis, a criteriology for an ethics of algorithms is proposed in a fourth step and finally the yield regarding the normative dimensions is summarised in a further interim result.

1 Problem-Oriented Description of Current Fields of Action

The selection of the following fields of action once again raises the question of the methodological approach, especially since each topic in itself would already be rich enough to be used as the subject of an ethical analysis. An analysis of the existing publications on self-driving vehicles or social networks or even digital education would provide sufficient material for this. A comprehensive presentation of the individual subject areas is therefore not possible. However, a brief introduction to each topic should not be omitted. The selection focuses on the diversity of those currently particularly relevant topics in our cultural sphere. From the present-day perspective, these areas already indicate sweeping societal changes, therefore a greater gain in knowledge for an ethics of algorithms is expected. This requirement is fulfilled by the following five subject areas:

C. Koska, *Ethics of Algorithms*,
https://doi.org/10.1007/978-3-662-71518-5_3

1. Self-driving vehicles
2. Knowledge transfer and news search
3. E-commerce and online marketing
4. Processing of financial, insurance and health data
5. Education and resource distribution

Building on the considerations from the previous chapter, the respective *process of algorithmisation* is at the centre of the observation and *not a specific algorithm*; it is therefore not about analysing the specific code of applications, to then evaluate them from an ethical perspective. Apart from the fact that the code of many applications is not freely available, such an undertaking would quickly exceed the scope of this book, since a multitude of algorithms work together in each of these areas. Moreover, the meaningfulness would be extremely limited due to the rapid innovation and update cycles. Therefore, it is more about exposing the general problem situation.

To what extent does the algorithmic search for numbers and values, which as a basic feature of human existence—as shown above, from the Presocratics through Aristotle's definition of the human being as *animal rationale* (gr. *zoon logikon*) or also Ernst Cassirer's *animal symbolicum*—runs through the entire history of philosophy, now in the context of comprehensive digitalisation suddenly change our understanding of the world, others and ourselves?

1.1 Self-Driving Vehicles

The term automobile was coined at the end of the 19th century. The two properties that were combined in this word, "self" (Greek *αὐτός*) and "movable" (lat. *mobilis*), originally referred only to the drive type of vehicles. This is also indicated by the common designation of a car as a motor vehicle. In contrast to carriages and all other land vehicles, automobiles were the first to have their own drive engine, so they no longer had to be pulled or pushed, but were in a certain sense self-driving. Terms like "self-driving cars" or even "automatically driving cars", which are often found in the context of current reporting, appear quite strange from this perspective due to the semantic doubling. On the other hand, the content repetition reflects the legitimate interest in finding a linguistic increase compared to the self-mobility of the first cars (cf. Koska 2018, p. 73).

Conventional and self-driving cars differ primarily in that it is now less about the driving force—although the current debate about electric drive may convey a different picture—than about the development of a so-called autonomous control for the vehicles. Talking about autonomous driving, under the sign of an independent control and steering unit, means illuminating the transition process from human to machine vehicle control (guidance).

The idea of driverless driving is not new. In a certain way, we are currently experiencing a renaissance of the vision of driverless driving and electronic propulsion, as the first driverless vehicles, which were presented to the world public at the 1939 World's Fair in New York, were also electric vehicles. Another commonality is the desire to make mobility more efficient and safer in a globally networked traffic control system. The implementation of the infrastructure, however, illustrates a significant difference: While the basic concept in the pre-digital machine age (similar to a Carerra car racing track) was based on inductive track guidance, digital networking promises autonomous vehicles that can move relatively freely on intelligent data highways (Fig. 1).[1]

The transition process from human to automatic vehicle control is carried out in up to six stages according to a definition by SAE International.[2] The traffic infrastructure necessary for fully autonomous driving aims, as already elaborated elsewhere (see Koska 2018), primarily at the idea of fleet learning. This initially involves collecting as much driving data as possible. In Tesla's customer data protection policy, among other things, camera data, e.g. video recordings of accidents or recordings from external cameras to recognise things like road markings, road signs and traffic light settings, braking and acceleration data, information about the use and operation of the autopilot to the vehicle-leading person, etc., are mentioned.[3]

With regard to the installed sensors and electronics, some vehicles already have the technical hardware equipment to capture all relevant data points for a level 5 classification (fully autonomous driving). However, the next step must also ensure a safe and fast transmission of this driving data to various data processing units within the traffic infrastructure. Although there has been a SIM card requirement in

[1]Interestingly, the so-called Trolley Problem (English for tram), which still dominates the ethical debate about self-driving vehicles, comes from the early days of the last century (cf. Engisch 1930, p. 288). The thought experiment, also known as the switchman case, describes a situation in which a switchman, through his active intervention (the track change of a train), could not prevent an accident with fatalities, but could reduce the number of victims. A theoretical discussion of the moral evaluation of such situations is omitted in this paper, as it does not yield any gain in knowledge for the current practice of car manufacturers—a more detailed justification of this assessment can be found in Koska 2018.

[2]In this context, SAE Level 0 stands for "no automation", which means that all driving tasks are performed by a human person at the wheel. Levels 1 to 3 distinguish different stages of assistance systems (such as cruise control, parking aids or lane keeping assistants) up to the conditional autopilot system, where the person leading the vehicle must always be ready to intervene in difficult situations. From Level 4 ("high automation") an appropriate intervention by the person at the wheel is no longer envisaged, but can occur after system request. The Federal Highway Research Institute classified SAE Level 4 as "fully automated" (Federal Highway Research Institute 2012, p. 7), while the American SAE still distinguishes a Level 5 for fully autonomous driving, in which the vehicle's operation under all environmental conditions "that can be managed by a human driver" (SAE international, p. 2) can also be fully executed by the computer system. Today, we are at the transition between SAE-Level 2–3 (assistance systems) and SAE-Level 4 (highly automated) (see Koska 2018, pp. 76–77).

[3]On some weblogs, it is repeatedly claimed that Tesla has been delivering vehicles with SAE-Level 5 since October 2016. However, according to Tesla, this classification only refers to the installed hardware. Because unlike Level 5, the person driving the vehicle must "maintain an overview and control of the car at all times, even in autopilot mode [Note: the new models]" (Frankfurter Allgemeine Zeitung 2016).

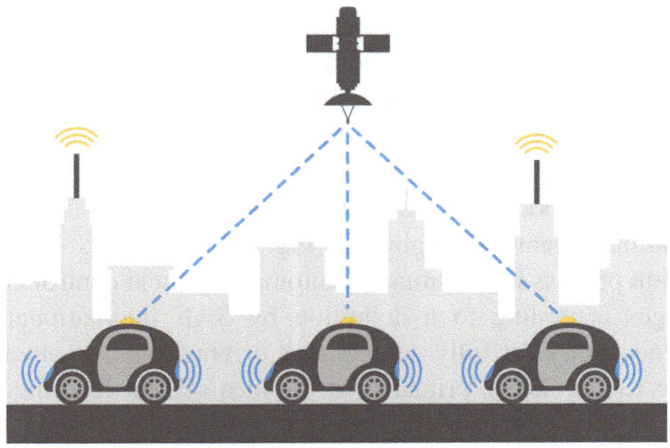

Fig. 1 Illustration of the digital infrastructure for the so-called fleet learning (Image source: Own representation based on animus81, Shutterstock)

Germany for all new cars since 31 March 2018, meaning that these vehicles could transmit their data to central servers via the mobile network, there is still a considerable need for action, particularly in terms of a nationwide expansion of the 5G mobile standard. But this is not the only reason why we are still in the transition from SAE level 2–3 (assistance systems) to SAE level 4 (highly automated). Crucial for the further development of autonomous driving is also to collect real data under real conditions with as many authentic users as possible.[4] Tesla calls this function shadow mode. In this mode, human vehicle drivers are asked to take over control in potential danger and conflict situations by a signal from the autopilot (SAE level 2–3). The existing technical hardware equipment is already sufficient to log all supposedly relevant driving data and then transmit it directly to the manufacturer, where it can be centrally evaluated. Insights that then contribute to an improvement of the autopilot can be transferred back to the vehicles by the manufacturer with a software update. In this way, so-called scenario databases can be assembled. If an autonomous vehicle now gets into a dangerous or accident situation, it can—provided the technical traffic infrastructure is also available—in the future look up in real time in the scenario catalogue which driving behaviour has the highest chances of success in a comparable situation to avert damage.

With the help of fleet learning, it will be possible over time, so the thesis, to recognise all driving situations that correspond to a certain pattern. In this way, the first (incremental) steps towards SAE level 5 are being taken in parallel with all other requirements. For example, Elon Musk, the founder and CEO of Tesla, argues that the first fatal traffic accident with a self-driving vehicle, which made

[4]This is also a major reason why Tesla does not test the beta version of the new autopilot in the lab (with a relatively small user group), but has already installed it in the vehicles.

headlines worldwide in July 2016, would not have been possible with a (not yet available at that time) software update of the autopilot (cf. Hull 2016).

According to a study by the WHO, 1.25 million people have dyed in traffic accidents every year since 2007 (cf. World Health Organization 2015).[5] In Germany (2015), 276,524 out of a total of 366,448 accidents with personal injury, i.e. a good 75%, could be directly attributed to the driver's misconduct (including influence of alcohol, incorrect use of the road, inappropriate speed, insufficient distance, mistakes in overtaking, disregard of right of way etc.) (cf. Federal Statistical Office 2016). Other sources even assume human error as the cause in more than 90% of all cases (Peitsmeier 2015; Becker 2016). In view of these figures, Elon Musk describes it as "morally reprehensible" (cf. McGoogan 2016) to further postpone the market launch of autonomous vehicles.

Against this background, the Federal Minister for Transport and Digital Infrastructure set up an Ethics Commission in 2016, which officially presented its report on "Automated and Networked Driving" to the public in July 2017. Many were surprised by the result. The first irritations were already caused by a passage in the preface in which the expert commission writes: *"it is not excluded that at the end of the development there will be motor vehicles that are inherently safe,* i.e. *can avoid an accident under all circumstances."* Florian Rötzer, the editor-in-chief of the online magazine Telepolis, describes this as an "interest-led fiction", *"after all, it can probably never be ruled out that a technical system will not suffer a breakdown or malfunction under all circumstances, which could cause an accident from internal or external causes"* (ibid.). With the qualifying subsequent sentence, it becomes visible where international research and development is currently focusing. The "reality of a heterogeneous and non-networked road traffic" (ibid.) is mentioned as the reason why "a complete avoidance of accidents" (ibid.) is currently not yet possible (besides the technical level not further elaborated at this point).

The somewhat paradoxical discussion of dilemma situations perhaps caused the greatest surprise.[6] Because, as already mentioned above, technology can and probably will never be able to guarantee one hundred percent that critical situations, as the Ethics Commission demands, "do not arise in the first place" (ibid.). Ultimately, the committee itself concludes that "technically unavoidable residual risks" (ibid.) exist, but "do not stand in the way of the introduction of automated driving if there is a fundamentally positive risk balance" (ibid.). This reference

[5]According to the EU, for every death there are four cases with permanent disabilities (for example due to spinal or brain injuries), eight seriously injured and fifty people with minor injuries (European Commission 2016).

[6]The introduction to the topic can be found in the second sentence of paragraph 5: "The technology must be designed according to its current state so that critical situations do not arise, including dilemma situations, i.e. a situation in which an automated vehicle is faced with the 'decision' to necessarily realise one of two evils that cannot be weighed up against each other" (ibid.). The restriction that accidents "should not occur as far as practically possible" (ibid.) refers to the statement in paragraph 3 "the avoidance of accidents is [Note: only a] guiding principle" (ibid.).

leads to the decisive consequence that arises both from the current practice of car manufacturers as well as from the recommendation of the expert commission. The question of ethical dilemma situations plays a subordinate role because on the one hand (i.e. in the past nearly 100 years), no satisfactory answer to the trolley problem could be given and in light of the possibilities of Big Data and artificial intelligence on the other hand.

With the introduction of shadow mode and fleet learning, there is rather an "outsourcing of morality"—from the experts (especially lawyers, philosophers and theologians) via the swarm intelligence of the vehicle-leading persons to artificial intelligence (Machine Learning). The Tesla Model S travelled 130 million kilometres accident-free with autopilot until the first fatal accident occurred in May 2016. Worldwide, a fatal accident occurs on average every 60 million kilometres. If this value proves to be stable, autonomous vehicles already have a (by a factor of 2.17) better risk balance compared to conventional vehicles. In addition, according to Tesla, the cause of the accident has since been addressed through a software update (keyword: fleet learning). The strategy therefore apparently consists of human drivers training the control software of self-driving vehicles in shadow mode.

Nevertheless, the accident draws attention to one of the most pressing problems: The handover of control between human and technology, especially in dangerous situations, also called "overruling" in the ethics report. Even if the legal basis for the fatal Tesla accident seems clear—it was a level 2–3 classified vehicle, meaning the driver should have reacted—experts criticise that the attention and anticipation skills of drivers, which are necessary to solve difficult situations, inevitably degenerate if they have been driving accident-free with the autopilot for long enough. In paragraph 17 the ethics commission notes the following rule:

> *"Software and technology of highly automated vehicles must be designed in such a way that the need for an abrupt handover of control to the driver ("emergency") is practically excluded. In order to enable efficient, reliable and safe communication between human and machine and to avoid overburdening, the systems must adapt more to the communication behaviour of humans and not demand increased adaptation performance from humans in return."*

Now one can ask how a human-machine interface can be designed to truly meet this requirement. How can overburdening and abrupt handover processes be avoided in an increasingly complex high-tech world? How can it be ensured that humans are not robbed of their own autonomy when driving autonomously? Can an increasingly powerful artificial intelligence be transparently integrated into the communication behaviour of us humans, so that we can seamlessly take over the control at any time in dangerous situations?

A look at the current investment strategies of the major technology companies shows how they envision the future of the human-machine interface. In addition to Facebook, Microsoft and many others, who are already experimenting with reading thoughts directly from our brain, Elon Musk's company Neuralink is also working on a brain-machine interface that should enable faster and smoother access to the machine control unit of robots. The human thumb as a media tool would therefore be meaningful (see media philosophical systematisation). Recent developments underline significant progress in brain-computer interface research: In January 2024, Neuralink successfully implanted its first human patient with an N1 chip, enabling him to operate computers solely through brain signals, for example, to browse the internet or play video games (Kleemann 2025). By January 2025, a total of three patients had received Neuralink implants, with plans to expand testing to 20–30 additional patients within the year (Fortune 2025). In parallel, the company Synchron has developed a brain-computer interface integrated with Nvidia technology, allowing paralyzed individuals to control devices by visualizing actions and selecting them through interfaces like the Apple Vision Pro (Mullin 2025). The symbiosis between human and machine, which Neuralink is currently researching with an invasive method for patients with brain damage, is intended by Elon Musk to be available as a mass-market product for non-disabled people in ten years. Because Musk apparently sees the direct networking of our brains with computers as the only possibility to protect humans from being incapacitated by artificial superintelligence:

> *"We're going to have the choice of either being left behind and being effectively useless or like a pet — you know, like a house cat or something — or eventually figuring out some way to be symbiotic and merge with AI"* (Urban 2017).

1.2 Knowledge Dissemination and News Search

The Arab Spring, the Brexit referendum, and Barack Obama's presidential campaigns in 2008 and 2012 are three prominent examples from recent history that put the "power of algorithms" in the focus of a changing information exchange. The actual role that social networks played in the occurrence of these events is still not conclusively clarified and is therefore still controversial. What is undisputed, however, is that the search for information, its evaluation and processing has fundamentally changed due to a shift in the classic gatekeeper function.[7] Since the election of Donald Trump as the 45th American president, there has been widespread talk of post-truth, fake news and lying press, and it almost seems as if a mediation between the different positions inevitably runs into the void, as the news monopoly of established media institutions to create a common public has simply been lost. It is now a truism that with the spread of

---

[7]The concept of the gatekeeper was originally introduced (in reference to the model by K. Lewin to explain the access of food to certain purchasing channels) by David Manning White in 1950 into communication science. As part of an individualised case study, White examined the influencing factors of the newspaper editor Mr. Gates, who "as a terminal gatekeeper" was responsible for the selection and dissemination of agency reports in a certain newspaper. He came to the following result: *"Through studying his overt reasons for rejecting news stories from the press associations we see how highly subjective, how based on the 'gate keeper's' own set of experiences, attitudes and expectations the communication of 'news' really is" and "that the community shall hear as a fact only those events which the newsman, as the representative of his culture, believes to be true"* (White 1950, p. 390).

social networks (or Web 2.0) all users not only appear as recipients, but can also act as senders of "news".

In communication science, the gatekeeper concept refers to the "hypothesis about an instance in the information and opinion formation process, which acts as a filter for the selection of the information reproduced in the mass media or orally passed on" (Brockhaus Encyclopaedia Online 2019). According to the classic understanding, this instance becomes "effective i) as an element of the professional role of journalists, who select information for their media, ii) as an element of the role of recipients, by setting certain accents of selection in the personal further processing of information" (ibid.). The Brockhaus, from whose online version this gatekeeper definition originates, was once considered one of those instances in the field of general education that determined what was to be considered worth knowing for the educated bourgeoisie and what was not.[8] Brockhaus is a renowned German encyclopedia, compareable to Encyclopedia Britannica. Compared to the (potentially) available resources and the free accessibility of content via the online encyclopaedia Wikipedia, the context of action of informing and looking up illustrates the success story of the so-called participatory web and the change of the classic gatekeeper function in an impressive way. With a view to the function of gatekeeping, the change in the influencing factors of social networks in the dissemination of news and information on the internet can be further specified. For this purpose, the thesis should first be questioned which can be found under the lemma "Gatekeeper (news research)" in the German-speaking Wikipedia. There it is proclaimed that *"with the advent of the internet, especially its collaborative applications such as blogs, online forums and networks [. . .] the gatekeeper function of the mass media [. . .] is increasingly being nullified in its effect"* (Wikipedia 2019).

This thesis is obviously based on the classic understanding of mass media and therefore primarily refers to the leading media of the 20th century, such as press, radio and television. If one recognises the characteristic of mass communication as a characteristic of mass media, then the internet is now itself to be considered a mass medium and thus also all internet-based services and platforms that reach a correspondingly large population. The statement that *"the gatekeeper function of the mass media has been overridden"*, is therefore ultimately misleading in this context.

The range of internet-based leading media such as YouTube, Twitter, Instagram, Facebook or Wikipedia has long since exceeded the reach of traditional mass media. Metaphorically, the moment of power shift can be formulated in analogy to the French herald's formula: "The gatekeeper is dead! Long live the gatekeeper!" The gatekeeper function is thus not fundamentally overridden but

[8]After about 200 years of gatekeeping history, Bertelsmann announced on 11 June 2013, however, "due to lack of economic prospects" (Wulff 2013) the gradual closure of the company and the associated publishing house. Under the leadership of the Swedish National Encyclopedia (NE Nationalencyklopædin AG), a small editorial team isstill working on the online version of Brockhaus.

rather shifted—from traditional mass media via social networks (Web 2.0), through semantic web concepts (Web 3.0), towards increasingly sophisticated AI models, like Large Language Models (see Fig. 2).

Naturally, the transition from Web 1.0 to Web 2.0 is also accompanied by ongoing ethical discourses. These address on the one hand (mainly under the term netiquette) the manners and behaviour of users in the participatory web. On the other hand, established reporters are accused of "reporting inadequately on relevant facts and unjustified scandalisation of individuals and institutions taking place" (Schicha 2019, p. 86). The latter was exploited by Donald Trump during his first presidency for his own benefit, by regularly portraying himself as a victim of the unbalanced reporting of the established media and labelling all investigative reports about his person as unjustified witch hunt of fake news. Donald Trump reached approximately 90 million followers at the peak of his Twitter account prior to its suspension in January 2021, rising again to about 102.5 million followers by March 2025 on X, while the New York Times increased its followers from approximately 50 million (2021) to about 55 million (2025). The subject of reporting thus gathered (in this comparison) a significantly larger audience behind his person than the traditional reporters. *"The role distribution between producer, distributor and recipient is therefore dissolving, merging in the non-professional produser"* (Rath 2016, p. 302).[9]

Particularly through the great success of the participatory web, the Big Data term spread in public perception as a designation for a phenomenon that is primarily associated with the strong increase in digital content by the so-called produsers. Thus, the disruptive innovation of making encyclopaedic knowledge online freely accessible and editable for everyone initially significantly increased

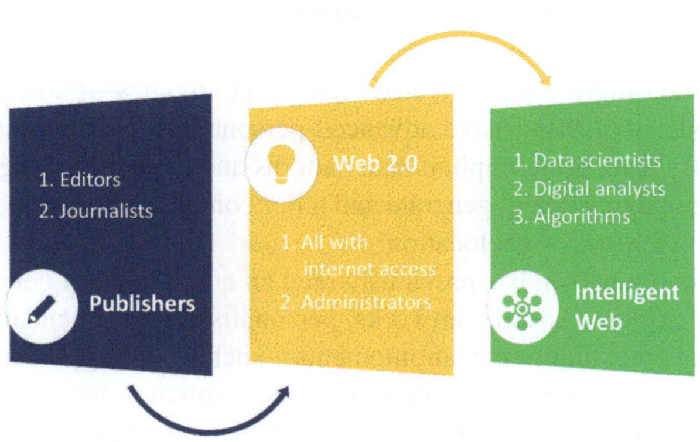

Fig. 2 The gradual change of gatekeeping using the example of general education: from Brockhaus or Encyclopedia Britannica via Wikipedia to so-called "Semantic Mashups" via the Linked Open Data Cloud towards Large Language Models (LLMs) (Image source: Author's own illustration)

[9]The term *Produser* is a portmanteau of *Producer* and *User* and originally comes from Axel Bruns (2006).

the volume of general knowledge.[10] Since March 2007, however, the exponential build-up of general knowledge in Wikipedia has significantly flattened.[11]

Studies on the declining growth after this period for the English version of Wikipedia, among other things, conclude that from 3 to a maximum of 4.5 million articles, the capacity of freely available editors may hit a limit, because the collective attention for maintaining and updating articles is exceeded (cf. Suh et al. 2009; Chi 2013). Therefore, the need for technological innovations for the quality assessment of articles was prioritised in the strategic plan of the Wikimedia Foundation as early as 2011 (cf. Wikimedia Foundation 2011, p. 10) and research regarding automated analyses and predictions of quality deficiencies within the so-called "User-generated Content" has been driven forward by data science (see e.g. Anderka 2013). The transition from the participatory web (Web 2.0) to the intelligent internet is not only announced inquality assurance: "Also some editions of the online encyclopedia Wikipedia [. . .] are largely written by algorithms" (Filipović 2013, p. 194). The computer-generated creation of content has already reached a level in some news departments, so that people no longer perceive a difference:

> *"Robot journalists consist of codes and are already being used in fact-oriented reporting, such as sports and stock market news. They are unbeatably fast. The US company 'Automated Insights', in which the American news agency AP is also involved, needs 9.5 seconds per report. According to a study by the Swedish researcher Christer Clerwall from Karlstad University, who examined the effect of automatically and manually created texts, most readers did not notice a difference, many of the participants even rated the automated reporting as more objective"* (Hackel-de Latour 2015, p. 4).

Semantically linked facts, for example, once formed the basis for early text-generating systems (see Fig. 3). These structured data points enabled automated content creation in fields such as sports or financial reporting. More recently, however, increasingly sophisticated AI technologies—particularly Large Language Models (LLMs)—have advanced personalisation and contextualisation significantly. By leveraging implicit data patterns and natural language processing, these models can dynamically generate and tailor content for individual users based on behaviour, interests, or geolocation.

For example if a person has previously read an article about Leonardo da Vinci (see Fig. 3) or explored specific artworks, personalised recommendations can now be provided at contextually relevant moments—such as during a visit to Florence. While such scenarios were once dependent on explicit semantic metadata and structured interfaces, modern AI systems, particularly LLMs, enhance these possibilities by inferring context and intent without relying solely on predefined data

[10] Just a few years after its foundation, there were more than 250 language versions, in early May 2019 the five largest language versions reached 5,846,165 (English), 5,367,473 (Cebuano), 3,747,886 (Swedish), 2,295,338 (German) and 2,100,511 (French) articles (see: https://meta.wikimedia.org/wiki/List_of_Wikipedias).

[11] See https://en.wikipedia.org/wiki/Wikipedia:Modelling_Wikipedia%27s_growth.

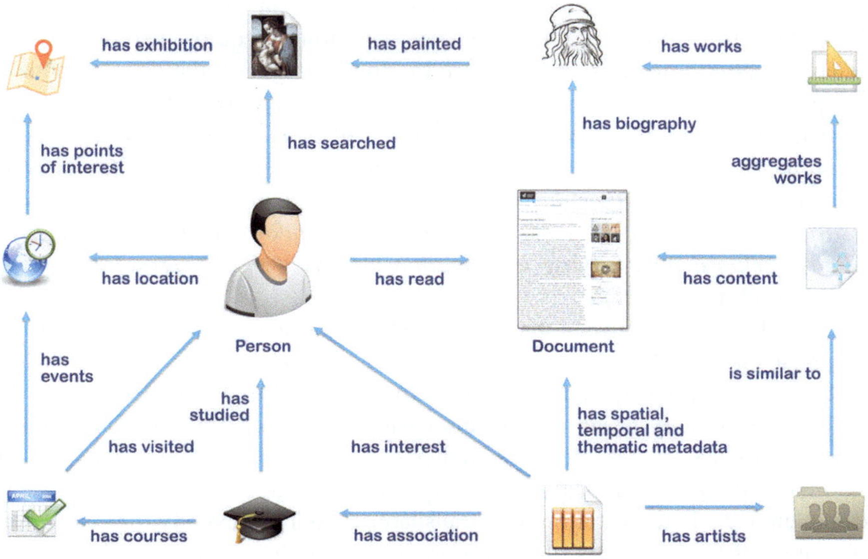

Fig. 3 Semantic contextualisation using the example of general knowledge (Image source: Author's own illustration)

structures. Recommendation technologies thus enable highly automated, affinity-based content delivery. This marks a significant shift in the cultural practice of information retrieval—from actively seeking out knowledge in static repositories to passively receiving personalised content from adaptive digital systems. The limitations of traditional print media—restricted storage capacity, limited networking capabilities, and slow updating cycles—are thus overcome by real-time, personalised digital knowledge dissemination.

Recommendation technologies, which, as in the above outlined application context, deliver content directly to the consuming target group (engl. *content consumption scenario*), can in principle be distinguished from models that serve the author of an article as an editorial tool by displaying content suggestions during the writing process (engl. *content creation scenario*). By extending the online editorial system (usually a plugin for the text editor), such a tool can analyse the lines written so far in real time and automatically provide suitable content for enriching the article.

Ten years ago, Altmeppen (2015) still assumed with regard to journalistic transformation processes, *"that digital technologies, if they are defined as tools of journalism, can be covered by existing dimensions of responsibility"* (ibid. p. 16).[12] Insofar as trained journalists use such editorial tools, the established dimensions of journalistic responsibility, such as audience ethics, organisational

[12]The audience ethics, the organisational and institutional ethics as well as the individual ethics are explicitly stated as established dimensions of journalistic responsibility.

and institutional ethics, and individual ethics, can therefore be applied. According to Altmeppen, however, the situation is quite different in the newly structured media system, where the focus is less on the development of independent journalistic products or the provision of journalistic services than on data-driven distribution of information: *"What is no longer present compared to journalism is a professional selection process,* i.e. *active topic selection, and forms of agenda setting, a high degree of organisation and institutionalisation in the sense of journalistic standards (topicality and periodicity, general accessibility and availability) as well as journalistic structures"* (ibid. pp. 28–29).

The relationship between the content selection criteria of journalists and the technical-formal selection mechanisms of news search engines was intensively analysed in German-speaking research by Beiler (2013). He determines the quality in this study based on four dimensions (cf. Koska 2014): transparency, diversity, topicality and relevance. Beiler's verdict already sounds sobering for the first three quality dimensions (transparency, diversity and topicality): news search engines do not offer optimal transparency, only a severely limited variety of content, they are susceptible to uniform reporting. In addition, the indexing of interest-driven sources blurs the boundaries between journalism and public relations, and the contributions are on average one and a half days old and thus only correspond to the daily summaries of daily newspapers in terms of their topicality. The determination of relevance, as the fourth quality dimension, occupies a particularly important position in Beiler's work and will therefore be briefly explained. As measurement criteria, the author introduces 19 journalistic news factors into the field of investigation, which he develops extremely revealingly through a historical reappraisal of the news value theory. He then confronts these content news factors with the mathematical-statistical ranking criteria of search engines and arrives at the result of a largely negative correlation between the two. The author clearly states at this point that news search engines are not capable of selecting according to the content-traditional standard of journalists. Rather, the author believes that the frame of relevance is increasingly shifting to the level of technical-formal criteria, which leads to "unforeseeable implications for users and journalism" (Beiler 2013, p. 389).

However, the careful juxtaposition of journalistic quality criteria and algorithmic filter criteria, according to the communication scientist Reineck (2014, p. 102), carries "the risk of comparing apples with pears." Thus, the criterion of transparency in journalism research is understood for example, as something completely different ("namely whether the conditions of origin and sources of journalistic contributions are disclosed", ibid.) than in the context of algorithmic decision systems. Also, the "severely limited diversity" that Beiler (2013, p. 372) attributes to the internet, according to Reineck, initially raises the question of the benchmark. Insofar as news aggregators do not produce their own journalistic products and services, but merely reflect the content of established media and news agencies, one could also suspect a deeper redundancy in journalism itself.

These foundational analyses by Beiler and Reineck have gained renewed relevance in light of recent international studies on algorithmic gatekeeping. For instance, Bandy and Diakopoulos (2019) found that human-curated news selections on platforms such as Apple News showed greater diversity and topical breadth than algorithmically generated "trending" sections. Similarly, Bhadani et al. (2022) demonstrated that including audience diversity in recommender systems can measurably improve the reliability of recommended news, particularly for users exposed to misinformation. These findings underscore the ongoing relevance of quality dimensions such as diversity, transparency and relevance, even as technical implementations continue to evolve.

1.3 E-Commerce and Online Marketing

Contextualisation and personalisation algorithms are also used to increase the turnover of online shops. The aim is to guide customers as quickly as possible to products that might interest them. The sentence: "Customers who bought this item are also interested in ... " is well known to most online shoppers. The magic word for this form of online marketing is: 360 °customer journey analysis. "First of all, it's about reducing fear" (Rickmann 2019, p. 15), explains the CEO of Deutsche Telekom. He then continues under the title "We take digital responsibility", "if we succeed in getting a 360-degree view of the customer, in giving the customer the right experience, the chances of success are good" (ibid.).

It may be surprising at first glance when the CEO of Deutsche Telekom is quoted in the introductory words to the chapter on E-Economy instead of an emerging internet visionary or a prominent representative of the Big Techs (Amazon, Google, Facebook, Apple or Microsoft). However, Rickmann's assessment, regarding the biggest challenges of digitalisation for companies, also recalls the foundation of digital consumption. Because a good 25 years after the privatisation of the German Federal Post (Post Reform II, 1994), the companies that emerged from it and its current competitors play a central role for the economic success of online trading—namely the provision and further development of the necessary infrastructure—from the nationwide availability of the internet, fast and secure data transmission, to the delivery of goods to the front door of the target group.

Among the electronic addresses, the top-level domain .com, with almost 152 million registrations, is by far the most frequently used address extension on the internet.[13] The abbreviation stands for the English terms commercial or commerce. Mainly, but not exclusively, the domain extension is used for the internet presence of companies. As early as the mid-90s, a gold rush mood developed on the digital path. Aggressive investors pumped up the so-called

[13]A top-level domain refers to the last section of an internet address (to the right of the dot). Following the .com ending, in second place is the country-specific top-level domain .cn for China, which recently had a total of 24.7 million registrations (see Verisign 2021, p. 2).

New Market until the dotcom bubble burst on March 10, 2000. For example, the internet address "business.com" changed hands in December 1999 for 8 million US dollars—under the assumption that the domain name (i.e., eleven letters) could be resold for 30 million US dollars by the end of March (cf. Borchers 2010). What was sold to shareholders at the time were mainly digital business visions. Even before the Corona crisis, the growth difference between stationary (+1.2%) and electronic commerce (+9.1%) had clearly turned in favour of e-commerce, and with an annual turnover volume of 58.5 billion euros, a tenth of all trade in Germany was conducted online (cf. Handelsverband Deutschland 2019).

It was recognised early on that business ethical problems and dangers, such as the reification of the human image, are intensified by e-business: *"Already in traditional economy, people suffer from the fact that business relationships are often no longer perceived as relationships between people, but are reduced to pure factual rationality. Where face-to-face communication is absent, where humans have lost their visible face, where web designers adapt foreign masks, even less of specifically human qualities remain. Through the latter determinations, e-business proves to be an intensification of an alienation already widespread in traditional economic life, namely the reduction of people to functions and things"* (Thorhauer 2003, p. 159). "You are not the customer of the internet corporations. You are their product," is the German subtitle for the insider view of internet pioneer Jaron Lanier, who was awarded the Peace Prize of the German Book Trade in 2014. In this work, he calls for the conception of a "humanistic information economy", in which the consumers—due to their function as data donors—participate in the profits of the internet corporations (cf. Lanier 2014). However, this would not prevent the instrumentalist reification of humans. The intrinsic value of privacy would also have to be bought through financial renunciation (by not participating in this form of information economy) and could thus become a luxury good.

While the loss of control over one's own data has been declared as a loss of privacy—as the end of informational self-determination (see e.g. Seemann 2014) and the starting point of the post-privacy era (cf. Heller 2013)—at the European level, the process for the EU General Data Protection Regulation (GDPR) has been initiated to counteract this development in a regulatory way. With the enforcement of the EU GDPR on 25 May 2018, there is now a legal framework for the collection and processing of personal data. The framework primarily defines the legal bases for data processing (Art. 6 GDPR) and is expanded by various national and EU-wide legislative packages (for more on this see Chap. 4, Sect. 2). The tension between the interests of data-driven companies and data-donating customers can no more be resolved by the current legal regulations than the danger of data-driven reification and instrumentalisation of humans. On the one hand, the initially quoted desire aims to enable a 360-degree view of the customer, because capturing the intention of the users is considered the most important basis for supplying them with as customised offers as possible or also to generate new target groups. On the other hand, the information obtained with the help of "User and Usage Mining"[14] refers to individuals and is therefore personal. Companies invade this personal sphere from the outside to create technical identity constructions (consumer profiles and affinity models) (cf. Greis 2003). This fact does not change even if companies then protect the data (e.g. through encryption or anonymisation) against third parties (employees, business partners etc.).

As a rule, individual consumers only have very limited power of disposal and control: They can either accept the terms and conditions to create their own data profile or install a certain app on their smartphone, or they try to resist this by not using corresponding offers.[15] With regard to the introduction of the EU Directive 2009/136/EC, Lobo (2018) already summarises: *"The contrary choices of yes and no appear identical in their effect, like a broken light switch. If you think deeper about it, there is a risk of a nervous breakdown."* Because even if individual internet users decide against the use of a certain digital application, they leave traces on the net from which dynamic temporary data profiles can be generated. Regardless of the currently used end device, in a next step, users can also be identified relatively accurately from inferenced information via a large number of temporary profiles, e.g. by using bridging technologies (see, for example, US patent by Sivaramakrishnan 2014).[16] For most people, the idea of informational self-determination is thus obsolete in both cases. Anonymity, privacy and transparency must, it seems, give way to the economic interests of targeting and retargeting strategies.

The concept of transparency in particular is extremely complex in the context of digitalisation. "No other buzzword dominates public discourse today as much as transparency" (cf. Han 2015). On the one hand, the term stands for the widespread fear of surveillance and the transparent human on the internet, for a threat to privacy and individual personality development (see, for example, Lück 2013). On the other hand, an ethical ideal is forming under the societal demand for transparency, which is cited as a panacea against opaque power structures, political and economic dependencies, conflicts of interest, corruption, data misuse cases and much more. The moral question that can be attached to this discussion is therefore: *Who* or what should be *transparent* to whom?

E-commerce platforms such as SAP-Hybris, PIWIK Pro and others promise sales staff a 360-degree view of their customers.[17] Although all these platforms assure that they work in compliance with GDPR, transparency is thus mainly established in one direction. This is because in the implementation of the GDPR,

[14]User and usage analyses are used to collect implicit information about the interests and behaviour of media users.

[15]Debatin (2012) has shown in the context of social networks that users, even with careful control of horizontal privacy settings, cannot gain control over the so-called vertical user profile—the introduction of the GDPR has so far changed this situation as little as the introduction of EU Directive 2009/136/EC—also known as the Cookie Directive—ten years earlier.

[16]The company "Drawbridge" by Sivaramakrishnan (about which I have reported in a previous publication, see Koska 2015a) has since been taken over by LinkedIn—also to optimise the cross-device measurement of their own business platform (see Lewanczik 2019).

[17]See e.g. SAP product video: https://www.youtube.com/watch?v=6AM1GK4aP2Q.

the concept of transparency is mostly reduced to the concept of *informational self-determination*. This concept is based on a minimal concept of autonomy, as the consent required for data processing is usually a one-time *informed consent* for a relatively general use of data, which many companies already consider fulfilled when they refer in general to the improvement of their products and services. The question remains problematic as to how much freedom of choice or action exists for users within the technical system or what conditions must be met when interacting with complex algorithmic systems to speak of transparency or personal autonomy—even after the time of the first consent.

The decision VI-Kart 1/19 (V) of the Higher Regional Court of Düsseldorf against the complaint of the Federal Cartel Office (2019) against the merging of usage data from different sources (including Facebook.com, Facebook Messenger, WhatsApp, Instagram, Facebook Payments, Masquerade, Oculus Rift and Oculus Gear, Onavo, CrowdTangle, ProtoGeo Oy) by Facebook Inc. shows how far removed from reality the concept of control is legally assessed. Thus, the finding of the Higher Regional Court of Düsseldorf reads:

> *"The collection and processing of this additional data takes place [. . .] on the basis of the terms of use provided by Facebook,* i.e. *with the consent of the Facebook user. In this situation, there can be no question of the user losing control over his data. The data processing takes place with his knowledge and will and thus very much under his control" (Higher Regional Court of Düsseldorf 2019, p. 10).*

The Higher Regional Court therefore only evaluates the informed consent at the time of the declaration of consent (i.e. the yes or no choice): *"This assessment can be made by the user, uninfluenced and completely autonomous, according to their personal preferences and values" (ibid.).*

Numerous practical examples, such as the data leak of the Bavarian Red Cross, known as "data transfusion",[18] show that users in practice only have very limited control and power over their data. The term "completely autonomous" by the Higher Regional Court of Düsseldorf may seem correct from a narrow perspective, as long as one only refers to the *moment of yes-no decision* before using a particular service. However, this interpretation is unsuitable for ensuring personal autonomy in digital times and therefore ultimately misleading. Because the effort that would have to be made to enforce the *no*—with regard to all background services—solely against the 5 Big Techs (Facebook, Amazon, Google, Microsoft and Apple) in practice is disproportionately high and would make working with digital media almost impossible, as Hill (2019) explains. Users who—in the words of Sascha

[18]A technical analysis by the Süddeutsche Zeitung has shown that health-related data of potential donors were sent to Facebook via the website of the Blood Donation Service of the Bavarian Red Cross, including intimate details about HIV infections, pregnancies, drug use or diabetes. According to the SZ—and here the inadequacy of the minimal concept of autonomy of the OLG Düsseldorf becomes particularly clear—it could be that *"the data could now be stored on Facebook profile-related, that is: they could contribute to assigning users to certain advertising target groups"* (Eberl 2019).

Lobo—do not want to operate a broken light switch, would therefore rather have to follow the sarcastically pointed call by Hans Magnus Enzensberger ("Whoever owns a mobile phone, throw it away", Enzensberger 2014) to further enforce their *no*. But even then, there would be no guarantee that friends or acquaintances would not exchange information about private matters (illnesses, birthdays, photos etc.) of digitally abstinent people on a social network. Measures to disguise one's own identity can therefore only reduce the 360-degree view of personal data—depending on the effort—by a certain range. The technical progress within the area of 'Artificial Intelligence, Big Data and virtual-augmented reality' (and here too Facebook collects data via the Oculus glasses and the associated platform and is allowed to merge this data according to the decision of the Higher Regional Court) will additionally increase the effort for the data sovereignty of the users, if this approach is not counteracted.

Well-intentioned applications like the project of the then 24-year-old student Catalin Voss from Heidelberg, who dealt with the question at the renowned Stanford University to what extent Artificial Intelligence can make people more empathetic, can quickly be turned into the opposite. Voss originally developed an app that determines the emotional state of the counterpart via camera glasses (Google Glass) to give children with autism access to the emotional state of their fellow human beings. The glasses blend in an audio-visual signal and according to Voss leads to sustainable learning and training effects: *"Parents of autistic children experience for the first time that their children look into their faces with the help of technology"* (Voss 2016). *"The real-time recognition of situations and emotional states also brings the possibility to automatically adapt communication strategies to the current emotional situation, and could bring completely new conditions of decision-making with it"* (Richter 2016, p. 212). The brain researcher Thomas Metzinger calls this "neuromarketing" against the background of the advertising industry, and in this context draws attention very specifically to the dangers for our mental autonomy (cf. Madary and Metzinger 2016, p. 235).

A look at the current investment strategies of large technology corporations shows how they imagine the future of the human-machine interface. As already explained in the context of self-driving vehicles, numerous companies such as Facebook, Microsoft, Google or Neuralink, are experimenting with brain-machine interfaces. On the one hand, to improve the control and management for their customers on the user interface (see p. 96). However, the presence of such technology could also be used to expand the 360-degree customer journey analysis by another axis, which illuminates the depth dimension of human inclinations and interests. After all, the advertising industry aims to offer selected products to consumers at a time when they seem to be particularly receptive to them.[19]

[19]Coming from behavioural economics, this paternalistic form of marketing communication is commonly referred to as "nudging" (cf. Thaler and Sunstein 2009; Lösch 2015; Schramme 2016; Drerup and Voloj Dessauer 2016). However, the paternalistic form of marketing communication involves much more than just nudging, as Jan-Hendrik Heinrichs (in a personal conversation) rightly notes, and nudging is, as already outlined above, not only used in marketing communication.

1.4 Processing of Financial, Insurance, and Health Data

Especially for established German companies in the financial, insurance, and health sector, innovative digitalisation projects are a tightrope act. On the one hand, digitalisation is associated with the demand that the processes should be as simple as possible for the users, on the other hand, particularly in these sensitive areas, there are urgent warnings e.g. about the “data hunger of health insurance companies” (Ackermann 2017, p. 954) and the associated dangers. This usually leads to the fact that renowned German companies approach the processing and analysis of financial, insurance, and health data very cautiously, and therefore regularly receive a poor report card in terms of digitalisation in international comparison (see ibid.).

The benchmarks are usually so-called FinTech, PayTech, Insur and HealthTech companies, which are increasingly taking market share from the established competitors through technological financial, payment, insurance, and health innovations. Especially with the promise to put customer benefit at the centre of their services, for example by saving expensive commissions for human advisory services through robo advisors, they are taking customers from the established banks and insurers within the digitally affine target group.

In addition to small innovative start-ups, the large technology companies Facebook (Libra), Apple (ApplePay) and Amazon are also pushing into the banking and insurance market and are trying to circumvent the strict government regulations and requirements within this industry.

Looking at the apparent shock paralysis of established companies in the face of the new market participants, various causes can be cited. In particular, banks are feeling a strong pressure to act due to the ongoing zero interest rate policy of the ECB, as this massively threatens their previous business model (collecting money and lending it to others for a fee). However, their scope for action is severely restricted by the legal regulations in place for them. Banks and insurance companies also look back on grown structures and hierarchies as well as extensive and differentiated advisory staff, who have little interest in cannibalising their own business through technological innovations, as long as their own existence is directly affected by it. That is, although Fin-, Pay-, Insur- and HealthTech companies are perceived as a disruptive threat, the established companies, in the words of Clayton Christiansen, are in an “Innovator’s Dilemma” (Christensen and Matzler 2013). The mechanisms that lead to established products or companies being seemingly surprisingly pushed out of the market, can be illustrated by the following two graphics.

To penetrate the market with a new product or a new technology, usually a very selected target group at the lower end of the market is initially addressed (Fig. 4: green arrow). After the product has gained a foothold in a certain market segment, evolutionary innovations are then attempted to meet the expectations of the clientele at the upper limit of the market (Fig. 4: black arrow), because the high-end market promises higher sales, stronger growth, a better differentiation from imitators and much more. Companies that have managed to establish themselves at the upper market limit, according to Christensen, however, face a serious problem

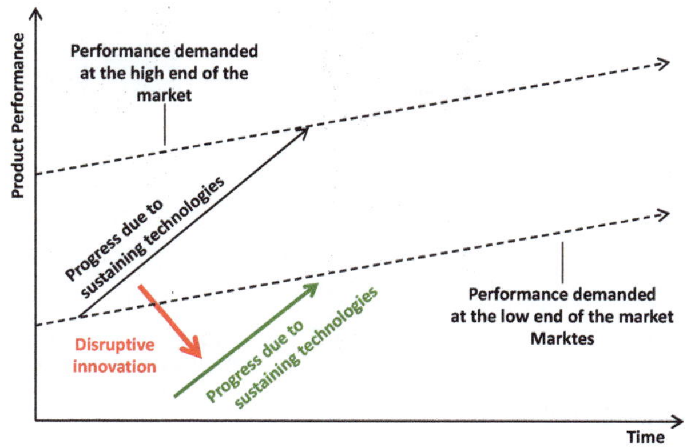

Fig. 4 The graphic describes the entry of a new product at the lower end of the market. The x-axis shows the time course, the y-axis the product performance. The expectations of the customers (dashed lines) regarding product performance, so the assumption, increases over time. The abbreviation KVP stands for continuous product improvement process (Image source: Adapted from Christensen (2013, p. 7), created by the author)

when a disruptive technology[20] pushes into the market (Fig. 4: red arrow). So what do established companies do when a disruptive technology reaches the upper end of the market (Fig. 5: green arrow)? According to Christensen, most companies tend to continue developing the product already established on the market—beyond customer expectations—through evolutionary innovations (Fig. 5: red arrow).

According to Christensen, the mechanics of the market or traditional management training forces managers to focus all their efforts on the existing product at the upper market segment (they have to achieve higher profits; among other things, because they are responsible for the livelihood of a much larger workforce). This results in a consolidation phase among the established companies, the number of market participants decreases, initial cost savings for the remaining market participants emerge, etc. In the financial sector, this has been causing branch closures for years and ultimately possibly an acceleration of the already much discussed death of banks.

Technologies, like Blockchain, however, severely limit the possibilities of the strategic development of banks through evolutionary innovations. Money—in the form of coins and banknotes—is losing its importance as the predominant means of exchange and payment due to digitalisation. The banks fear for their central role as

[20]A disruptive technology is an innovation that may completely displace an existing technology, product or service. Disruptive innovations are usually found at the lower end of the market and in new markets. These new markets usually emerge unexpectedly for established companies and are uninteresting for them, especially due to their initially small volume/target group segment. Because the responsibility of a manager of a company worth 1 million euros has a different dimension compared to that of a colleague from a 10-million or 100-million-euro company. Let's assume he has to generate a 20% return then that's 200,000 euros for the first manager, 2 million for the second and 20 million for the manager at the high-end market.

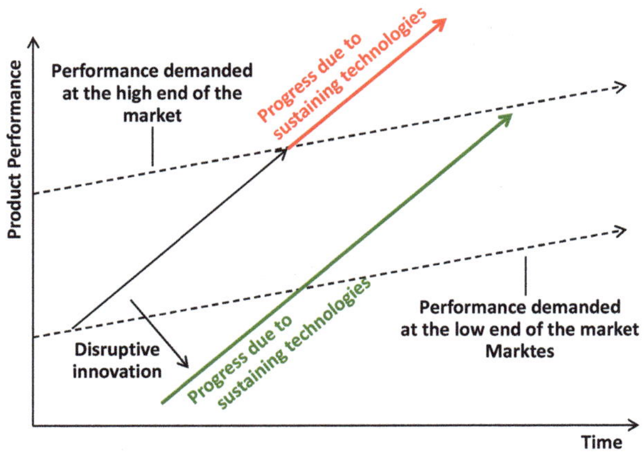

Fig. 5 The graphic shows why established companies usually lose the competition for groundbreaking technologies according to Christensen (2013) (Image source: Adapted from Christensen (2013, p. 7), created by the author)

intermediaries in the digital exchange business. Indeed, the advancing digitalisation in this sector thus requires fundamental economic policy reorientation, organisational rethinking and bureaucratic reforms.

Estonia is often cited as a role model in this context within the European Union. After the country separated from the Soviet Union in 1991, a consistent digitalisation strategy was soon pursued at the state level, which was intended to enable the administration of the state independently of its territorial integrity. Consequently, in 1999 the Estonian cabinet decided to completely abandon paper and extensively reduce stationary file mountains. Since the year 2000, the Estonian constitution guarantees all citizens access to the Internet to continue to ensure the exchange of information with the population. The country has since been considered a digital pioneer in many areas.[21] Today, Estonia has an extensive data treasure of its population and (especially after the annexation of Crimea by Russia in 2014) also via the so-called concept of the "data embassy" to secure this data outside the country.[22]

[21]Among other things, Estonia has had an "e-Tax Board" since 2000 and nationwide "m-Parking" (a parking ticket system that is controlled via smartphones). Since 2001, there has been a "Population Registry", a digital database of the population, which forms the basis for numerous other digital services and which every resident can access. Since 2002, there has been an "e-School" (web application, via which not only learning content and homework for students, but also grades, attendance information etc. are provided for parents), in addition, elections have been completely conducted online since 2005 via "i–Voting", a "Mobile-ID" was introduced and from 2008 an "e-Health System" etc. (cf. Piperal 2016).

[22]See online: https://e-estonia.com/estonia-to-open-the-worlds-first-data-embassy-in-luxembourg as well as the OECD report under https://www.oecd.org/gov/innovative-government/Estonia-case-study-UAE-report-2018.pdf.

What sounds like a totalitarian surveillance state or the end of democracy to some, sets incentives for others to apply for e-residency in the country. With the e-citizenship programme, the Estonian government is particularly targeting technology start-ups, but also all other business operators outside its own national borders, who desire a target group-oriented alignment of all state administrative necessities.[23] For this, they receive a digital identity, which among other things enables them to establish a company in Estonia, open a bank account there and—according to their own statements—submit a tax declaration online within three minutes. The country's former Chief Information Officer (CIO), Taari Kotka, describes the Estonian digitisation strategy as "a completely new type of benign disruption—and this time the category is government" (Kühl 2017).

A health information portal was also connected to the underlying data exchange platform "X-Road", which is used by 100% of all doctors, specialists, hospitals and pharmacists in Estonia (cf. Thiel et al. 2018, p. 103). The "patients have complete control over which doctor can access which health data and which cannot" (ibid. p. 101). Nevertheless, the available resources should be utilised. By 2020, for example, personalised health data should be available for risk analyses to shorten treatment paths and facilitate diagnoses or decision-making for doctors. "Furthermore, the manufacturers of digital health services should provide their data for evaluation programmes and quality controls" (ibid. p. 99).

A comparable analysis of financial, insurance or health data is currently unthinkable in Germany due to organisational restrictions. For example, the data of bank customers is usually still distributed across the numerous data silos of the various bank branches, where customers are individually cared for by their personal advisors. But even if there was an agreement between the branches and the customers' consent regarding the consolidation and evaluation of their data, it would still be questionable to what extent individual companies can stand up to the market power of American and Asian platforms. After all, data has been collected and consolidated here from all areas of users' lives for years. If it is not possible to break up the increasing market power of global technology corporations, then "Europe [. . .] is in danger of becoming the Africa of the information age in terms of the use of private data", as Meixner (2016, p. 2) states in a reference to colonial times.

Under the guiding principle of "digital sovereignty", the Federal Ministry for Economic Affairs and Energy (BMWi) has therefore initiated the design of a platform-based ecosystem for European companies. Because without digital sovereignty "Europe loses the ability to control data flows and value creation potentials in many fields of digital transformation, which threatens to have fundamental consequences for value creation and prosperity", as the BMWi (2019b, p. 3) also states. In addition, "democratic values and the stability of our political system [. . .] are potentially in danger in the face of the rapidly changing and sometimes almost unpredictable geopolitical shifts, if only platforms that cannot be controlled in Europe are used for communication, goods or information exchange" (ibid.).

[23]See online promotional video: https://www.youtube.com/watch?v=H4QLzQGMI3k.

The time is now obviously pressing. Thus, at the Digital Summit in October 2019, the concept of a networked data infrastructure named "GAIA-X-Cloud" was introduced, which had already started operations by the end of 2020 (see Stegemann 2019). Various application scenarios of GAIA-X are presented using demand examples—including the linkage of the Financial Big Data Cloud (FBDC) with other industry ecosystems to strengthen the German and European financial marketplace or to network the German health infrastructure to derive added value for economy, science and society from this (see BMWi 2019a, pp. 26–33).

Although the project's target image states that "the infrastructure [. . .] is provider-neutral and [. . .] takes into account the interests of data producers, providers and users equally" (BMWi 2019a, p. 11), it remains to be seen how this will be specifically implemented. It is still open whether GAIA-X increases the digital self-determination of consumers, or whether the project only increases digital sovereignty for politics and business, thus actually only enabling added value from the perspective of the providers. Clearly, the processing—and especially the networking—of financial, insurance and health data is associated with fundamental risks for our societal value system. Specifically, the principle of solidarity, which as a basic principle of statutory health insurance, for example, ensures that the weak and sick are supported by the community of solidarity, could be undermined by additional knowledge gained from user and usage behaviour. As soon as individuals are assigned to a certain affinity or risk class, for example to pay either lower or higher insurance premiums, it "merely" plays a legal role whether the data donors have consciously consented to such an evaluation, these insights were gained from anonymised data sets (affinity models) or neither the one nor the other legally prescribed procedure was used.

In addition to the technical requirements and a brief reference to further regulations, the concept paper for GAIA-X—even if this is not further elaborated—already addresses the educational prerequisites for competent citizens: "Germany and Europe must develop the infrastructural and regulatory framework in the coming years and create the prerequisites for the education of correspondingly competent citizens" (BMWi 2019b, p. 4).

1.5 Digital Education and Media Competence

Digitalisation has become an integral part of contemporary learning and education approaches. This realisation became particularly clear in 2020, during the worldwide Covid-19 crisis and the associated school closures or the temporary shutdown of face-to-face teaching. However, it is not just about expanding the necessary infrastructure for online education offers nationwide, so that in a resource-poor country like Germany, the economic connection to technical progress (or the contact of students to teachers) is not lost. Because in addition to imparting technical skills, it is also necessary to reflect on the effects and impacts of digital world construction (see above). Viewing digital education merely as a tool to increase societal human capital in the world of work 4.0 inevitably leads to a dangerous reduction of the societal educational mandate. Building on the historical foundations from Chap. 2, the phenomenon of digitalisation, as we encounter it through the increasing algorithmisation and datafication of our environment, is also used in this section as the subject of educational-theoretical and resource-technical investigation.

Continuing the thought at this point therefore first takes us back to the roots of algorithmic thinking and action and reminds us of the mystical-theological origin of the term. Against this background, the image we have of the world is deeply connected with mystical introspection or the creative power of the divine.[24] Even the namesake of the term algorithm (al-Ḫwārizmī) refers, as already explained, at the beginning of his treatise directly to the "wisdom and knowledge of God the Lord." Looking back at the historical path of rational and purposeful thinking, fundamental motives for the digital measurement of the world have already been revealed and current development trends outlined. Thus, educational responsibility does not exhaust itself in reactively evaluating the implicit direction of digital technologies, but focuses primarily on shaping this process in a creative and value-oriented way.

With the DigitalPakt Schule, the German federal government and the German Bundestag declared their intention in 2018 to further advance digitalisation in general education schools in Germany. Because a standstill in terms of digital education was not only talked about in professional circles since the publication of the results of the "International Computer and Information Literacy Study (ICILS) 2018". The Corona crisis, however, became a magnifying glass for the inadequate digitalisation of the German education system. Before the Corona-related school closures, only four percent of German eighth graders used digital media in class every day—compared to 91% in Denmark (cf. Eickelmann et al. 2019, p. 19). According to the ICILS study, before Corona, only a good quarter (26%) of all German schools had WLAN access—in Denmark, in contrast, 100% (ibid. p. 14). The demand to anchor computers and computer science education in general education in Denmark can be traced as far back as the mid-1960s. The computer pioneer and co-founder of the Copenhagen datalogy tradition[25], Peter Naur, shared

[24]In the Historical Dictionary of Philosophy, Lichtenstein (2017) further explains: "*The origin of the B.-concept in philosophical use lies [. . .] not in the humanistic and pedagogical, but in the mystical-theological and natural philosophical-speculative field of meaning. The Old High German basic word, with the physical meaning 'depict, image' and 'formation, shape', already has a reference to 'imago' and 'forma' as well as to 'imitatio' and 'formatio', but etymologically already to (symbol, sign). As a cipher of a spiritual process, it belongs to the abstract philosophical neologisms of late medieval mysticism and is probably a conceptual creation of Meister Eckhart [. . .].*"

[25]Naur introduced the concept of "Datalogy" (Danish: datalogi) as the science of the nature and use of data, to distinguish it from other aspects of computer science; for example, "Datamatics" as the part that deals with the automatic processing of data, or the term "Datamaton" for a device for the automatic processing of data (cf. Naur 1966, p. 485).

his insights as early as 1966 via the radio with a broad public (within the framework of the Rosenkjrer lectures):[26]

> *"Thus if one has realized that on the one hand computer science unites a large number of vital human activities and concepts in one overall point of view, and on the other hand is capable of inspiring and renewing ideas in an equally great number of subjects, one can be in no doubt as to its place in general education. To arrive at a reasonable view of this position, one must of course make comparisons with similar disciplines and one will arrive at the conclusion that language and mathematics lie closest. Computer science and these two subjects deal with signs and symbols as tools invented by human beings. The three subjects have also in common the fact that they are tools for many other subjects. Therefore they enter education in two ways; both as auxiliaries in the study of many other subjects and as majors where specialists are trained in these subjects themselves. All of us have had to learn a considerable amount of languages, arithmetic and mathematics in school, without many of us subsequently becoming linguists or mathematicians. In the same way we must bring computer science into the school and prepare ourselves for life in the era of the computers, just as reading and writing are regarded as necessary prerequisites for life in a society characterized by the printed word."* [Translation from Danish into English by Sveinsdottir and Frøkjær (1988, p. 457)]

And further on the positioning of computer science in schools:

> *"Computer science can enter the school curriculum either as an independent subject or as a part of mathematics; what is crucial is the contents of what is taught. The emphasis should be on data, data representations, and data processes. These fundamental concepts must be illustrated by means of a number of concrete examples which can easily be taken from areas that the pupils are familiar with - arithmetic, spelling, looking thinys up* etc. *Simple examples of the use of mechanical and electrical phenomena for data representation should also be included. These examples should be illustrated by simple experiments. Computers should also be mentioned, not as the most important element in the subject, but rather as a final point of information."* (ibid.).

The importance and significance of computer science education have been discussed in the context of school and university curricula for more than 50 years internationally (see, for example, Forsythe 1963). Consequently, there is no shortage of concepts for the integration of digital competencies into the general education canon. Only in the consolidation and widespread implementation of digital education concepts too little has happened in Germany until the lockdown of school lessons, beginning of 2020,—exemplarily, at this point, the heated discourse following the announcement of the Thuringian State Data Protection Officer Lutz Hasse is reminded, in which he threatens fines of up to 1,000 euros for possible violations of data protection by teaching staff.[27]

---

[26] I owe the reference to this text to Ludger Humbert, whom I had the opportunity to meet during a lecture at the 2nd Symposium Informatics Learning for Understanding the Digital Media World at the Bergische Universität Wuppertal on 1 February 2019.

[27] *"When Mr Hasse talks about the necessary communication tools being available in Thuringia, he overlooks the actual situation. The HPI-Schulcloud was initially only open to the 25 pilot schools, so the GDPR-compliant platform was only available to a small part of the teaching staff. If, out of creativity, despite a lack of further training and with the extensive use of private devices*

The establishment of the technical infrastructure for distance learning or homeschooling therefore moved even more into the foreground due to the Corona-related predicament. Given the high demand, the financial aid from the federal and state governments, which came into effect on 17.05.2019 with the DigitalPakt School,[28] may therefore only be sufficient to finance what Naur described in 1966 as the "last information point" (see above) of digitalisation, i.e. for the purchase of hardware.

A main subject that addresses the structural properties of computer systems and makes the design space of digitalisation (not only, but also in depth) comprehensible, is currently not in sight. "Because the music is not in the piano," so Humbert et al. (2018, p. 67) quote from an interview with the American Turing Prize winner Alan C. Kay. In his work for the Xerox Palo Alto Research Center, Kay dealt earlier than many others with the conceptual and practical prerequisites for a "Personal Computer for Children of All Ages" (1972). The subject known as "computer science" in the Anglo-Saxon language area, in most European countries (including Germany, France, Netherlands, Italy, Poland) referred to as "informatics" and in the Scandinavian countries as "datalogy" (see above), should not aim to operate computers according to Kay, but to realise one's own thoughts and ideas.[29]

According to Humbert and Losch (2019), computer science education is therefore always essentially about three dimensions: i) applying, ii) designing and iii) deciding. Between "applying" and "designing" Humbert and Losch initially draw a line, to distinguish between "digital education" (note: presumably a kind of elementary media competence) and "informatics literacy" or between the "operation" and the "control" of computer systems (see Fig. 6).

However, this is an idealised model, as the dividing line between "operating" and "controlling" can only be located in practice in relation to specific applications. On the one hand, the number of graphical user interfaces for the design of digital media is rising, and on the other hand, the complexity of algorithmic decision-making systems is also increasing.

Computer science education is usually not a linear process in the sense of "i) apply → ii) design → iii) decide." Humbert and Losch address this fact with a second model (ibid.), which represents the three dimensions (i–iii) as three

for official purposes, teachers now face a fine, this will do a disservice to the digitalisation push" was the reaction of the state chairwoman of the Education and Science Union (see: Vitzthum 2020).

[28]For details on the objectives and content of the DigitalPakt School and the purpose of the financial aid, see https://www.digitalpaktschule.de/files/VV_DigitalPaktSchule_Web.pdf.

[29]*"Most schools define computer literacy as the ability to use Microsoft Office and perhaps do a bit of web design. They miss the point. It is like saying: 'If you know which end of the book to hold on to, and you know how to go to chapter three, then you are literate.' Literature is first and foremost the existence of sufficiently important ideas for discussion and writing in one form or another."* Extract from the interview "Computers are instruments whose music is ideas" available online at https://sudonull.com/post/12350-Alan-Kay-Computers-are-instruments-whose-music-is-ideas (last checked on 10.06.2020).

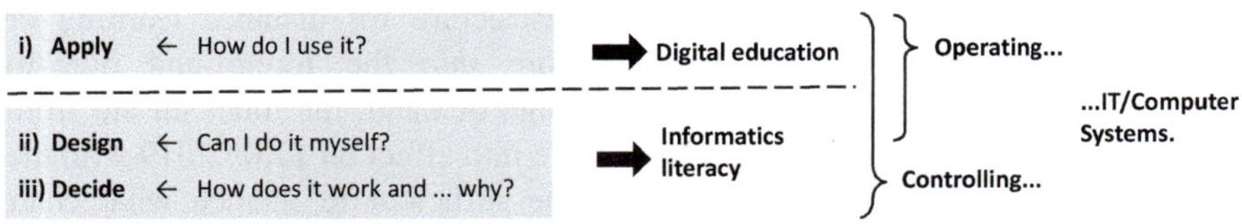

Fig. 6 Core of computer science education according to Humbert and Losch (2019) (Image Source: Author's own illustration)

intertwined phases of a continuous improvement cycle (see base in Fig. 7). If one combines the two models of Humbert and Losch in a third model by erecting a vertical time axis on the proposed cycle to also take into account the implied hierarchy from the first model (Fig. 6), the three recurring phases (i-iii) can be determined as the base of a superordinate development process—this is the process of lifelong learning.

This model (Fig. 7) clarifies that drawing a boundary between the teaching of application knowledge and the design of computer systems offers no added value

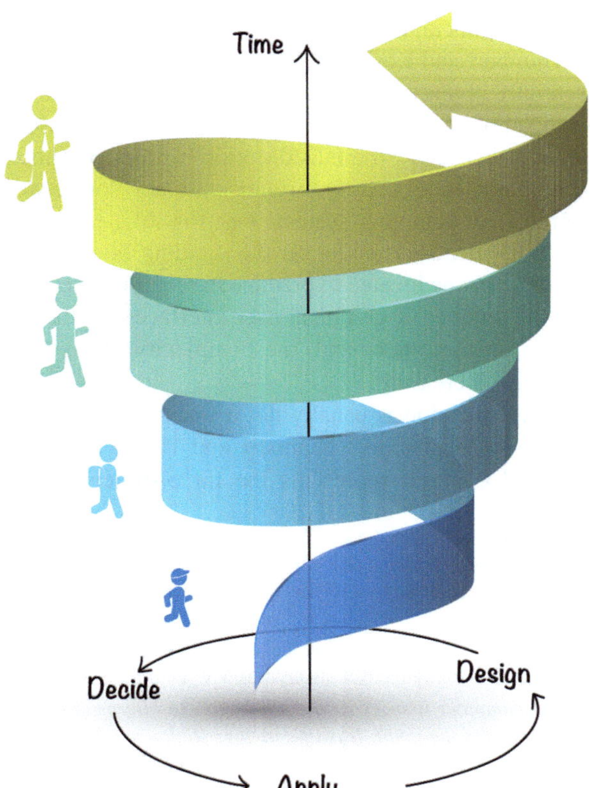

Fig. 7 Projection of lifelong learning onto the dimensions or phases of computer science education proposed by Humbert and Losch (2019) "i) apply, ii) design and iii) decide." (Image source: Adapted from Humbert and Losch (2019), modified by the author)

from a pragmatic perspective. In the dispute over the "right dosage" of computer science education in the school context, the "unspoken message of most non-specialist teachers" is, as Lautebach (2018) proclaims: "Computers cannot be understood, [. . .]" is unmistakably supplemented by: " . . . but they don't have to be." Among the advocates of delimitation of computer science education, this analogy is also very popular: "Not everyone who uses a computer has to be able to code. After all, I also drive my car without having any relevant car knowledge." This sounds very plausible to most people—especially when such sentences are spread by socially established educational authorities. However, these arguments are often based on false assumptions (or completely different motives). This includes, among other things, the mistake of limiting "coding" solely to the programming of computers, and the non-understanding (or unwillingness to understand) of the extent of the risks associated with the divergence of technology and education.

Chapter 2 has already extensively explained how algorithmic thinking and action has shaped our cultural history long before the invention of electronic computers, as the two most important prerequisites for a good algorithmist are deeply rooted in our human nature.[30] On this superordinate level, an algorithm can therefore be qualified as an elementary part of our thinking that we have understood so well that we can outsource it in signs or symbols. The historical foundation of digital and computer science education can therefore also be understood as a process of becoming aware of our own inherent knowledge (in the sense of anamnesis). This means that we do not need laptops and tablets for the introduction to the topic, especially in early childhood development (see e.g. Geldreich 2019). Rather, it is about thematising the process of understanding. That this should be a superordinate and primary educational goal, no one can seriously dispute.

Of course, the next step is also about bridging the gap between education and technology. The above mentioned analogy to controlling a conventional motor vehicle is dangerous because it trivialises the problem (whether intentionally or unintentionally). Firstly, it quickly becomes apparent that apples are being compared with pears, as the handling of commercial vehicles (cars) is on a completely different organisational level than the handling of information technologies (media). The automotive industry is not a category that exists alongside information technology, but it is—like all other economic sectors—permeated by it (see Sect. 1.1 in this chapter). A more fitting comparison in the media context refers to the media revolution that was triggered in the 15th century by the printing press, therefore as a reference for the current situation. With the technology of printing, not only the understanding of texts, but also the independent storage of knowledge in a linear language became an elementary part of education. Before the book as the

[30]What is meant here is the ability to reflect (the ability to think about one's own thinking) and the ability to abstract (the ability to organise or structure this thinking in a clear sign system) as the two most important prerequisites (see second chapter) for a detailed explanation.

leading medium of the "Gutenberg Galaxy" (McLuhan 1962) could fully unfold its effect, a widespread literacy of the population was necessary.

Even with regard to digitisation, it is not just about understanding how digital media are to be used, not just about the conveyance of correct consumption (of a few selected media), as is offered, for example, with the acquisition of a "media driving licence" from the Media Education Foundation in Bavaria (within 4–5 lessons), to reiterate the problem of this analogy. This may be well-intentioned—but sticking to the pure application level falls short, as a responsible and self-determined use of digital media also requires participation in shaping our virtual world. Digital expertise requires continuous and progressive practice of application, design and decision-making skills (see Fig. 7).

This thesis can be further substantiated, based on the already presented changes, (especially in knowledge transfer and news search and against the background of interest profiles that internet services like Google or Facebook create—see Sects. 1.2 and 1.3). For this, I have already proposed the concept of a "digital educational identity"[31] elsewhere, the necessity of which I have initially justified epistemologically with reference to the ever larger and faster growing mountains of data. Because against the background of the ever larger and faster growing mountains of data, the right access to information becomes increasingly crucial. The "big data" phenomenon can be compared with a maximum dense information point: Without technical aids, like algorithmic filters, it destroys thinking. Because for humans, there is simultaneously too much and too little information in large data mountains. The maximum information density is so to speak identical with the maximum absence of information—maximum bright light or darkness lead to the same result: In both cases you see nothing. So if you try to download the entire mass point of information, nothing reaches the individual. Therefore, we need machine filters in the big data age, i.e. algorithmic gatekeepers, to make relevant information for the individual visible in the first place (see Koska 2015b, p. 82).[32] An extension or even outsourcing of the gatekeeper function, which aims at outsourcing the filter and selection mechanisms of information, requires targeted educational measures. When technologies from outside invade the personal sphere of individuals to create technical identity constructions, then the focus of digital education shifts from the personalised (learning and education) content to the administration of the personal learning, education and research profile.

[31]A digital educational identity is a virtual representation of a person's knowledge in relation to certain knowledge domains, an individualised learning or research profile, on the basis of which so-called recommendation technologies filter and provide personalised further learning or research content (see Koska 2015b, p. 81). The concept is further elaborated in the 4th chapter of this book.

[32]The social and media scientist Danah Boyd and Microsoft researcher Kate Crawford put this fact in the following way: "Taken out of context, Big Data loses its meaning" (Boyd and Crawford 2012, p. 670 f).

2 Conscious and Unconscious Value Inscriptions

With a view to the descriptive analysis of the five exemplary fields of action, the normative dimensions of algorithmic technologies will be examined in more detail below. The beginnings of the normative discourse can be found in the dystopian science fiction literature of the 1920s and 30s, whose one-sided monotony, among other things, prompted Isaac Asimov to start writing stories between 1939 and 1941 in which robots were no longer portrayed as villains, but as machines that perform certain tasks for humans based on ethical principles (cf. Asimov 1994, p. 439 f).[33] In light of technical progress, not only scenarios with conscious, but increasingly also with unconscious value inscriptions were discussed: *"[...] one thing that is apparent [...] is that intelligent machines will embody values, assumptions, and purposes, whether their programmers consciously intend them to or not. Thus, as computers and robots become more and more intelligent, it becomes imperative that we think carefully and explicitly about what those built-in values are"* (Waldrop 1987, p. 38). The first systematic investigation of algorithmic biases (engl. *bias* "prejudice, tendency, inclination, distortion") comes from Friedman and Nissenbaum (1996):

> *"In its most general sense, the term bias means simply 'slant.' Given this undifferentiated usage, at times the term is applied with relatively neutral content. A grocery shopper, for example, can be 'biased' by not buying damaged fruit. At other times, the term bias is applied with significant moral meaning. An employer, for example, can be 'biased' by refusing to hire minorities. [...] we focus on instances of the latter, for if one wants to develop criteria for judging the quality of systems in use—which we do—then criteria must be delineated in ways that speak robustly yet precisely to relevant social matters. Focusing on bias of moral import does just that. Accordingly, we use the term bias to refer to computer systems that systematically and unfairly discriminate against certain individuals or groups of individuals in favor of others"* (ibid. p. 332).

Friedman and Nissenbaum distinguish (ibid. pp. 333–336) three main categories for bias effects in computer systems: i) "preexisting bias", i.e. existing biases that have their roots in pre-existing structures, attitudes and practices and can then also be found in the algorithmic systems, ii) "technical bias", these are bias effects that are based on technical considerations, limitations or constraints, iii) "emergent bias", i.e. emerging or newly arising bias effects that arise in connection with the practice-related system application by individuals (this bias effect typically arises some time after the completion of a system, as a result of changing societal knowledge, population numbers or cultural values). The findings from the analysis by Friedmann and Nissenbaum are cited in numerous publications as an entry point into the topic (among others by Wallach and Allen 2009; Shilton 2013;

[33]This first creative phase led Asimov in 1941 to the famous three laws of robotics: "1) A robot may not injure a human being or, through inaction, allow a human being to come to harm. 2) A robot must obey the orders given by human beings except where such orders would conflict with the First Law. 3) A robot must protect its own existence as long as such protection does not conflict with the First or Second Law."

Spiekermann 2015), in order to describe the problem situation based on this (see also Bozdag 2013; Mittelstadt et al. 2016) or to develop their own approaches and solution concepts that range from the unconscious to the conscious inscription of values in technologies (value-based IT-design) to the vision of implementing morality into the machine (artificial moral agents).

The following considerations aim to narrow down the moral actors of algorithmisation. The classification by Friedmann and Nissenbaum (see above) is dissolved in favour of a processual view to gradually shift the focus from the phenomenon of digitalisation to the decisive actors. For this purpose, Krämer's model of flattening is first expanded with a view to the fields of action. Based on the insights gained from this, it will then be shown how the inherent dynamics of self-learning systems can be understood using so-called system images and how these can be used to address the moral actors of algorithmisation.

2.1 The Model or the Process of Flattening

Building on the intellectual and historical foundations, we have developed a multi-layered concept of algorithms within the framework of our media-philosophical considerations. To determine the moral actors of algorithmisation, it is helpful to recapitulate our previous considerations against the background of the just completed inventory. First, we outlined the process of algorithmisation as a process of rational and purposeful thinking. At this fundamental level, algorithmic thinking was determined as an elementary part of our thinking that we have understood so well that we can outsource it in signs or symbols (media). It was then shown that the outsourcing of algorithmic thinking and action using artificial artefacts could be successfully mechanised and electrified to minimise human computational or thinking errors, as Leibniz intended.

As part of the intellectual and historical in-depth study, it was shown that algorithms can also be understood as basic structural and ordering principles of reality (natural laws). In the context of our media-philosophical considerations, we then explicitly pointed to the tipping or turning point, at which natural processes and phenomena become anthropogenic algorithms through a media manifestation. Following this short ontological reflection (what are algorithms?), we turned to the epistemic question (what do algorithms describe?) and distinguished between reality and virtuality. We concluded that algorithmics provides a formal sign system to virtualise reality. It was shown that this virtual reality is not a value-free sphere, even though science is oriented towards the ideal of value neutrality and objectivity. Finally, with regard to the ethical dimension (what do algorithms aim for?) we introduced a further differentiation, with the distinction between epistemic and moral errors or failures.

Furthermore, in our previous considerations, we have already pointed to an essential dimension of meaning of algorithmics, which in the traditional scientific understanding consists in inferring events in the future based on data from the past and the present (e.g. the calculation of the total solar eclipse of 28 May 585 BC). In the context of our media-philosophical thoughts, it was then further explained that humans, due to their special predisposition (ability to reflect and abstract), also aims to overcome mere observation and description of nature in order to penetrate the basic structure and normative order of the cosmos with his own dimensions of meaning. So it is not just about a theoretical description of reality, but increasingly also about actively shaping the virtually possible with the help of algorithmics. In doing so, the human puts himself in a normative-desiring relationship to his own goals, desires and ideas and thus also the risk of moral failures.

If we now turn our attention to the five exemplary fields of action to verify our previous statements about the ethos and the implicit direction of algorithmics, it can be immediately seen that an increase in efficiency and effectiveness is sought in all subject areas. According to an observation by Krämer (2020b), this is based on a universal need for simplification or flattening of human activities. From this need a separate cultural technique has emerged, as Krämer explains in her cultural history of digitalisation. The technique of flattening, as she named it, is compatible with the intellectual and historical roots of algorithmisation outlined in the first part of this book: *"From cave painting and skin tattooing, through the invention of images, graphs, diagrams, tables and maps to the computer screen, tablet and smartphone, the thread of flat representation practices runs"* (Krämer 2020a, p. 1). She immediately goes on to explain that *"contrary to the rhetoric familiar to us [. . .] the 'cultural technique of flattening' is of immense productive power in the field of sciences, arts and technical-architectural design. An intersubjectively accessible workshop for computation, composition, cognition and communication has emerged"* (ibid.). If one follows this view, then behind the two-dimensional graphical user interfaces of digital media on the one hand there is an inscrutable and uncontrollable "artificial special space, whose depth is annulled" (ibid.), but on the other hand it is "overseeable, controllable and manipulable from a bird's eye view" (ibid.).

If we embark on the search for traces in our five exemplary fields of action to test Krämer's theory of flattening, then the question arises, for whom this artificial space is overseeable, controllable and manipulable and for whom not.

If we look at our first example of self-driving vehicles, it is noticeable that the cultural technique of flattening (in the sense of a projection of three-dimensional reality onto a two-dimensional user interface) seems to be only partially viable in this context. Because on the one hand, the vehicle-leading person is currently primarily asked to take over the steering through an acoustic-tactile signal (e.g. haptic steering wheel or vibrating seat) and on the other hand, more emphasis is already being placed in this area on voice recognition and the exploration of brain-machine interfaces than on two-dimensional computer screens, as the latter (even if they are embedded in the windscreen) could distract the human driver. The model of flattening would therefore only apply in this context if we understand the acoustic-tactile signals, as they are used, for example, in navigation belts for the blind and visually impaired (cf. Walter 2016), as a further step of flattening (from two-dimensionality to one-dimensionality). Neuronal impulses would be just like tactile, acoustic or simple electrical signals therefore only a projection onto the dimension of time. Let's assume for example, that we use a navigation app on our smartphone with headphones while cycling and let ourselves be guided solely by the announcements through a completely unfamiliar city. In this thought experiment, we cycle by the shortest route through the city, without taking our smartphone out of our pocket and looking at the two-dimensional map, solely by following the navigation voice at the right moment. In contrast to the tactile signal in the above-mentioned navigation belt, which shows the blind and visually impaired the right way, the acoustic signal falls silent as soon as we are back on the right track. So the navigation voice fades away as soon as we can orient ourselves independently again, whereas the tactile signal in the belt only disappears when the blind or visually impaired person has reached their destination. The added value of the navigation solution is shown in both cases not only in the disappearance of the two-dimensional user interface, but also in the silencing (becoming invisible) of the medium. At least when using a medium successfully, we are therefore actually already moving in zero-dimensionality.[34] The media property of 'self-withdrawal' and 'self-neutralisation' is not new, as Krämer points out, referring to Aristotle's speech about the 'transparent medium' via Niklas Luhmann's concept of 'loose coupling' or Dieter Mersch's 'withdrawal of media in their execution' up to her own media-philosophical design of the 'disappearing messenger'. (see Krämer 2008, p. 273 f). Krämer's model of two-dimensional flattening, in view of the further development of human-machine interfaces, as we have just seen in the example of acoustic-tactile controls, is not entirely unproblematic. Likewise, further thinking towards zero-dimensionality leads to problems. Thus, acoustic or tactile impulses can only be reduced to a temporal dimension in our thoughts, but not in empirical reality, since a voice naturally also needs a space in which the sound can spread in the form of a sound wave. This space usually eludes the sensory perception of media users: But what have we gained from this consideration?

The model of flattening initially points to two opposing centrifugal forces in connection with the control and management of machines. Because on the surface, the human-machine interface obviously follows the paradigm of flattening, insofar as it is increasingly contextualised and optimised for the users through the reduction of complexity. But below the user interface (in the 'artificial probe space, whose depth is annulled') complexity increases. Transparency and opacity thus form two sides of the same coin. This insight is important in order not to formulate a blind demand for transparency in the context of algorithm ethics, among other things, and should therefore be further elaborated. Building on this knowledge, the model of flattening also enables a target group-oriented differentiation of moral actors. The mechanism we use for this has been used several times in the course of this treatise. If we look again under the bonnet of the virtual world and descend layer by layer deeper into the engine room of digitality, we find different forms of

[34] The term 'zero-dimensionality' as further thought in the context of flattening is to be distinguished from the term 'zero-dimensionality' by Vilém Flusser (as he developed it among other things in the context of techno images).

letter algorithmics. On the lowest level, the symbols '1' and '0' (in electronic circuits) symbolise the current states 'on' and 'off'. When we flatten binary logic by using symbols, signs, graphics or illustrations, for example by making notes on a two-dimensional sheet, writing down an algorithm and starting to calculate, we gain access to logic at the level of machine language. By using images, graphics or illustrations to flatten certain facts, we can also give letter algorithmics a visual representation that, in the best case, not only provides logicians but also non-experts with a superficial insight into the basic functioning of an electronic computer.[35] If we therefore make the medium the object of consideration, for example by inscribing certain functions in a two-dimensional user interface, then this "inscribed surface"[36] can be understood as a demarcation line between media users and media producers. The terms "frontend" (for the user interface of media users) and "backend" (for the user interface of media producers) commonly used in the context of numerous IT applications illustrate the two characteristic perspectives on this dividing line in the context of digital media: On one side are the users and on the other side the administrators of the application; behind one's own user interface (the frontend), so the associated idea, there is an unmanageable backside (the backend). By realising that the flattening of functions takes place on both sides (frontend and backend), the naive notion of the impenetrable black box can immediately be somewhat demystified. Because ultimately, the backend of one application, from the perspective of the next deeper level, is again the frontend etc.: layer by layer, down to the lowest level of letter algorithmics, with which the computer's processor architecture is commanded (e.g. "OFF, ON, OFF, OFF, OFF, [. . .]"), as we already know. Therefore, flattening occurs at all levels, insofar as it is a structuring principle of software systems.

Within the so-called layered architecture, the formal language elements on the lower layer limit the space of possibilities on the next higher layer. This means that the concept of flattening can be understood in a double sense. In a graded navigation system or user cockpit, the complexity ideally decreases upwards. Thus, in ontology-based adaptive user interfaces, as we have demonstrated in the field of knowledge transfer and news search, information is increasingly personalised and provided in a context-sensitive manner. In one case, the increasing complexity reduction can be ideal, for example, when it comes to an acoustic-tactile navigation system for certain application scenarios (self-driving vehicles) or user groups (blind or visually impaired people). In another case, for example when it comes to the formation of a critical public, a flattening in this further sense of the word, as we have particularly observed in the political context in recent years, leads to a problematic narrowing or restriction of the information offer.

---

[35]Gottlob Frege already used numerous illustrations or diagrams in his concept script (1879) to visualise certain logical relationships.

[36]Important: The pages of this script are also to be considered as inscribed surfaces according to Krämer (2017) (in the sense of a flattening into the alphanumeric space).

2.2 On the Dynamics of Self-Learning Systems

Before we differentiate the moral actors in the next step, the following digression is about the aspect of the creativity of self-learning systems, which was raised in the interim conclusion of the media philosophical considerations. We remember that Krämer's "Small Metaphysics of Mediality" (2008) proclaims, that especially in the context of computer-aided media "it is less about data transmission than data processing: not about the preservation of an order, but about its transformation" (ibid. p. 11). Krämer's question of whether transmission can be creative, we have for our purposes already transferred into the question, to what extent creativity can be attributed to algorithms. Against the background of our inventory, the following is therefore about an interpretation of the creative dimension of digital media, especially in the context of self-learning systems.

For this, a differentiation between physical, organic and machine self-organisation systems is necessary. Basically, modern self-organisation research, which developed from the end of the 1950s or beginning of the 1960s, is based on chemical (Ilya Prigogine, Manfred Eigen), physical (Hermann Haken), mathematical (Edward N. Lorenz, Benoit Mandelbrot) and cybernetic (Heinz von Foersters) questions, as Paslack (1991) explains in detail.[37] The upswing that the self-organisation research or also synergetics has experienced since then, is closely related to the invention and further development of computers and their computing capacity. Because essentially it is, "when you think about it, about a systematic application of analogies and the search for general principles", as Haken (2017) summarises; and for this purpose, machine learning methods are particularly suitable.

The primary characteristic of machine learning methods is that they enable a computer to learn from experiences in order to solve certain tasks and make predictions, without having been explicitly programmed for this function (cf. already Samuel 1959). Or to use a more formal definition following Mitchell (1997): "Machine learning is the study of algorithms that improve their performance *p* with respect to some task *t* based on their experience *e*". (Sudmann 2018, p. 10).

In the second chapter of this book, we have already dealt extensively with the outsourcing of algorithmic thinking and action (especially in Sect. 1.3). Using the example of cellular automata, we have also already learned about a simple mechanism of dynamic self-organisation with evolutionary algorithms (see Sect. 1.3.2) and subsequently reflected on the functioning of self-learning systems (see Sect. 1.3.3). In doing so, we concluded that the question of how self-learning systems work usually culminates in an analysis of the functioning of the human brain. However,

[37] Similarly, Passlack (1991) provides an introductory overview of ancient, pre-Socratic (including Hesiod, Heraclitus, Thales, Anaximenes) and philosophical precursors (such as Plato, Aristotle, Descartes, Kant, Schelling) of self-organisation concepts. The concept of self-organisation thus becomes compatible with the ideological and intellectual historical foundations, as they were outlined in the second chapter in this book.

there are numerous nuances between self-organising systems and self-learning systems that are hardly taken into account in the analogy to the human brain. According to Mainzer (2020, p. 45), human learning, in contrast to learning in animals and also to machine learning, is characterised by the ability for causal learning and inference.[38] In the introductory chapter, we already pointed out that machines cannot autonomously establish a normative-desiring relationship to certain values. Now it is necessary to further illuminate the spectrum of technology-based value inscriptions with a view to specific application scenarios.

The exemplary inventory in the various fields of action shows that application-related models of machine learning lead to a differentiation of self-learning systems. With self-driving vehicles, the aim is to resolve dangers and accident situations as safely as possible using so-called fleet learning algorithms (experience values are collected in the so-called shadow mode). In knowledge transfer and news search, the focus is increasingly on personalising information and preparing it in a context-sensitive manner (the relevance is not only calculated from the interaction behaviour of the users, but also modelled by using software ontologies, among other things). The objective is similar in the field of e-commerce and online marketing, with the focus in the latter primarily on increasing the conversion rate (for this purpose, companies create, for example, 360-degree views of their customer base). In the processing of financial, insurance and health data, established German companies are much more cautious, mainly due to strict legal regulations (however, the numerous FinTech, PayTech, Insur and HealthTech start-ups are increasing the pressure for innovation in this application context, so that self-learning systems are now also being considered beyond fraud prevention; economic policy adjustments, as have already been made in other countries, therefore appear indispensable in this area). The field of digital education and media competence takes on a prominent role against the backdrop of machine learning, as sticking to the pure application level falls short of enabling responsible and self-determined handling of self-learning systems. Especially when technologies penetrate the personal sphere of individuals from the outside to create technical identity constructions, such as the 360-degree views, the focus of digital education shifts from the use of proactively provided information to the administration of personal data profiles. Machine learning can be compared to the mechanism of self-organisation with regard to our exemplary fields of action.

To better understand the dynamics of self-learning systems and to be able to assess the emergence of technology-based value inscriptions more differentiated, we want to consider the model of synergetics according to Haken (1969). As per Haken, structures are created in principle even without an organising hand from the

[38]"*In causal reasoning, properties of data and observations are derived from causal models, i.e. law assumptions of causes and effects. Causal reasoning thus enables the prediction of the effects of interventions or data changes* (e.g. *through experiments). Causal learning, on the other hand, attempts to derive a causal model from observations, measurement data and interventions* (e.g. *experiments), which presuppose additional law and structure assumptions. Causal learning and reasoning from causal models would be the first steps towards a strong artificial intelligence, which is not observable in animals but in humans*" (Mainzer 2020, p. 45).

outside. If we look around in our current environment, we find structures that were designed by humans (like the text you are currently reading, as well as the book or the screen on which this text is located, etc.). In addition to these structures created by humans, structures form in nature, but also without our intervention, structures and patterns that can be described using algorithms, as we already know from the second chapter. The problem of natural self-organisation and structure formation is compared by Haken (2017) to the dilemma of Munchausen, who has to pull himself out of the swamp by his own hair. The question that Haken sought to answer fifty years ago (using the example of laser radiation)[39] is: Where does the blueprint for these structure formations come from if no organising hand (from outside) intervenes? Are there general principles for self-organisation that exist independently of the nature of the objects?

The theory that Haken proposes to answer these questions, he himself refers to as the "doctrine of cooperation (synergetics)" (1969) in complex systems. Because according to Haken, all these systems consist of individual parts, elements and subsystems. The parts, elements and subsystems can be of different nature, starting from the atoms in a gas (laser light) to the molecules in a liquid and the nerve cells in a brain to the people in a certain population. The doctrine of cooperation (synergetics) states that macroscopic structures (complex systems) arise through interactions between these parts, exceeding the dimensions of the individual elements (see Fig. 8).

Macroscopic structures can be observed as temporal, spatial or functional manifestations everywhere in nature. The general mechanism of self-organisation can be understood with Haken as follows: First, the intrinsic dynamics of complex systems are fixed by a control parameter (from the outside or inside). A prerequisite for a system change is then an instability of the individual parts, elements or subsystems. This leads to a fluctuation and triggers a competition between different configurations of the elements. Only one or a few configurations manage to prevail. According to Haken, this configuration is determined by a so-called order

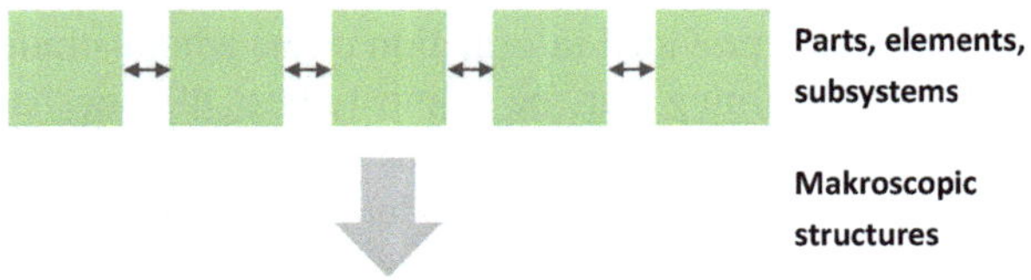

Fig. 8 Emergence of complex systems through the interactions between parts, elements and subsystems (Image source: Adapted from Haken (2017), created by the author)

[39]Hermann Haken showed in the 1960s, first using the example of the laser, how from disordered (chaotic) light waves a single highly ordered wave train (the laser beam) is created through a specific type of self-organisation. Later, he developed his theory of self-organisation also outside of physics, e.g. for chemistry, biochemistry and biology, as well as sociology and economics (see Haken 1990).

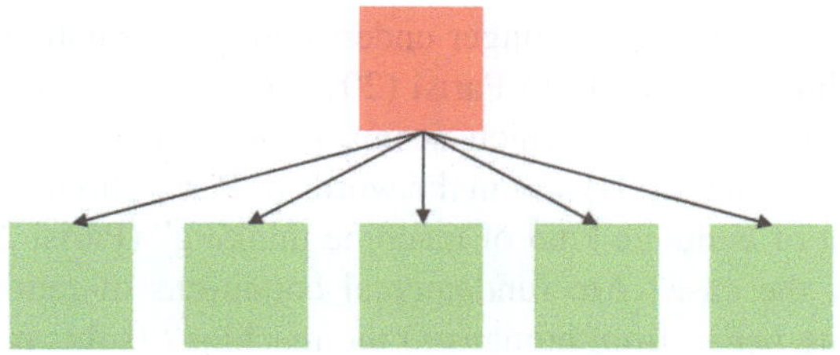

Fig. 9 Principle of enslavement (Adapted from Haken (2017), created by the author)

parameter. The function of the order parameter is to describe the configuration (the blueprint) and to enslave the individual parts, elements and subsystems (see Fig. 9).

The principle of enslavement is crucial in the context of self-organisation systems and will therefore be further explained using a generally understandable example from Haken (1990), namely the learning of a language in a certain language community:

> *"In the terminology of synergetics, languages are order parameters that enslave subsystems, namely humans. A language changes little over the span of a single lifetime. After his birth, a person learns a language,* i.e. *he is enslaved by it, and he contributes to the survival of the language during his life. A multitude of facts about a language such as competition, fluctuations (changes in the meaning of words* etc.*) can now be investigated with the methods provided by synergetics"* (ibid. p. 371).

The individual human being in this example is therefore an element or subsystem, which is imposed with a macroscopic structure (in language acquisition) from the interaction with his environment. At the same time, and here we can return to Munchausen, the relationship between order parameters and parts is, however, a circular causality, as the individual elements of complex systems can also change the structure by in turn changing the order- or control parameters.[40]

Let's now return to the differentiation of self-organising systems and self-learning systems to determine the range based on the degree of self-legislation (autonomy). In the context of self-driving vehicles, incorrect environmental conditions can lead to a malfunction of the vehicles (including accidents). Through so-called overruling, the human vehicle operator can also override the machine and optimise the model or the configuration of the order and control parameters again. The actual problem, however, lies deeper: Because the outsourcing of the order system to the functional logic of the machine leads, according to the opinion of

[40]According to Haken (2017), folders represent certain objects or generally certain ideas or plans. Therefore, the folder, as he believes, belongs to the mental realm on the one hand. On the other hand, the neurons are the individual parts in the brain, as Haken further explains, which is why the folder also plays a physical role at the same time. The folder thus takes on the role of the two-sided coin in Haken's view, which we have already considered in the context of our media-philosophical preliminary considerations: "Depending on which side you look at, you see different things—but ultimately it is the same coin" (ibid.).

some experts, to the fact that we no longer understand the normative principles of self-learning algorithms. According to Parisi (2018, p. 103), a "blind spot" arises when machines "learn to learn", which seems to fundamentally elude human rationality (see also Matthias 2004) *and* in the words of Parisi should be understood as the "starting point of a unique kind of machine thinking" (Parisi 2018, p. 103).

But is this really the case? Are fundamental conditions of rational decision-making really shifting here—from humans to the machine? Is this really a unique kind of structure formation, which is to be understood as machine thinking?[41] Can structural changes within the framework of self-organisation already be understood as a moment of creativity in the sense of Krämer? Or is this about those language confusions that we have already discussed in the context of the algorithmic composition of music and paintings. According to Haken, the individual elements of self-organising systems due to their embedding and interaction with the conditions in their environment, are always also determined by others (heteronomous) to a certain extent. Thus, as we know, humans can escape enslavement (in the sociological sense) by consciously deciding, in the case of language refusal, for example, to emigrate to another country. However, Haken's crucial point is: As soon as you live in a social system, you are always also subject to the *principle of enslavement* (the general rule is: "Long-lived systems enslave short-lived systems", Haken 1990, p. 207). In the context of digital self-organisation, it is therefore less about whether machines appear as the (autonomous) origin or source of a creative activity, but rather about developing a basic understanding of the dynamics. As can be seen from our exemplary fields of action, it is primarily about creating transparency regarding the interaction of the individual elements, parts and subsystems with the order and control parameters to consciously influence the configuration of complex systems.

But how can transparency regarding the dynamics be created? Matthias Vogel has presented a media concept that ultimately leads to a theory of the mind and which we can use for this purpose.[42] Vogel advocates *"building a media theory on the basis of the intentionalist vocabulary and to decidedly take the perspective of methodological individualism"* (Vogel 2003, p. 115). Media codes (Vogel exemplarily mentions the ASCII code) according to Vogel, presuppose "individualised intentional states" (desires, intentions, beliefs etc.) of their producers (cf. Vogel 2001, p. 348 ff). Algorithms can therefore be interpreted as prescriptions or rules for a specific set of rational behavioural possibilities (*possibility space of M*) that were implemented by the producers into a machine (cf. ibid. p. 161).

---

[41] See also Nassehi (2019, p. 255): *"Acting algorithms [. . .] are thus those that actually have to start somewhere. This does not mean that they are switched on with a switch. They have to start themselves, which is why I speak of acting algorithms in this case."*

[42] Like Sandbothe, Vogel shares the view that pragmatism is an effective therapy for overcoming the physicalistic concept of media. Unlike Sandbothe, however, he advocates for an intentionalistic vocabulary, in which expressions for (mental) contents, desires and beliefs occur (see Vogel 2003, pp. 114 & 213).

The inherent dynamics of digital self-organisation can be understood in Vogel's typology on the one hand as a physical means (in the already known sense of "ordinary tools", ibid. p. 352) for realising intended world states. On the other hand, Vogel distinguishes media codes, similar to what we already know from Krämer and Haken, as a medium of "higher order" (ibid.) from the physical realisation.

To understand the emergence of such a higher order, we can refer in a further step to the analysis by Krotz, which explains that so-called "artificial companions" do not exhibit intentionality in the sense that they pursue their own goals, but nevertheless have *"something like an inner reality"* (Krotz 2018, p. 16) that can in principle be understood by a human observer. This inner reality, which arises through the outsourcing of intentional states from humans to the machine, was also referred to as "system image" by Norman and Draper (1986) more than thirty years ago. System images consist of the mental model of the designers (Design Model) and the mental model of a specific user (User Model). First, the developers design the "Design Model" in the form of a functional concept of the system (cf. ibid. p. 489). Users develop their understanding of how the system works, the so-called "User Model", based on prior knowledge and their own expectations, but primarily through their direct experience in dealing with the system (cf. ibid. p. 496 f). Ideally, the image of the functioning and behaviour of the system is compatible with the conceptual design of the developers and the assessment of the users (see Fig. 10).

It becomes particularly tricky for the attribution of responsibility when the *inner reality* of the machine no longer matches the original intentions of the developers.[43] A very obvious explanation is that the users have used the medium incorrectly or differently than originally intended by the producers.[44] The inherent dynamics in complex self-learning systems arise, as could be shown with reference to the exemplary fields of action, from the interaction of its individual parts and thus point to the *collective dimension of algorithms*.[45] Nassehi (2019) extends this view by a system-theoretical approach that leads to a change in perspective, by

---

[43]The observer-relative experiences, which are always embedded in a social and historical context (see Vogel 2003, p. 388: "principle of productive restriction"), characterise Vogel's methodological individualism—Vogel assumes "that everything there is to say about the principal role of media can be explained by analysing the relations between two, but at most three interacting beings with intentional states." (ibid. p. 115). On the one hand, he positions the "content of a media constellation" in the experience, "which its producer connects with its performance (realisation)" (M8) and on the other hand in the experience that the reception of the media constellation causes in its recipients (M9) (cf. Vogel 2001, p. 292). Finally, "the content of a media constellation" is determined as "the experience that goes along with the comprehension of its compositional identity" (M12) (ibid. p. 387).

[44]A well-known example is the racist derailment of the Microsoft chatbot "Tay": *"Users brought Tay among other things to praise Adolf Hitler, to deny the Holocaust and to insult black people"* (Heise Online 2016).

[45]The aspect of the collective dimension of algorithms is also addressed by Jaume-Palasí and Spielkamp (2017, p. 2): *"The current ethical debate about the consequences of automation focuses on individual legal aspects. However, algorithmic processes, which primarily constitute*

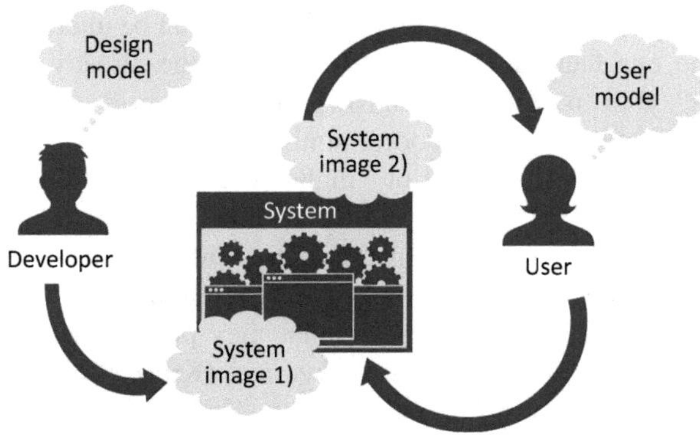

Fig. 10 Ideally, system image 1) is compatible with system image 2) If this is not the case, for example because the functional logic changes in an incomprehensible way through interaction with the system, a gap arises between the system and the users according to Norman and Draper (Image source: Adapted from Norman and Draper (1986), modified by the author)

interpreting the self-referentiality of the data world in such a way that it is no longer humans, but the "data as observers" (ibid.) of their environment that appear.

In light of recent advances in generative artificial intelligence, such as large-scale language models, Nassehi's (2019) thesis of 'data as observers' takes on new relevance. These systems not only observe their environment through vast amounts of training data, but also actively shape perceptions, meanings and even realities through the outcomes they generate. This leads to a new kind of reflexivity in which data-based observers are no longer merely descriptive, but increasingly performative entities that influence and transform the environments they were originally intended to describe. This performative dynamic may also contribute to the ongoing shift of trust from human actors towards algorithmic systems (Koska et al. 2024).

2.3 Differentiation of Moral Actors

Now that we have gained a general understanding of the mechanics of conscious and unconscious value inscription, we can further differentiate the moral actors of algorithmisation in the next step. Building on the model of flattening, we have learned to distinguish (reciprocally) between media users and media producers in a multi-stage process. We have designated the demarcation line between the two groups of actors (in the words of Krämer) as "inscribed surfaces" and at the same time pointed out that human-machine interfaces are not necessarily a graphical user interface that we operate using a screen. In view of the transparency problem, we want to maintain the term of the "inscribed surface" but distinguish it from the just

automation, primarily have a collective dimension. This can only be partially addressed in terms of individual rights."

developed concept of the "system image". The system image consists, as we have just seen with reference to Donald A. Norman, of the mental model of the media users (User Model) and the mental model of the media producers (Design Model). The User and the Design Model represent in this context the intentional states (intentions, desires, goals, beliefs, values etc.) of the two groups of actors. With the help of the media-theoretical considerations of Matthias Vogel, we have hinted at the outsourcing of the human mind and rationality to artificial artefacts and outlined the collective dimension in complex systems with reference to the theory of self-organisation (synergetics).

The following section initially involves examining the process of product development more closely to further concretise the actors from the group of media producers. Subsequently, the role of the media users is integrated into the processual view and an overview of further groups of actors is given. The processual view on software development projects allows us to think beyond the confines of the IT department. The aim is firstly to clarify the dialogical character between the various business areas of companies (strategy, marketing, sales etc.) and the development teams. Secondly, the next step is to demonstrate how the usage behaviour of media impacts the design and functionality of software solutions. As already explained elsewhere in collaboration with Filipović et al. (2018, pp. 40–44), a technical and organisational separation between Demand-IT units and Supply-IT units has proven effective in practice. The so-called Demand-Supply model (see Fig. 11) illustrates the organisational environment of software development projects in companies.[46]

The model serves the purpose of tracing the flow of information in the formulation of software requirements. Initially, certain functionalities are proposed by employees of a specific business or specialist area (in agile development processes e.g. as an "epic", as a sketch or very roughly formulated "user story"). The Demand-IT unit then takes up this requirement in the so-called "product backlog" (a collection pool for all product requirements) and decides which requirements should be implemented in the next development sprint. As soon as an epic has been assigned to a sprint, the Demand-IT breaks down the epic with the Supply-IT into several user stories. This results in a first transformation from the abstract to the concrete, which already provides the developers with the most important functional details for implementation and offers the Demand-IT unit the opportunity to align these functions with the respective specialist or business area. In this model, the Demand-IT unit therefore coordinates the requirements of the various business areas and translates them into a project specification. The Supply-IT unit or also the IT delivery department, on the other hand, is responsible for the implementation of

[46] The schematic representation of the organisational environment (see Fig. 11) makes no claim to cover all organisational variants of Demand-Supply management. Not every company has its own development department, for example. In smaller companies, individual IT professionals may also be directly assigned to a certain business area. Often the internal IT or digital department only acts as a Demand-IT unit and has the entire development process outsourced or it supplements the internal development team (Supply-IT) with external developers etc.

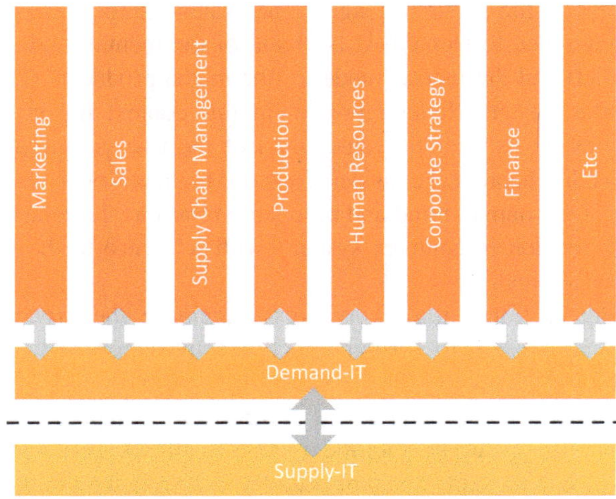

Fig. 11 Demand-Supply model (Image source: Author's own illustration)

a corresponding solution.[47] The model emphasises the dialogic character between the individual business or specialist areas, the technology-savvy intermediaries (Demand-IT), who coordinate IT project planning and project control (innovation management, IT controlling etc.), as well as the developers (Supply-IT). If we zoom in further on the key roles and functions involved in the conception, modelling and development of algorithms or software, then the following job titles can be mentioned in particular: Product Owner, Business Analyst, Project Manager, IT/Solution Architect, UI/UX Designer, Coder/Programmer, Test Engineer, Data Scientist, Citizen Data Scientist.[48] However, the field of activity of algorithm design cannot be limited to a homogeneous group (cf. Filipović et al. 2018, pp. 45–47).

The Demand-Supply model thus primarily illustrates the requirement coordination between the operators and the developers of a specific IT solution (ideally including consideration of industry-specific best-practice solutions and the economic policy regulatory framework, see orange marking in Fig. 12).

In addition to the developers and the operators, however, there is also the user in the inner ring of this "responsibility onion." The transitions between these groups of actors are often fluid and extremely dynamic, as can be further explained by the processual perspective on product development and by using our exemplary fields of action. Because even if the users—in contrast to the developers and operators—usually only have an indirect influence, for example by having their wishes and goals formulated by a specialist department in the form of so-called user stories, the

[47]In order to be flexible in the market, but also due to the high rate of self-employed IT professionals, the Demand and Supply-IT units are usually supplemented by external service providers or even completely provided by external digitalisation agencies.

[48]A detailed description of the activity profiles of these roles can be found in Filipović et al. (2018, pp. 42–44) and therefore will not be repeated here.

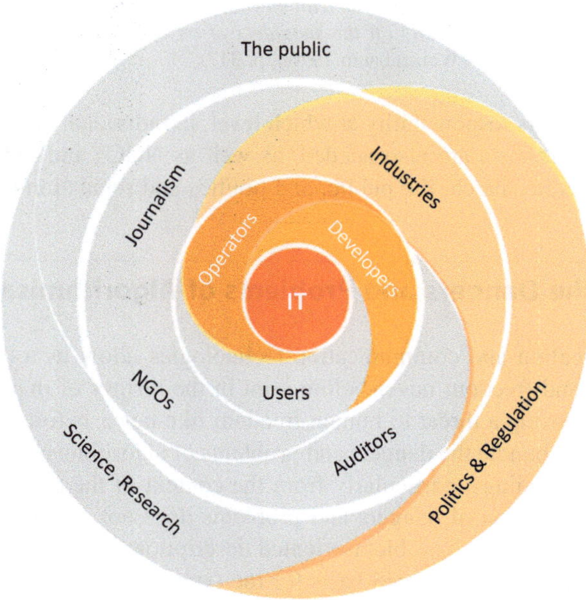

Fig. 12 Overview of the groups of actors who can be considered as moral responsibility bearers (Image source: Adapted from Saurwein (2018, p. 43), modified by the author)

term "user story" already provides an important clue that the needs of the customers or users should actually be made the first link in the Demand-Supply chain. With a view to the implementation of self-learning systems and algorithmic decision-making processes, the process of target group-oriented personalisation, for example in the context of context-sensitive recommendation technologies and adaptive ("ontology-based") user interfaces, as we can already see in online marketing, reaches a whole new quality.

Building on the problem-oriented description of current fields of action, it has been shown how the algorithmic search for numbers and values changes through interaction with the environment. Initially, (conscious and unconscious) value inscriptions are usually defined in the specialist departments and implemented by the algorithm designers into an IT system (see Demand-Supply model, Fig. 11). After the go-live, these initial values—especially in self-learning systems—can be changed by the interaction behaviour of the users (consciously or unconsciously). Finally, self-learning systems develop a certain dynamic of their own, which we find increasingly difficult to understand with increasing complexity and therefore also refer to as technology-based value inscriptions. In view of this we have also spoken of the zero-dimensionality of the media; in connection with the model of flattening, however, we have at the same time referred to the layer model, which leads to the question of who has access at which level to the control and steering options of the underlying layer ("inscribed surface").

"The myth of technical, political and societal inevitability is an effective sedative [. . .] Its function is to take responsibility off the shoulders of anyone who believes in it. But in reality, there are actors" (Weizenbaum 1976b, p. 317).

To clarify who bears responsibility at which level, in individual cases, auditors and investigative journalists are also needed, as well as NGOs and industry associations, science and research, the public, and politics and regulation (see Fig. 12).

3 On the Dangers and Problems of Algorithmisation

Modern information and communication technologies allow us a degree of self-determination and freedom never before seen in the history of mankind, while at the same time posing a threat to human freedom like never before. The following primarily aims to bundle the dangers and problems of algorithmisation. As we draw on our previous findings, particularly from the context of the exemplary fields of action, this compilation of dangers and problems does not claim to be complete. The aim is rather to offer a problem-oriented description of current challenges that can be used as a practice-oriented basis for the criteria in the next chapter.

In the context of digitalisation, two essential drivers are primarily mentioned: power and capitalisation, which are noticeably complementary to each other. The social and media ethicist Alexander Filipović (2015, p. 12) sums up this connection as follows:

"The capitalisation of our personal activities stops at nothing. The data economy as a paradigm for all communication and media products leads to our communication and our media reception taking place in a purely economic, data-driven infrastructure and thus being dependent on economic interests. Because power is always at stake in the economy, political interests are also involved, and big data companies become political actors whose know-how and technology enable them to influence political decision-making in their own interest: 'Technology companies', as Yvonne Hofstetter puts it, - i.e. *commercial organisations - want to influence the political decision-making of society, without losing sight of the goals of economic activity: sales revenues, profits, profitability, efficiency'. The technology companies have the means to change capitalism politically entirely in their favour."*

The Internet of Things takes on a whole new, originally unintended meaning through the reification of humans for commercial purposes. Jaron Lanier, who was awarded the Peace Prize of the German Book Trade in 2014, emphasises this problem in the title of his monograph with a single question: "Who owns the future?"[49] (Lanier 2013).

The all-encompassing datafication of society has long been recognised as a means of exercising power. Europe finds itself caught in the struggle for digital supremacy between two extremes: "Commercially driven digitalisation (USA) on the one hand and state-controlled digitalisation (China) on the other" (Nida-Rümelin 2021, 10:40).

[49] German title: "Who owns the future? You are not the customer of the internet companies. You are their product" (Lanier 2014).

Although the numerous regulations issued by the European Commission are intended to strengthen the European economic area, they are often perceived in the everyday work of employees in data-driven companies as a brake on innovation. The following section will therefore examine the ethical reasoning behind the need to subject technological progress to critical moral reflection.

3.1 The Problem of Social Construction

Greis (2003, p. 144) neatly summarises the phenomenon of social construction as follows:

> *"The virtuality of the internet allows, on the one hand, to initiate identity processes without having to consider an external perspective, on the other hand, it simultaneously results in identities being organised from the outside, which in turn do not have to take into account the person to whom they are attributed."*

The latter, i.e. the attribution of identity characteristics (goals, interests, needs) by third parties, is usually justified by highlighting the customer benefit through the provision of high-quality information and personal offers. However, what is often forgotten is that no one has such privileged access to their own desires, goals and interests as the person concerned. Therefore, if the aim is truly to put the benefit of the customers first, it should also be possible to provide the users with information about their profile—so that they can optimise the offer according to their own ideas. What is recorded and why? What is not recorded and why? Is it possible or desirable for users to compare the interests of the operators of data-driven services with their own interests?

Looking at the fields of action of e-commerce and online marketing, it can be initially stated that the advertising industry has so far not managed to create transparency out of its own motivation. In order to strengthen the interests of European citizens, an ePrivacy regulation will therefore come into force, in addition to the EU GDPR (General Data Protection Regulation) which has already been in force since May 2018. The mere fact that, in addition to the *lex generalis* (EU GDPR), a *lex specialis* (ePrivacy) is needed, is an indication that there is not yet a common understanding of the correct data usage practice. The permissions to process usage data are managed by the data processing companies in so-called consent management systems. However, these primarily aim to increase the disposal and control power of companies by centrally managing consents. Thus, a conflict of objectives arises between the interest of companies, i.e. to achieve as high a consent rate as possible, and the interest of their customers in a transparent presentation of data usage practice. This conflict of objectives is reflected in the product design of leading consent management providers for over 20 years.[50] Although the GDPR provides for a duty of disclosure for all data

[50]This is also the case in the current IAB framework (TCF 2.0), where the focus has shifted to the "legitimate interests" of companies. Only after the third click in TCF 2.0 do you get to these purposes, which you then have to actively object to via opt-out. The Interactive Advertising

processing (state or non-state) institutions, so that those affected must be informed on request about which personal information is held. “In practice, however, the right to information is rarely claimed [. . .] It is also questionable what significance isolated data have when it remains unclear how this data is processed and on what basis it is used for decisions” (Kammerer 2016, p. 192).

When it is no longer just about the personalisation of product offers, but also about targeted information or disinformation campaigns in the context of knowledge transfer and news search, then the information asymmetry between media users and content suppliers carries additional explosive potential. In this sense, we have found in our inventory that all media presuppose a gatekeeper function. Even “in capitalist, liberal societies, information is, so to speak, ‘sieved’ through institutional filters before it can become news” (Zurstiege 2016, p. 146).[51] The gradual change in the gatekeeper function exacerbates this problem and leads us to the phenomenon of so-called echo chambers and filter bubbles: “Digital media offer highly personalised information, which is aligned with individual rather than societal relevance structures and offer each individual more of the same” (ibid. p. 150).

With regard to conscious and unconscious value inscriptions, we have found (in the problem-oriented description of current fields of action) that personalisation and contextualisation are less about the analysis of individual interests and needs, as individual desires and goals are dissolved in the “numerical generality” (Heesen, 2018) of affinity models and anonymisation methods. The phenomenon of echo chambers is therefore more of a danger of synchronising people with similar interests (for more on this, see Sect. 3.5). Especially in the context of financial, insurance and health data, it is not yet foreseeable what personal disadvantages and long-term societal risks would be associated with distributing individual needs and services according to the principle of numerical generality.

Some data-driven enterprises construct a reality that is increasingly inescapable for those affected, as the complexity of the emerging information spaces far exceeds human comprehension in certain application areas. Since the image we make of the world and ourselves is increasingly influenced by digital technologies (e.g. by pre-sorting learning and educational content for us), it is not just about administration, but also about the self-responsible design of a personal educational identity (see “Design Perspectives” in the fourth chapter); to continue to make our own decisions and not to be controlled from the outside more than before. The music is not in the piano, to return to the quote from Alan C. Kay. It is therefore not

Bureau (IAB) is an international trade association of the online advertising industry based in New York.

[51]Referring to the propaganda model by Herman and Chomsky (2002, p. 298) “»[A] propaganda model suggests that the ›societal purpose‹ of the media is to inculcate and defend the economic, social, and political agenda of privileged groups that dominate the domestic society and the state«“, Zurstiege (ibid. p. 147) sensitises to the fact that “the content offers that the mass media distribute society-wide, for everyone, essentially only serve the interests of the political and economic elites.”

just about the transmission of application knowledge or the competence to operate a certain medium (instrument), but about expressing our own thoughts, i.e. the realisation that we set the tone ourselves.

3.2 The Danger of Discrimination

The phenomenon of discrimination is primarily discussed in its negative connotation, as a danger of exclusion and rejection of certain people based on algorithmic selection criteria. Specifically, access restrictions to certain information and services, attractive offers and privileged social positions due to implicit or explicit identity characteristics of people are considered unjust (cf. Stoecker et al. 2011, p. 290). Characteristics that characterise people in their identity, such as religion, origin, sexual orientation, gender "can be immutable, but also temporary, such as age, unemployment, physical or mental deviation from a standard accepted as normal" (ibid.).

Looking back at our inventory, the danger of discrimination, in connection with self-driving vehicles, can easily be seen in relation to the possibilities of social construction, using a utilitarian approach. With the mass collection and processing of personal data, a highly sensitive differentiation in terms of "cost-benefit maximisation" would theoretically be conceivable. Because the more we know about the potentially affected victims, the more precisely the utilitarian control of self-driving vehicles could of course be programmed. As soon as a self-driving car would have access to the personality traits of the affected persons, specific behavioural rules could be established in dangerous or accident situations for the vehicle, for example, whether the survival of a group with a doctor, a female executive and two elderly ladies should be preferred to a group with an elderly woman, an elderly man and a homeless person—or whether the life of a male compared to that of a female executive is more worth protecting, etc.[52]

In the context of e-commerce and online marketing, the primary concern is whether consumers are shown different product or price offers based on implicit or explicit identity characteristics. In the case of knowledge transfer and news search, the question of participation and educational justice arises, as it has, for example, in a case of university place allocation in France. Discriminations in the processing of financial, insurance and health data are particularly concerning, as they could easily undermine the principle of solidarity in our society.

> *"Characteristics that give rise to discrimination are relatively stable and real identity characteristics, even if their social reality, such as racial affiliation, partly depends on false beliefs. Normatively speaking, identity characteristics should be irrelevant for the social situation of the characteristic bearers"* (Hermann 2011, p. 290).

[52]The Massachusetts Institute of Technology (MIT) has developed a "Moral Machine" (MM) for an online survey, which in its variety of human life trade-offs is hard to surpass.

Building on the media-philosophical considerations, I have shown in the previous chapter that ultimately every form of data processing and representation is based on conscious or unconscious value inscriptions. Every form of information visualisation presupposes a relevance mechanism so that individual data become visible to us. Regarding the phenomenon of social construction, it was shown that the selection criteria for algorithmic relevance calculations are mainly set from the outside. In the context of self-learning systems, it was explained that software developers often only define the initial conditions of the system. Especially in connection with the supposed distortions on social platforms, it can therefore be shown that the complex network information algorithms usually only reflect the behaviour and existing resentments of the users, i.e. not the algorithms, but the users are discriminatory. In view of this, the question arises whether the algorithmics should not be used in a positive-discriminatory[53] manner. The answer of libertarian paternalism is clear in this respect, especially when it comes to the aspect of justice. Particularly when it comes to creating equal opportunities, a gentle nudge (engl. *nudging*) seems justified here. *"In health and geriatric care or assistance, such effects are even desired when alternatives and exit options from system support are concealed. Under the term persuasive computing (persuasive: persuade), paternalism even gains a strategic concept"* (Wiegerling 2013, p. 375). Justice, participation and involvement are therefore central guiding principles in the discourse on algorithmic distortions and discriminations.

3.3 The Problem of Responsibility Gaps

Already in the introduction, three minimal conditions (control, transparency and freedom of action) for the attribution of moral responsibility were defined, following Hans Jonas (1984).[54] In addition, attention was drawn to the fact that (oder: it was pionted out that) responsibility in the traditional ethical understanding can only be assigned to human actions or their intentions and consequences. For "a specific feature of the responsibility-ethical approach is its starting (point?) from the actor's perspective" (Funiok 2016, p. 74). Therefore, "as a catchy short formula, the W-question 'who (subject) is responsible for what (object: action/omission), to whom (addressee), before which instance, why (norms) and in which time perspective?' is taken" (ibid.). In the differentiation of moral actors in the context of

[53]*"Positive discrimination refers to the preference of members of groups in the allocation of social goods, such as the filling of positions, the allocation of posts in politics and economy, of study places. Examples of a policy of positive discrimination are quota regulations"* (Hermann 2011, p. 290).

[54]Similarly, Matthias (2004, p. 175) argues: *"For a person to be rightly held responsible, that is, in accordance with our sense of justice, she must have control over her behaviour and the resulting consequences 'in a suitable sense'. That means that the agent can be considered responsible only if he knows the particular facts surrounding his action, and if he is able to freely form a decision to act, and to select one of a suitable set of available alternative actions based on these facts."*

conscious and unconscious value inscriptions, an initial overview of the potential bearers of responsibility in algorithm ethics was presented.

Building on the findings regarding the dynamics of self-learning systems and the collective dimension of algorithms it is necessary to confront the "individual, corporate and societal subjects of responsibility" (ibid.) now with regard to the question of practical implementation. For this, our problem description starts again with the field of action of self-driving vehicles. The responsibility discourse in the context of "autonomous driving" is often conducted in public against the background of the so-called "Trolley Problem". This originally involves a situation in rail traffic, where a switchman through his active intervention—the track change of a tram (engl. *trolley*)—could not prevent an accident with fatalities, but could reduce the number of victims (cf. Engisch 1930, p. 288). However, the discourse about supposed dilemma situations obscures the view of the actual complexity of responsibility attribution. To hold only the software developers accountable, as Bartlett (2019) suggests, does not do justice to the topic, just as if one only targets the superiors of technology corporations.

As outlined in the previous chapter, developers and operators have a particularly privileged access to the functioning of complex network information algorithms, as they are in the inner circle of the so-called responsibility onion (cf. Fig. 12). Therefore, they naturally have a particularly high degree of responsibility. But in the inner circle of the responsibility onion are also the users. Especially with regard to the collective dimension of self-learning systems, as is the case with fleet learning in shadow mode, it is therefore also necessary to hold the software users (as well as all other actors) accountable. Because in the context of complex self-organising systems there is not *the one* switchman.

This applies to all fields of action. An outsourcing of human morality—from the developers and operators via the swarm intelligence (e.g. of the car drivers in shadow mode or the so-called prosumers in the context of information and knowledge transfer) to the supposed artificial intelligence of machines—is an expression of a pragmatism that promotes a utilitarian benefit calculation, without necessarily demanding visible evidence for specific individual situations (cf. Koska 2018, p. 88). Ethics in this context is therefore called upon to expand the traditional understanding of responsibility and trust. Starting from the personal responsibility of the singular switchman, an expansion is usually first thought in the direction of "collective responsibility" (see Isaacs 2017) or towards "corporate and cooperative responsibility" (see Bratu 2017). Focusing on the task or shared responsibility, both of these conceptions ultimately aim at the traceability of different aspects of responsibility to natural persons.[55] However, problems arise when the attribution

[55] *"Division of labour in the group or team means that the individual is no longer responsible for all aspects of solving a task, but focuses on partial aspects and completely ignores certain challenges because others are responsible for their resolution. It is easy to imagine that in this context a tendency towards responsibility diffusion in groups has arisen. Each group member can benefit from the membership by ignoring certain challenges that are (supposed to be) handled by other group members"* (Bierhoff and Rohmann 2017, p. 928).

is not fully successful, when gaps emerge because not all aspects can be fully captured, when the system's interaction with the environment produces decisions or reactions that (in relation to the three minimum conditions) cannot meaningfully be conceived as the action (in the sense of task or co-responsibility) of a particular person. "In such novel 'networks of accountability', conditions of responsibility such as causality, knowledge or freedom of choice are difficult to estimate and consequential responsibility is often not clearly assignable" (Heise 2016, p. 206). Wilhelms (2017) advocates the concept of system responsibility in view of this situation:

> *"Person-bound responsibility is visibly losing its importance and legitimacy and needs to be supplemented by a regulatory responsibility that can be related to structures and to subjectless, anonymous processes. The term 'system responsibility' can help to educate the acting persons about such processes and to design corresponding options for action"* (ibid. p. 501).

Against this background, the system-theoretical approach of Nassehi (2019) also gains attractiveness.

However, an "outsourcing of morality" into self-learning systems carries the risk that we then only talk about responsibility in the context of correlations and no longer in the context of causalities.[56] In the media public, the supposed "power of algorithms" is often discussed against the background of diffuse responsibility relations. For example, Ranga Yogeshwar notes: *"And then we would experience something very contradictory, namely a modern technology with an almost regressive attitude of our culture, which goes back into the Middle Ages, into the fate of the algorithms"* (Fulde 2016). The problem of responsibility gaps thus leads to the danger that humans retreat behind technology.

3.4 The Danger of Digital Incapacitation

Until the end of the 20th century, incapacitation was generally "a judicial act by which the legal capacity of a person was abolished or restricted for his protection, the protection of his family or third parties" (Brockhaus Encyclopaedia Online 2021). To incapacitate a certain person, (in Germany until 1992) the incapacity of this person had to be determined by a court procedure. The reasons why a person could be declared incapable and incapacitated were laid down in § 6 BGB (mental illness or weakness, wastefulness, alcohol or drug addiction). However, since incapacitations often led to a conflict with the right to human dignity (Basic Law) in practice, the law was abolished. The feeling of incapacitation continues, however, based on the perception of one's own powerlessness and is thus closely related to a lack of responsibility, a restriction of personal autonomy and the idea of paternalism as a response to this deficiency.

[56] *"While 'causal responsibility' is always retrospective, the normative responsibility relationship has a prospective and a retrospective side"* (Werner 2013, p. 39).

From the context of medical ethics, we are familiar with the question of whether the well-being against the will of the person concerned, i.e. from outside (e.g. by the doctor or a legal guardian), may be enforced. Especially in situations where one can no longer face responsibility because one is no longer able to take a position, usually only a patient directive prepared in advance helps to express one's own will. The desire to die with dignity or—in the context of advancing digitalisation—to step down, as the American philosopher Dietrich (2011, p. 537) suggests, is a symbol of the process of creeping incapacitation, which is associated with the emergence of responsibility gaps.

For self-driving vehicles, it can be observed in relation to our five exemplary fields of action that the human being always has the possibility to overrule. Since the current models (for legal reasons) are usually only equipped with assistance systems (SAE-Level 2–3), the person leading the vehicle must even be able to take over control at any time. Experts criticise, however, that the attention and anticipation ability of the person at the wheel, which are necessary to solve difficult situations, inevitably degenerate if they have been on the road with the autopilot for long enough without an accident.[57]

The experience that machines—even in complex situations—act better, i.e. faster, more accurately and more efficiently than humans, can not only be observed in the context of self-driving vehicles,[58] but also in many other application areas. Access to relevant information is becoming more important than ever in view of the ever larger and faster growing mountains of data. To make this information visible to the individual, we need algorithmic gatekeepers, as shown in the field of knowledge transfer and news search. The human being consciously gives up a piece of his freedom of action to be able to orientate himself in artificially intelligent environments at all. However, this creates an information asymmetry between the data donors and the data processors. In the context of e-commerce and online marketing, this loss of control (over one's own data profile) carries the risk of manipulation and instrumentalisation for commercial purposes. Especially when processing financial, insurance and health data, a risk decision must also be made between individual and social interests. This inevitably leads to conflicts of objectives. Precisely because the added value of intelligent systems lies in the fact that users do not need to understand all the technical details to use a system, it is all the more important that we learn to assert ourselves under these conditions. The tension between predictability and responsibility is summed up by Wiegerling (2016, p. 222):

> *"If our life becomes predictable and supported by systems in this predictability, it no longer needs to be led. The relief provided by system support can go hand in hand with*

---

[57]Depending on the previously performed activity, experiments show that human vehicle drivers take up to 40 seconds to re-engage in a traffic situation—in any case longer than the average reaction time of 1 to 2 seconds in typical accident situations (cf. Lin 2015, p. 72).

[58]Section 1.1 of Chap. 3 states that up to 90% of all accidents with personal injury can currently be attributed to human failure (more on this see Koska 2018, p. 78 ff).

incapacitation and disempowerment of the individual and society if action dissolves into behaviour."

In the current debate about the dangers of digital incapacitation, the European Commission has also now put forward a proposal to protect personal freedom of action. On the basis of a risk-based assessment system, AI systems are to be banned *"that are considered a clear threat to the safety, livelihoods and rights of people [. . .] This includes AI systems or applications that manipulate human behaviour to circumvent the free will of the users"* (European Commission 2021). Article 5 (paragraph 1a) further states *"the placing on the market, putting into service or use of an AI system that deploys subliminal techniques beyond a person's consciousness in order to materially distort a person's behaviour in a manner that causes or is likely to cause that person or another person physical or psychological harm"* (European Commission 2021, p. 43).

Whether Europe will succeed with this initiative in positioning itself between the two extremes, the commercially driven digitalisation (USA) and the state-controlled digitalisation (China), remains to be seen. While in the press release of the Representation of the European Commission in Germany, for example, AI systems, "that manipulate human behaviour" and "enable a social behaviour assessment (Social Scoring)" are still explicitly referred to as an "unacceptable risk" (European Commission 2021) that needs to be prohibited, in the official regulatory proposal, only a prohibition of subliminal techniques that significantly influence or "materially distort" a person's behaviour (European Commission 2021, p. 43) is mentioned—with the proviso that no physical or psychological harm is or can be inflicted on individuals. However, this wording leaves open the initial (medical-ethical) question of whether paternalistic manipulation of human behaviour might be allowed in certain situations. But where would the boundary of significance be drawn and who can ultimately decide what serves the well-being of the users.

According to Wiegerling (2016, p. 222), comprehensive IT systems imply "potential for incapacitation and paternalistic effects when they are used in a controlling and steering manner in all spheres of life to contribute to the rationalisation and optimisation of existing conditions" (ibid.). The product design has a particularly strong influence on the control over one's own data, as we have already seen with regard to consent management systems. Mühlhoff (2019) also sees product design as a central lever to counteract digital incapacitation. Especially when it comes to assessing risk decisions involving trade-offs between security and personal freedom of choice, when optimal system support is accompanied by a loss of control for the individual and people are no longer trusted to make decisions in certain situations, then the mechanisms of paternalistic disempowerment and incapacitation come into play. Wiegerling (2016, p. 223) states:

"Privacy is seen as a component of personal expressions to be minimised [. . .] Individual expressions that cannot be assigned to typical behaviour may be considered suspicious from a security perspective. With the intrusion into the private sphere, there is a restriction of self-determination when comprehensive IT systems take decisions away from us, no longer allow us to perceive decision-making spaces and do not support certain volitions.

Thus, we are forced to adapt our volitions to system preferences, resulting in a reverse adaptation according to the aforementioned imperative" (Wiegerling 2016, p. 223).

This is also why "the use of interfaces is being discussed that allow users better insight and control over the collection and transmission of data as well as a flexible adjustment of filter and personalisation algorithms [...] as Nele Heise already noted in 2016 (p. 207) referring to Schuster et al. (2015) and Filipovic (2013).

3.5 On the Disintegration of the Public Sphere

The question of the disintegration or structural change of the public sphere is closely related to the discourse on media-technical innovations and changes. The fear of a systematic influence on democratic opinion formation is therefore not new, but accompanies the debate on the concept of the public sphere, ever since the conditions of free decision-making and the possibilities of collective power control have been considered. "The concept of the public sphere plays a central role in debates about the significance of media communication for the political process" (Bieber 2016, p. 67). For the legitimacy of modern systems of rule depends on the approval of the public.

"The development of a democratic public sphere involves all citizens and not just the holders of political offices in such a way that a state with the minimal goal of external peacekeeping formulated by Hobbes can still be made with radical egoists, but hardly one that is good and appropriate to meet the modern challenges posed by the scientific-technological society, which must be understood as part of the global society" (Brenner 2011, p. 281).

The problems and dangers outlined above (of social construction, discrimination, responsibility gaps, and digital disenfranchisement) mark central cornerstones that are discussed in the course of advancing algorithmisation, digitalisation and datafication from the feuilleton to science, politics and the economy. The analysis of the problem situation, as to be expected, varies greatly. Recently, the talk of the "power of algorithms" and "artificially intelligent systems (AI)" has intensified again. With this headline and the buzzword "AI", it is usually suggested that the transfer of power from humans to machines is imminent or has already been completed in certain areas. The actors recede behind the nebulous and unleashed power of algorithmic processes and effects. The behaviour of algorithms is then described as biased, discriminatory, distorting, reinforcing, etc., while the behaviour of the people who influence the behaviour of the algorithms is usually inadequately reflected.

"It is not 'the people at Facebook' (or at Twitter, Google, Instagram and all the other providers) who bring approaches of order and productive dynamics into the individual experiences of the users, but it is routinised protocols and procedures, in short: algorithms, that take over this performance. And not only that: Here, there are no rigid structures at work that stubbornly repeat once established processes, but self-learning

agents that can adapt and change their 'behaviour' along a constantly growing data corpus" (Bieber 2019, p. 156).

An *AI ethics*, an *ethics for algorithms* or *data ethics*, so the universally cherished hope, is supposed to alternately put a stop to this unleashing by imposing moral boundaries on the *behaviour of algorithms*. However, the discourse as to whether self-learning algorithms actually appear as a "source of certain behaviour" should not be limited to individual professional ethics (e.g. to computer science or software development, journalism, etc.). Because algorithmic thinking and action, as we have seen, is fed from the ideological and intellectual historical stock of rational and purposeful thinking with which we collectively try to understand and shape the world. An understanding of the normative dimensions of an algorithm ethics should therefore not be removed from the public sphere. It is necessary to create transparency, open the discourse space and initiate deliberative processes beyond specialist circles. Integration and participation are prerequisites for the creation of a public sphere and this in turn is a condition for societal discourse about the behaviour of algorithms.

The social and media ethicist Alexander Filipović clarifies (referring to the challenges in times of digitality) that we need "alternative theories for an ethics of public communication" for this: *"Holding on to the ideal concept of the deliberative public sphere in this situation seems like the sign 'Forest dieback forbidden!' in a dying forest: well-intentioned and correct—but apparently not the means of choice to improve the situation"* (Filipović 2019a, p. 220). The behaviour of algorithms and artificially intelligent systems must rely on democratic consent. If this is not successful, then the question arises as to whether an ethics of algorithms is still an ethics in the classical sense—or merely a technocratic elite or a "pure" machine ethics.[59]

"It's about the analysis and clarification of the infrastructure of the contemporary political public sphere in the era of digitality" (Filipović 2019a, p. 229). The feuilletonistically invoked decay of the public sphere can be described much more differentiated after a detailed examination of the infrastructure. This can be further elaborated using the example of social construction in view of the problem of the so-called filter bubbles. The phenomenon of filter bubbles, and here we can tie in with the initially mentioned fear of a systematic influence on public opinion, is not new. The prehistory of digitalised filter bubbles is located by Bedford-Strohm (2019) in monasteries, political parties and established press organs.

"Liberal as well as authoritarian governed state alliances are characterised by different contexts in which like-minded or functionally allied groups of people come together to jointly pursue a specific activity. This applies to functionally elite classes in the feudal

[59]The differentiation that matters at this point concerns the media-philosophical interpretation practice with which statements, such as those by Bieber (see above), which refer to the "behaviour of algorithms", are structurally classified. Does the genitive in Ethics of Algorithms refer to a *genitivus objectivus* or a *genitivus subjectivus* in the author's view? (I will return to this at the end of the investigation).

> *system just as much as for economically organised groups in the industrial age and milieu-based demographics in the service-oriented market economy. Filtering is also not new in the media system. On the contrary: The pluralistic press landscape was created from partisan publications, which were built as a means to an end of a political or societal goal. The idea that individual media should be committed to objectivity and diversity of opinion is a relatively new idea of the 20th century"* (ibid. p. 202).

The digital version of the filter bubbles came into the focus of public perception with Eli Pariser (2011). As "digital propaganda" and "greenhouses of radicalisation" Zurstiege (2016, p. 150) refers to the "echo chambers" of digital media and immediately opposes Eli Pariser's analysis with the thesis of Cass Sunstein (2007): *"Not the decay of the public sphere is the primary problem, but the radicalisation of existing and potential members of societal splinter groups."* However: *"what can be theoretically plausibilised with the concept of the filter bubble, is empirically not yet clearly verifiable"*, Bedford-Strohm (2019, p. 202) counters. From his point of view *"a more fundamental theorem is needed that integrates the yields of the filter bubble theory with the socio-political influences of media forms beyond personalised news feeds"* (ibid. p. 214). For both analogue and digital filter bubbles, he refers to the concept of "confirmation bias" (ibid.) from psychology. This consideration leads us back to our media philosophical preliminary considerations through the process of conscious and unconscious value inscription.

4 Criteriology for an Ethics of Algorithms

Following the preceding overview of the current debate, this chapter aims to develop a criteriology for an ethical evaluation of algorithms based on the problem-oriented description. The goal is to create an approach for dealing with the dangers and problems of algorithmisation that goes beyond the analysis of the current situation. The time- and culture-specific aspects of algorithmisation should be arranged in view of an overarching structure. The path from the ideational and intellectual historical foundations via the media philosophical preliminary considerations and the ethos of algorithmic thinking and acting to the current debate about algorithms finally leads us to the question of whether a common criteriology can be found for the advancing algorithmisation at all.

The outsourcing of algorithmic thinking and action is often not a substitution, but an extension of the material infrastructure. However, with the transfer of technical functional logic, a certain ideological mindset is also transferred. Although the directional tendency of algorithmics seems to be moving towards the machine simulation of an ethical consciousness at this level, at the beginning of the 21st century, predominantly negative voices can be heard in Europe against such an undertaking.

In recent years, a multitude of ethical guidelines and corporate self-commitment codes have been created, which are intended to provide guidance in the general handling of data and specifically with applications from the field of artificial intelligence. Empirical studies show that almost all data ethics and AI guidelines

Fig. 13 Word cloud with a rough overview of currently dominant values, norms and principles in data ethics and AI guidelines (Image source: Author's own illustration)

published so far refer more or less to the same terminologies (cf. Zeng et al. 2018; Jobin et al. 2019; Fjeld et al. 2020; Hagendorff 2020). The reason for this could be that a broad ethical consensus already exists (or the authors of the guidelines tend to copy from each other, for example, to save time and resources). However, if one looks more closely at the geographical assignment of the guidelines (see Jobin et al. 2019, p. 391),[60] this rather suggests that the currently prevailing values, norms and principles (see Fig. 13) are also an expression of a cultural bias.

Differences and differentiations can only be observed in the current codes and guidelines with regard to the weighting and semantic interpretation of these values, norms and principles.

Within the context of the Western-influenced frame of reference, it is therefore less about defining further ethical criteria, but about how these values, principles and norms can be integrated into everyday work. Such a pragmatic approach is certainly helpful for the perception of digital corporate responsibility and is therefore to be welcomed. The aim is, within the scope of this paper and in general, to look beyond one's own horizon and not only to know but also to understand other perspectives. After all, datafication and algorithmisation is a global phenomenon that requires an intercultural moral philosophy. Any attempt to justify the general validity or universality of a position, in the words of communication and media scientist Roger Silverstone, also presupposes *"a form of coercion"* (Silverstone 2008, p. 20), so *"that the proposal to search for the conditions of a morality of the media can at any time attract the accusation that it is at best ethnocentric and at worst an expression of that form of cultural imperialism that it wants to prevent"* (ibid.).[61]

[60]Most ethical guidelines are published in the United States and within the European Union according to Jobin et al. (2019, p. 391), followed by the United Kingdom and Japan. Canada, Iceland, Norway, the United Arab Emirates, India, Singapore, South Korea, and Australia are (at least) represented with one document each.

[61]Against this background, Silverstone advocates a new form of polis, which he refers to as "Mediapolis" (ibid.). Silverstone considers the concept of mutual recognition as the basis for

The following criteriology is intended to propose a position between relativism and universalism. Since the dimensions of the criteriology are determined by the preceding analysis of the problems and dangers, it can be considered relative on the one hand. It is related to the exemplary inventory resp. the selection of fields of action, the current technical possibilities, the Christian-Western culture, my personal experiences and value systems, among other things. At the same time, building on Silverstone (2008) and in reference to Christians (2019), a contribution to understanding a cross-cultural criteriology is also to be made. For this purpose, the proposed criteriology is divided into four sections.[62] The first section is about identifying time- and culture-independent elements for an ethics of algorithms. Subsequently, in the second step, two thematic fields are taken up, which result from the descriptive analysis of the fields of action and for which it is necessary to develop contemporary guidelines. The third step also involves updating existing values, norms and principles with a view to the societal opportunities and dangers of digitisation, this time, however, from the aspect of weighing up. In the fourth and final step, three application-related criteria are specified.

4.1 General Ethical Aspects

Building on the previous analysis, two paths can be taken in the search for universally valid criteria for an algorithm ethics. The starting point for both paths is the question "What is morality?" The first way to encounter this question is the normative one. Such a path is taken by those who ask which actions in the context of algorithm design (or which applications with regard to a certain data usage practice etc.) are morally allowed, which are forbidden, and which are indifferent (cf. Scarano 2011, p. 25). A normative theory of algorithm ethics thus presupposes an idea of what is morally right or wrong, which entities are considered legitimate or illegitimate from a moral point of view and which are beyond the scope of moral evaluation. In the course of this study, we have, for example, already encountered the thesis of the value neutrality of scientific knowledge and the theory of use of media. We have found that common statements like "technology as such is neutral!", "media are tools" and "in the end it only matters how we use media or tools" are usually based on false beliefs. Anyone who only takes this path, therefore, runs the risk of slipping into a dysfunctional black-and-white thinking, of overestimating the validity of their own moral convictions and of no longer perceiving the shades of grey (diverging moral views). In addition to the normative

a cross-cultural moral minimalism: *"The forms of visualisation and representation of the other in the media are crucial for our morality today [. . .]. But it's not just about appearance and visibility. It's about being heard. And not just as a source of sound, but also in terms of content. So it's about understanding"* (Silverstone 2008, p. 161 f).

[62]The assignment of autonomy and digital self-determination to the second section of the criteriology refers (with regard to the central importance of autonomy in Western philosophy) to the fact that the four dimensions of the criteriology are not (necessarily) to be understood hierarchically.

path, there is another approach to the question of morality with a completely different intention. This second approach does not aim to search for the right morality. Rather, it aims to maintain neutrality towards normative questions. The *"goal is to describe the [note: shades of grey] various aspects and manifestations of this phenomenon and to prepare explanations for them"* (ibid. p. 25 f). This second concept, where the focus is not initially on what the right morality is regarding the phenomenon of morality, is the descriptive one. In principle, both paths can be taken to gain access to the following general ethical considerations.

4.1.1 The Principle of Human Dignity

Any serious conversation about universal norms in media ethics necessarily includes the name of Clifford Christians according to Cortes (2020, p. 131): "'Necessarily' because Christians was at the inception of this conversation. Indeed, he is considered one of its 'precursors', since he began to make an appeal for 'normative approaches to media ethics' as early as 1979" (ibid.). In his late work "Media Ethics and Global Justice in the Digital Age", Christians (2019) summarises all his considerations for a cross-cultural communication and media ethics. He shows how a normative approach to morality can be complemented by a descriptive one. Based on his considerations for anchoring media ethics in the "the sacredness of life" this will first be explained in relation to the principle of human dignity.

The challenge, according to Christians, is to develop a universalistic model that keeps ethics close to people's everyday lives, emphasising the diversity of cultures and not homogenising them through abstractions (cf. Christians 2019, p. 76). In almost all data and AI ethics codes published so far, the human being is at the centre of technological progress. This human-centred perspective is compatible with Christians' observation that the philosophy of technology traditionally tends more towards an ethics of being than an ontology of absolutism (cf. ibid.). Referring to Thomas Nagel, he further argues i) that moral values are more likely to be located in human existence than in metaphysical constructs[63] ii) that we can, however, (due to our ability to abstract and reflect) form overarching conceptions of the world with us in it. At this superordinate level, Christians anchors the sanctity of human life ("sacredness of human life") as a universal norm. Reverence for life and recognition of human dignity is understood from this standpoint as the transnational and cross-cultural crystallisation point of ethical decisions. Whenever the principle of human dignity is introduced in application-related discourses, it is usually about exploring the limits of the unbearable: *"The appeal to human dignity is primarily an attempt to prevent the worst, and only secondarily to optimise the quality of life"* proclaim Andorno and Christensen (2014, p. 198) in the handbook "Ethics and Law of Research on Humans."

[63] "Norms and values are not something a culture has, but something it is" (McDonald, 1986, p. 3).

> *"The concept of human dignity refers to the intrinsic value of each human individual, who, as a human being, deserves unconditional respect in the same way,* i.e., *regardless of special characteristics, features, or achievements. The concept emphasises that there is no worthless human life and that every human being counts equally. Ultimately, the invocation of human dignity expresses the idea that all humans are persons, that they have the right to have rights"* (ibid. p. 197).

The special feature of Christians' anchoring of human dignity in the "sacredness of life" compared to the predominantly legal foundations (e.g. by Andorno and Christensen)[64] is that it is only limitedly accessible to the rational considerations of human reason. Rather, it refers to an existentialist experience of being human and allows, on the basis of this experience, to resolve absolutist claims to validity and moral disagreements—ideally without drifting into moral relativism (cf. Christians 2019, p. 237 f). For secular readers, however, the reference to the sanctity of human life will cause strong irritation. Especially when it comes to resolving absolutist claims to validity. Accordingly, Andorno and Christensen locate the principle of human dignity in a codified ethics: *"The first and most important function is to absolutely prohibit certain actions. Here, no trade-offs with other goods are allowed"* (Andorno and Christensen 2014, p. 198). As examples of absolute prohibitions that must not be restricted under any circumstances, the authors mention the prohibitions of torture or slavery. With regard to medical research on humans, (referring to the International Covenant on Civil and Political Rights 1966, Art. 7 and 8) the necessity of voluntary consent of the subjects or their named legal representatives is emphasised. On a second level, human dignity can then indeed be weighed against other goods according to Andorno and Christensen.[65] In view of the dangers and problems of advancing algorithmisation, the principle of human dignity can be invoked to counteract the instrumentalisation and reification of humans. Specifically, the problem of social construction, the danger of discrimination and digital disempowerment can be excellently discussed against the backdrop of human dignity. For it is not uncommon for both consumers and employees to be seen as an object in the digital development process and thus as a means to an end. Against such an understanding, Kant's third version of the categorical imperative can be cited from the perspective of Western philosophy, for

[64]The authors of the article on human dignity in the Handbook of Ethics and Law of Research on Humans, Roberto Andorno and Birgit Christensen (the latter is to be distinguished from the communication scientist and ethicist Clifford Christians due to the similar surnames), were working and researching at the Legal Institute of the University of Zurich at the time of publication.

[65]*"For example, an optimisation of health care or education, which also base their demands on the idea of human dignity, are limited by the actually available financial means of a society. Here, human dignity does not formulate an absolute, but a relative demand. Measures in these areas do not have an imperative character, but mark a desirable goal and may therefore be weighed against other protectable goods"* (ibid.).

example.[66] Kant bases the dignity of humans on their ability to give themselves laws, i.e. on their autonomy.[67] At this point, I am not interested in discussing the pros and cons of Kantian philosophy (further details on the extensional and intensional determination of human dignity in Kant can be found, among others, in Wils 2011, p. 560 f). Rather, I would like to take this opportunity to point out that our legal conception and our legal system are also shaped by this thinking. While the European-enlightened judiciary traditionally anchors human dignity in the awareness of autonomy and in the moral capacity of humans, it has long since overwhelmed most media users with this claim. For a meaningful weighing of the chances and risks is in many cases neither possible for the users nor for the developers or legislators. Also, because the principle of human dignity occupies a prominent position in many constitutions—including in the Federal Republic of Germany (Art. 1, para. 1)—as well as in the Universal Declaration of Human Rights of the UN, it is necessary to translate the concept of human dignity into concrete guiding principles for action. While Western thinking will probably primarily strive to establish and ensure personal autonomy—Luhmann (1965) associates the concept of dignity, for example, with the condition "of the success of a person's self-presentation as an individual personality" (ibid. p. 61)—Silverstone (2008) proposes concepts such as truth and justice, which "play a role in every known society, [...] as abstract building blocks of a general—albeit narrow [...]—moral basis" (ibid. p. 32). The initial proclamation by Christians of the rooting of human dignity in the "sacredness of life" is therefore not a necessary, but merely a sufficient condition—which, when spelling out what is to be understood as dignified or undignified existence, has always given humanity more breadth and depth across cultures (not only in a positive sense).

4.1.2 The Principle of Responsibility

Building on the principle of dignity and against the background of the associated discourse (e.g. about the unavailability of the person's centre or also the inviolability of life), the principle of responsibility moves into the centre of general ethical consideration next. With the human ability to live according to one's own laws (awareness of autonomy), the necessity to take moral responsibility for one's own actions also gains in importance. Already in the differentiation of the moral actors, we have seen that the traditional practice of giving account and response (ger. *Für-etwas-Rede-und-Antwort-stehen,* Werner 2011, p. 541) quickly reaches its limits in the context of complex network information algorithms and self-learning systems. For the attribution of responsibility, we have defined three

[66]"Act in such a way that you treat humanity, whether in your own person or in the person of any other, never merely as a means to an end, but always at the same time as an end" (Kant: AA IV, p. 429, online https://korpora.zim.uni-duisburg-essen.de/kant/aa04/429.html).

[67]*"But the legislation itself, which determines all value, must therefore have a dignity,* i.e., *an absolute, incomparable value, for which the word respect alone gives the appropriate expression of the estimation that a rational being must make of it. Autonomy is therefore the ground of the dignity of human and every rational nature"* (Kant: AA IV, p. 436, online https://korpora.zim.uni-duisburg-essen.de/kant/aa04/436.html).

minimal conditions (control, transparency and freedom of action) in reference to Hans Jonas (1984) and outlined the problem of responsibility gaps that arise when these three conditions cannot be met.

We have discussed one strategy to counter the problem of responsibility gaps in connection with the collective dimension of algorithmics. From the developers and operators to swarm intelligence (e.g. of drivers in shadow mode or the so-called prosumers in the context of information and knowledge transfer) to the supposed Artificial Intelligence of machines, this approach aims to make ethics itself (to a certain extent) machine-operable. The attempt to gradually transfer responsibility for certain decisions step by step to a self-learning system ("out-sourcing of morality") raises many questions. Because the paradigm of any responsibility is traditionally the responsibility of the individual (cf. Gerhardt 2017, p. 432). To attribute individual responsibility, for example, based on the previously presented Demand-Supply model, it is necessary to make a statement about the actor status of collective entities. Because in everyday language we already speak in this context of the responsibility of individual departments (collective responsibility), of corporate responsibility or also of co-operative responsibility (in cross-company development projects). Whether the primacy of individual responsibility can be maintained in view of the complexity of increasing networking is controversial in the face of advancing globalisation and digitalisation—while Isaacs (2017, p. 474) warns, for example, that in many cases we can no longer take a normative stance if we abandon the collective actor status and the model of collective responsibility, Bratu ultimately advocates "ontological parsimony" (2017, p. 498) and for expanding the concept of responsibility for a gapless attribution of responsibility instead:

> *"A broad concept of responsibility, on the other hand, allows (individual or collective) actors to also be responsible for the unintended, but foreseeable consequences of their actions as well as for their omissions. In its most comprehensive form, a broad concept of responsibility understands responsibility as care, so that actors can also be responsible for ensuring that certain desirable states of the world occur in the future, provided they can contribute to their realisation"* (ibid. p. 497).

In this context, recent research suggests that these so-called "responsibility gaps" cannot be addressed by relying solely on classical models of individual or collective responsibility. Instead, a shift toward a relational understanding of responsibility is required—one that foregrounds shared accountability, answerability, and stakeholder participation throughout the AI lifecycle (cf. Koska, forthcoming). This perspective not only addresses the distributed nature of agency in socio-technical systems but also questions the ideal of a neutral observer, which still underpins many current attempts at bias mitigation.

According to Gerhardt (2017, pp. 445–449), the merit of such an "overstretched conception of responsibility" (ibid. p. 447) is primarily to remind people of the limits of their actions (ibid.). Because the price we pay for an "overstretching of the concept of responsibility" (ibid.) often leads (in the last step, for example, also with Hans Jonas) to overburdening people: "And he who wants too much, wants, according to a line of poetry often quoted by Kant from one of his students, nothing" (ibid. p. 446). Also with regard to the current debate about an ethics of algorithms, it is not just about locating the subjects of responsibility (actors) in any goal-oriented organised collective or in a particular company or in the respective department (see above), but primarily about a meaningful limitation of what can be made responsible.

In view of the increasing complexity and risk richness Wilhelms (2017) therefore proclaims: "The question of who should bear the responsibility is losing importance compared to the search according to the structural conditions of responsibility" (ibid. p. 517). Without wanting to completely abandon the concept of individual responsibility, he further explains: *"The 'classic' person-related responsibility, including its usual expansions in the sense of 'collective' or 'corporate' responsibility, is to be supplemented by a regulatory responsibility that refers to the structural conditions of the possibility of responsibility"* (ibid. p. 522). The programme associated with the term system responsibility aims, according to Wilhelms, to "reflect and bridge the gap between subject and system" (ibid. p. 518). A discussion of whether such a system could or should be capable of taking on the actor's perspective goes far beyond the classic concept of moral responsibility or actors; for example, the assignment of responsibility relations in the subjectless dynamics of self-learning systems (cf. Nassehi 2019) would be less based on causality, but rather more than before on the basis of correlations and so on. A central problem that has already been discussed in the context of the current discourse is that such a system could even increase the risk of digital incapacitation. "That is, the debate in the responsibility discourse is ignited by the central question of whether and to what extent such a form of responsibility represents an ethically deficient development" (ibid. p. 503). In Wilhelms' view, it would not be so "if it proved to be the better and more successful way to secure and develop human existence" (ibid.).

4.1.3 The Enforcement Problem

The insight into the correctness of a certain practice does not necessarily mean that humans actually act according to the standard of this knowledge. Various reasons can be given for this. Aristotle had already dealt with this phenomenon in the Nicomachean Ethics VII 1–11 under the term of Akrasia (ancient Greek ἀκρασία *akrasia*, lat. *incontinentia*, "weakness of will, incontinence"). In everyday life, it often requires willpower (ancient Greek ἐγκράτεια *enkrateia*) and attitude (or resilience) to actively pursue one's own "subjective purposes despite all difficulties, especially to control opposing inclinations and feelings" (Thiess 2011, p. 554). From a purely pragmatic point of view, weak-willed people who capitulate to internal and external resistance therefore need additional motivation or compulsion to do the right thing.

The enforcement problem refers to akratic actions, that is, acting against better knowledge. Let's first recall the examples of absolute prohibitions in the context of a legislated ethics by Andorno and Christensen (2014, p. 198). From a constitutional perspective, it was necessary to draw a clear line on the issues of torture and enslavement in order to uphold human dignity. Analogous to medical research on humans, the need for voluntary consent from consumers or their legal representation is also associated with the digital illumination of humans. The so-called "Privacy Paradox" (Barnes 2006) is a much-discussed example of a (supposedly) akratic action by consumers in this context. It describes a situation in which people share personal information (especially over the internet) against their better judgement. However, an akratic action only occurs here if the acting person actually considers the protection of their privacy as an absolute good that should always be preferred over all other things (e.g. the need for self-presentation)—and yet shares private information. Insofar as visibility, embodiment and personality, as Lück (2013) has shown, is understood as an anthropological characteristic of human existence, the question is raised under what circumstances the disclosure of personal information can be described as akratic at all.[68]

A complete rejection of the private disclosure of information would be necessary, for example, from a constitutional perspective, if we were certain that the release of our data would lead directly to torture and enslavement. According to Aristotle, this would already be the case if the knowledgeable person allowed himself to be dominated and dragged around like a slave by hasty desires such as pleasure or anger (cf. Aristotle: Nicomachean Ethics: VII 5, 1157b18-19). If the desire for visibility and recognition drives us into a dependency relationship and we share our data for this reason alone, then we should seriously consider how we can break this cycle. In the context of the inventory, the vision of "neuromarketing" was already discussed, which could bring completely new conditions of will formation (especially for the advertising industry), insofar as communication strategies could be adapted in real time to the respective emotional state of the customer. In order not to exacerbate a problem that is already 2,500 years old through the use of digital technologies, it is necessary to counteract this in good time.

Countermeasures are being taken in the European Union in particular through joint legislative initiatives, such as the GDPR or the "Harmonised Rules on Artificial Intelligence" (European Commission 2021). To build sustainable trust in digital services, the purely legal concept of responsibility must be expanded. Because what is already provided for in theory is unfortunately rarely correctly implemented in practice—as was explained with reference to the IAB framework TCF 2.0.[69] It turns out that the enforcement problem, upon closer inspection, has not only an individual but also a systemic, collective dimension. In the introductory section on the dangers and problems of algorithmisation, the two driving forces of

[68]At this point, I am primarily concerned with the question of whether akrasia is possible and only secondarily with the privacy paradox.

[69]Addendum to the original text (dissertation from July 2021): In February 2022, the Belgian data protection authority declared the "Transparency and Consent Framework—TCF 2.0" to be illegal and asked the European branch of IAB to delete all collected personal data (cf. Dachwitz 2022). IAB Europe has rejected the assessment of the data protection authority on the one hand, but on the other hand has already announced the implementation of an action plan to ensure the further use of the TCF in the market (cf. IAB Europe 2022). As long as the underlying conflict of interest is not resolved, the race (between the hare and the hedgehog) is thus heading towards a TCF 3.0.

the system, power and capitalisation, were already mentioned. The conflict of objectives between the protection of privacy and the capitalisation of our personal activities, to stay with the above example, therefore needs to be reflected on from both the inside and outside perspective of this system.

4.2 Guiding Directives

Algorithmic thinking and action always takes place under a sense of orientation. The main focus is on creating values. In the search for suitable criteria for an ethics of algorithms, we have already named two ways (the normative and the descriptive) to find common values in the previous section. Based on Christians' (2019) anchoring of media ethics in the "sacredness of life", we have so far aimed to reveal something about the general reference points of an ethics of algorithms, not only with regard to a specific time and a specific culture. The following guiding values also aim to identify central criteria for an ethical evaluation of algorithms. Unlike the general ethical aspects, however, this section aims to uncover ideal guiding principles that consciously allow for cultural differences in terms of content. Just as star constellations provide common points of orientation for seafarers, the following guiding directives should provide a common basis for discussion for continuous search and understanding processes.

Building on the enforcement problem, the principle of responsibility and human dignity, the following section will only initiate the necessity of a contemporary differentiation of these criteria. To begin with, this concerns the topics autonomy and digital self-determination and subsequently the topic area education, participation and justice.

4.2.1 Autonomy and Digital Self-Determination

Extensive discussions have taken place in recent years about a loss of personal autonomy against the backdrop of the dangers and problems of algorithmisation outlined above.[70] Until the introduction of the EU GDPR, much suggested that the idea of personal autonomy was being overrun by the digital revolution (see e.g. Pauen and Welzer 2015). The critical witnesses of this development usually pointed to the increasing loss of control of consumers, the problem of social construction as well as the danger of digital incapacitation and discrimination etc. (see e.g. Bunz 2012; Pariser 2011; Morozov 2013; Mayer-Schönberger and Cukier 2013; Lanier 2013; Filipović 2013; Seemann 2014; Hofstetter 2014; Schirrmacher 2011, 2013). The sceptical analysis of the current situation was further intensified with regard to a temporal vanishing point, which is celebrated by the apologists of technical progress as transhumanism and singularity, but which critical voices claim would be equivalent to the end of humans as independent and self-determined people. The concept of autonomy is thus an elementary—in

[70]Therefore, I will also tie in with my analysis in Koska (2015b, p. 85 ff) here.

Europe possibly even the central—anchor point for an ethical confrontation with the digital revolution.

> *"The concept of autonomy, although its history goes back two and a half millennia (cf. Pohlmann 1971), has become a central concept of modernity. In ethics, it stands representative for that modern moral consciousness of freedom, in which the normative responsibility of the human being as an insurmountable prerequisite for normative obligation systematically comes into effect"* (Bielefeldt 2011, p. 311).

In the context of digitalisation, autonomy is often synonymous with (informational) self-determination, sovereignty, freedom, self-governance, self-regulation and self-creation. Other values, such as security or privacy, are often negotiated in relation to digital innovations under the concept of autonomy or ultimately traced back to this concept. A central criterion in the evaluation of digital technologies is therefore the way in which these technologies enable, preserve or corrupt personal autonomy. An evaluation of the question of whether a technology ensures the personal autonomy of the users is, however, only meaningful if it is visible which concept of autonomy underlies this evaluation. For this, it is necessary to enter into dialogue with each other as the debate has become highly differentiated and specialised in recent decades (see Rössler 2011, p. 93).

Autonomy functions in the context of comprehensive digitalisation as a partial element of the ethical idea of human freedom. But what makes an action autonomous? Betzler (2013) names two basic intuitions that we associate with personal autonomy—control and authenticity: *"Whoever is autonomous controls his immediate given motives or controls himself through self-chosen goals, by accepting them, approving them, identifying with them, valuing them or rejecting them, not letting them become effective, disapproving them and distancing himself from them"* (ibid. p. 12). The condition of authenticity adds that, *"what a person approves and by which she controls herself, should be something that is really 'her own' and that really 'distinguishes' her"* (ibid. p. 13). As already explained elsewhere (see e.g. Koska 2015b, 2018; Koska and Filipović 2019; Koska 2020), it is necessary to supplement these two minimal conditions in view of the increasing datafication and algorithmisation of reality with a third condition, otherwise it is not possible for the data donors to control whether, for example, the filter criteria—in the case of personalised information and knowledge processing—really correspond to their own motives and self-set goals. To ensure personal autonomy in times of AI and Big Data, I have proposed a transparency condition in addition to the control and authenticity condition of Monika Betzler (cf. Koska 2015b). The value of transparency (and control) is closely related to the concept of the gradual degree of autonomy (as we will see in more detail in the context of the balancing criteria); because in the literature, as Rössler (2011, p. 93) explains:

> *"[It is] rightly distinguished between the categorical attribution of autonomy, which is due to every person qua person; and autonomy as ability (in the sense of a possibility and the actual exercise of autonomy). Autonomy in the categorical sense is due to persons then and only then when they in principle have the unrestricted ability to autonomy,* i.e. *not children*

or demented people; above a certain threshold, persons are therefore referred to as autonomous. Below this threshold, however, persons can have the ability to autonomy to a greater or lesser extent: hence we speak here of a gradual concept."

Against the background of this gradual progression, the two extremes of the transparency condition can also be defined: *"i) A maximum transparency condition would be fulfilled if an insight into all personal data for the affected person is possible at any time, ii) a minimum transparency condition would be fulfilled if the data profiles, which consist of raw data with countless correlations, are arranged for the user in such a way that he can do something meaningful with this information"* (Koska 2015b, p. 86).

Transparency is—just like autonomy—not a binary concept. While the idea of autonomy in ethics is associated with the idealised ability of the human being to understand himself completely out of his freedom at some point in his development and to act morally out of this freedom, complete transparency in many situations appears neither desirable nor achievable, as will be further explained.

4.2.2 Education, Participation and Justice

In the context of the problem-oriented inventory, it was explained, that the topic of digitalisation can no longer be ignored from contemporary learning and education offers. In general, the ethical problem of education and training can be divided into two contexts according to Mandry (2011).

"Since education is an intentional, formative action of people for people, which typically includes a power gradient, one must firstly ask about the legitimacy of education: Who may educate whom with which means and with which objectives? Justification is needed for both the educational or training objectives and the methods used for them as well as the groups of people who are active in education, and finally the circle of those who are legitimately the addressees of educational action. Secondly, the education and training system must meet ethical requirements of justice, as it is a significant factor within the overall societal distribution of goods and burdens and is closely linked with it in the allocation of chances for social recognition and social rank" (ibid. p. 248).

The fundamental aim of education is to impart knowledge and skills that contribute to the preservation of human life. From an economic perspective, this involves an education that enables citizens to provide for their basic needs (such as food, clothing, housing, health) and also educates them to be contributors in a community of shared labour and solidarity. Only *"at an advanced stage does the expansion of human life's richness (and not just the abundance of goods) in the sense of diverse, autonomously selectable cultural development opportunities for free individuals come into focus"* (Ulrich 2011, p. 300). Due to the logic of the situation, in a resource-poor country like Germany, the initial focus is on increasing societal human capital through education (to avoid losing economic competitiveness). Along with imparting basic technical skills, it is also important to reflect on the impacts and effects of digital world construction (see inventory).

"The media 'literacy' of citizens is a prerequisite for their participation in the Mediapolis, i.e., late modern society as a whole," Silverstone (2008, p. 274) assists.[71] In the context of school and university curricula, the importance and significance of computer science education have been discussed internationally for more than 50 years, as specified above. It was also shown in this context that a multitude of concepts and ideas for integrating digital education into the process of lifelong learning already exist. Against this background, a model was presented based on Humbert and Losch (2017) that differentiates between i) application ii) design and iii) decision-making (see Fig. 7) and is compatible with the minimal conditions of personal autonomy just discussed.

Digital expertise requires—just like autonomy—a continuous and progressive practice of application, design, and decision-making skills. The more technologies penetrate the personal sphere of individuals from the outside to create technical identity constructions, the more the focus of digital education must also shift from learning and educational content to the administration of a personal learning, education, or research profile. Because the virtual space is already overcrowded with "virtual zombies," as Yvonne Hofstetter calls the usage profiles that users themselves have no access to and of whose existence they still have no concrete idea even after the introduction of the EU-DSGVO.[72]

The only control option, and here we can return to the privacy paradox that we just discussed in connection with the enforcement problem, usually consists for those affected in agreeing to or opposing the processing of their own data. This concept is based on a minimal concept of autonomy, as the consent required for data processing is usually a one-time informed consent for a relatively comprehensive data usage, which many companies already consider fulfilled when they generally refer to the improvement of their products and services. The question remains problematic as to how much choice or freedom of action exists for users within the technical system or what conditions would have to be met in interaction with complex algorithmic systems to actually be able to speak of transparency or personal autonomy—even after the time of the first consent (see Koska and Filipović 2019).

As long as autonomy is considered a central guiding value in our society, citizens must also be empowered to become masters of their own data. It was pointed out that the current implementation for consent management (IAB Framework TCF 2.0) due to a conflict of objectives (between the protection of privacy and the capitalisation of our personal activities) does not create sufficient conditions for this. Therefore, a central task of state regulatory and educational bodies is to reflect the minimal conditions (transparency, control and authenticity) from the inside and outside perspective. Finally, the participation opportunities of the users in shaping the horizon of responsibility play an important role (see Fig. 12), as also proven by Silverstone (2008, p. 168 f):

[71]Silverstone refers to a form of the polis shaped by media as "Mediapolis".

[72]In addition, let us remember the wooden head by Raul Hausmann (Chap. 2, Fig. 15).

"Therefore, even if it seems banal or cumbersome, I will speak of viewers and users as contributors [. . .] The term however, has a catch, as it implies something else. Any kind of participation and collaboration presupposes an action, an own activity. [. . .] If participation is an activity, and that is of crucial importance [. . .] then it implies a form of responsibility [. . .] Otherwise, the individual in the Mediapolis would only be left with the role of the zombie."

Another aspect that needs to be clarified in connection with the complex of education, participation and justice is the question of distribution and financial participation. Controversial is how far the data donors should participate in the profits of the "siren servers" (Lanier 2014), and if so, how and why: e.g. due to the communal production of economic goods, to ensure equal opportunities and rights or, to build a new system of "information economy" (ibid.) and much more.

4.3 Criteria for Consideration

The so-called privacy paradox has been mentioned several times as an example of value consideration, insofar as the value of privacy is set in relation to (an) other value(s). For the sharing of data, the desire for visibility and social recognition as well as (following the information economic considerations of Jaron Lanier) the possibility of a monetary participation[73] were cited as motives.

A continuous repositioning of existing values, principles and norms is necessary when values compete with each other. If the realisation of one value impairs the realisation of another value, then a balance of interests is needed. For this, the relationship between competing values can be determined using hierarchies. In complex situations, which are to be expected in the context of digitalisation, static value hierarchies can however be counterproductive. Because a too rigidly fixed value structure from the philosophical ivory tower cannot do justice to the situation-related dynamics due to its general character. Exactly for this reason, a balancing competence is needed. To consider the relationship of values case-appropriately, i.e. taking into account the specific circumstances and in the context of a particular individual case. In analogy to spatial orientation, it could therefore be about, for example, choosing the shortest, fastest or most economic route from a navigation system in a certain situation. Depending on the context (is there a hurry or do I have time to also look at the landscape, etc.) the choice of route varies. The rank of a value "A" compared to another value "B" can therefore be made according to various aspects, as Horn (2011, p. 392) shows using some generally known rules of thumb:

"For example, if an actor has to choose between two evils, it is plausible to advise him, ceteris paribus, to prefer the lesser to the greater, the short-term to the long-term, the one-time to the recurring, the less consequential to the more consequential, the few people

[73]It quickly becomes clear that such an approach runs the risk of making privacy a luxury good (the non-sharing of data must be affordable).

affected to the many people harmed, the reversible evil to the irreversible, and finally the less likely to the more likely."

To justify such preference rules, Horn suggests at least four different theories*: "(1) based on calculations of expected utility sums, (2) in view of the categorical priority of moral goods, (3) based on a conception of basic needs, and (4) using an anthropological-essentialist procedure"* (ibid.). In addition, Horn (following Thomas Aquinas) shows how a factual weighing of goods can succeed in moral dilemma situations using (5) the doctrine of double effect. However, the following is not about discussing the advantages and disadvantages of the various moral philosophical theories, but rather about demonstrating the existence and the right to exist of different views, to open up the discourse space for a societal confrontation at very specific points.

4.3.1 Individual Goods vs. Societal Goods

The word cloud (see Fig. 13) in the introductory words of the criteriology provides a rough overview of currently dominant values, norms and principles in data ethics and AI guidelines. At first glance, it is noticeable that "data protection, transparency and security" are dominant themes in guidelines. The "orientation towards people" or the orientation towards the "needs of the clientele (in an economic context)", but also the topics "sustainability, fairness, avoidance of prejudices or non-discrimination" are central aspects (cf. Zeng et al. 2018; Jobin et al. 2019; Fjeld et al. 2020; Hagendorff 2020). As Zeng et al. (2018, p. 3) shows, however, differentiation can also be observed with regard to the weighting and semantic interpretation of these values, norms and principles—it is exemplified that for companies the topic of "collaboration" currently has a significantly higher value than for state or scientific institutions, whereas the topic of "privacy" is exactly the opposite (see ibid., p. 3).

Guiding principles, which based on the mission and vision describe the self-understanding of companies, institutions, associations and other organisations for stakeholder communication internally and externally, aim in the context of advancing digitalisation primarily at building or strengthening trust in a company (more on this in the next chapter). On a very general level, mission statements describe the ideal points of orientation of the company towards customers, business partners, investors and society. For most employees, however, they provide little practical value in times of digital upheaval and change—due to their generality.

To bridge the gap between theory and practice, the primary aim is for employees to learn how to relate certain values to each other. Because as actors (developers, users, operators, etc.—see Fig. 12), we sometimes find ourselves in dilemma situations where one good can only be achieved at the expense of another good (see "Privacy Paradox") or where one evil can only be avoided by accepting another evil (see "Trolley Dilemma"). Jaume-Palasí and Spielkamp (2017) have also pointed out that the collective dimension of algorithms can only be addressed to a very limited extent with individual legal criteria. To avoid conceptual confusion (e.g. on topics such as privacy and discrimination), they have therefore proposed a more differentiated taxonomy that distinguishes between individual goods and societal goods.

Using the example of "predictive policing", the two authors show how the topics of data protection, privacy, security and non-discrimination—without clear differentiation or structuring—quickly become confused. For example, data anonymisation is carried out not only to protect the privacy of those affected (but usually only justified on this basis), but also because the evaluation of so-called anonymised affinity models no longer falls under the special protection for personal data in the GDPR. What is usually kept quiet is that the collective character of algorithms can easily undermine this individual legal logic: *"discrimination occurs individually, but not ad personam. The assignment to a collective is both the reason and the basis"* (ibid. p. 13). In the case of predictive policing (or also when calculating creditworthiness), this means that it is often enough to live in the wrong district of a city to be assigned to a certain collective. *"Paradoxically, the social construction of collectives is both the trigger for discrimination and the reference parameter for checking discrimination patterns"* (ibid.). The concession of individual rights (such as data protection) can therefore *"throw an entire city into social imbalance, as these algorithms de facto contribute to so-called no-go areas, because excessive police presence can suggest a massive security problem instead of additional security"* (ibid.). Therefore, it is necessary to weigh up carefully. What personal disadvantages and long-term societal risks are associated with individual interests or actions being dissolved in the "numerical generality" (Heesen 2018) of affinity models. *"An ethic that focuses on collective goods and collectives follows a different logic than the logic of individualistic interests"* (Jaume-Palasí and Spielkamp 2017, p. 12). Even the balancing between individual and collective goods sometimes leads to complex deliberation processes. If individual legal or technical criteria such as data protection or data anonymisation are also confused with ethical criteria such as privacy or autonomy, guidelines quickly become smoke candles that, in terms of their practical effectiveness (especially among the workforce), mainly lead to ignorance, cynicism and rejection. In the context of the balancing criteria, checkbox policies are therefore usually counterproductive. What is needed instead is a transition from a more deontologically oriented, action-restricting ethic, which insists on the universal observance of principles and rules, to a situation-related ethical approach, which is based on virtues and personality development, knowledge expansion and freedom of action. This in turn requires (as we will see shortly) a stable basis of trust.

4.3.2 Trust vs. Transparency (Control)

"Trust is a troublesome thing because it presupposes that we ask about the purposes and means of those we are supposed to trust" (Silverstone 2008, p. 196). Against the backdrop of pervasive digitisation and datafication, however, trust is indispensable. The added value of algorithmic systems would ultimately be rendered absurd if the consuming target group had to understand every technical process in detail themselves.

> *"Functionally considered, norms stabilise interaction patterns. This reduces social complexity and relieves the individual. Often, one must rely on the norm-conforming behaviour of other people,* i.e.*, be able to trust them. Trust requires a high average compliance with norms and institutions. Established behavioural expectations and trust, economically speaking, reduce the transaction costs of interactions."* (Ott 2011, p. 475).

Every relationship of trust is therefore based on information asymmetries. Since data-driven enterprises depend on the trust of consumers, numerous AI and data ethics projects primarily aim to build or strengthen trust in their own enterprise. The basic problem, which Silverstone refers to as "troublesome" (see above), was pinpointed by the sociologist Georg Simmel over a hundred years ago: *"The completely knowing person does not need to trust, the completely unknowing person cannot reasonably even trust"* (Simmel 1908, p. 346). When and why do we trust data-driven companies with our data? Transparency can create trust. In ethical guidelines, companies therefore primarily advertise with transparency (and data protection) to gain the trust of the consumer target group. In 73 out of 84 examined guidelines, the term transparency is addressed according to Jobin et al. (2019). The study by Fjeld et al. (2020) also states that transparency and explainability are found in 94% of all guidelines. However, most developers cannot relate to this term in their daily work. Transparency, as Schneider (2013) also notes, only exists as a futuristic vanishing point: "It shows that 'transparency' can always only be promised. There is no transparency here and now." An increase always seems possible. On the other hand, data protection is usually easier to implement. An increase in data protection seems possible at any time due to changing technical possibilities. However, the arms race is usually kept within previously defined limits by the question of justifiable effort. A company that makes a particularly high effort in terms of data protection should not automatically be trusted more, as we have seen in the previous chapter.

Neither data protection nor transparency serve a purpose in themselves. Already in the balance between individual and collective goods, we have seen that data protection is not an ethical, but a technical criterion that can guarantee the protection of privacy in certain situations—but in other situations (due to the collective dimension of algorithms) can also lead to social disadvantages (e.g. discrimination). The question also arises with regard to the concept of transparency: Who or what should be transparent to whom? Is the company aiming to improve the data sovereignty and digital self-determination of consumers? Or is the company more interested in getting a 360-degree view (see inventory) of the consumer target group? The concept of transparency is extremely complex in the context of digitalisation. *"No other buzzword dominates today's public discourse as much as transparency"* (Han 2015). On the one hand, the term stands for the widespread fear of surveillance and the transparent human being on the internet, for a threat to privacy and individual personality development (see e.g. Lück 2013). On the other hand, an ethical ideal is forming under the societal demand for transparency, which is cited as a panacea against opaque power structures, political and economic dependencies, conflicts of interest, corruption, data abuse cases, etc.

The value of transparency (and control), as outlined in the context of the orientation directives, is closely related to the concept of the gradual gradation of autonomy. In view of the three minimum conditions proposed above, the horizon of transparency is spanned by two extreme points. As already explained elsewhere (see Koska 2015b; Koska and Filipović 2019), the maximum concept of transparency is excluded from the list of meaningful measures, as it is generally counterproductive for the establishment of autonomy, data sovereignty or digital self-determination. The same applies to minimal transparency. The maximum information density is in some respects even identical to the maximum absence of information—even maximum bright light or darkness lead to the same result: In both cases, you see nothing. So what is the right trade-off? How much trust, how much transparency and how much control are necessary? Who determines the selection criteria of the data filters, what changes the parameter spaces and automated selection mechanisms? Who should we trust specifically? Can complex relationships be visualised in a generally understandable way? Personal autonomy, data sovereignty and digital self-determination can be located at the level of abstraction where transparency and control can be established. On all other levels, only more trust helps.

4.4 Formal and Technical Criteria

In the fourth and final step, the focus is on the application-related criteria of criteriology. This specifically involves an analysis of the formal and technical criteria that can contribute to the realisation of an abstract value structure. A crucial moment to build trust in a digital service lies, among other things, in the *guarantee of data and information security*. However, if it is about respecting the *privacy* of users in order to respect the value of *personal autonomy*, then privacy-by-design can be a solution. Also, ensuring a sufficiently high *data quality* falls under the category of formal and technical criteria. All three criteria provide an indication regarding the perception of responsibility in view of practical implementation. These criteria are therefore a means to an end, a tool to realise higher-level values, principles and norms. In practice, technical procedures, organisational structures and legal regulations are used to realise these criteria.

4.4.1 Data and Information Security

First, it is necessary to distinguish the field of data and information security from the topic of data protection. The European Union understands data protection as "in particular the protection of the privacy of natural persons in the processing of personal data" (Art. 1 para. 1 Directive 95/46/EC).[74] With the GDPR, the primary right to data protection in Europe has been further specified. As already shown, the term is misleading *"because data protection is not—as the wording of the term*

[74]Available online at EUR-Lex—31995L0046—EN—EUR-Lex (europa.eu).

suggests—exhausted in the protection of data. The object of protection is rather the individual affected" (Gola et al. 2017, p. 135). In contrast, data and information security primarily aims to ensure the completeness and correctness of data by taking preventive measures, e.g. to avoid data and information losses, data theft or information falsifications. "Data protection is therefore—primarily—personality protection and not a second property right or copyright" (ibid.). The subject of data and information security, on the other hand, is primarily the latter—i.e. it mainly refers to formal and technical criteria as well as the organisational or legal protection of data and information, for example to minimise economic damage and risks.

The assurance of data and information security is often ensured in companies by establishing an *IT & Data Governance* structure. The protection objectives of EU data protection already show that data governance concepts, i.e. strategies for controlling data flows, are important not only for companies, but also at the state level. Article 1, paragraph 2 of Directive 95/46/EC mentions the objective of "free movement of personal data between Member States". Through a historical analysis of further legal texts, Gola et al. (2017, p. 135) show that at the political level the focus has shifted from ensuring free data traffic to ensuring fundamental rights—although the equal importance of the two protection objectives remains in the EU GDPR.[75] Data protection in Europe is therefore an integral part of data governance organisation both at the state (macro level) and at the corporate level (micro level). According to Tiedemann (2020), there are four core areas that fall under the term Data Governance:

- "***Data Quality:*** *This is about ensuring that data is fully captured, that data is current, suitable for further processing and appropriately prepared, and that access is ensured and regulated.*
- ***Data Maintenance:*** *Aims at data enrichment, correction of data and maintenance of master data.*
- ***Data Privacy:*** *Ensures that all relevant standards in terms of security aspects and confidentiality towards the customer are met.*
- ***Data Compliance:*** *Compliance with legal standards, ethical and moral guidelines as well as company-specific standards and guidelines."* (ibid.)

Data and information security is in a way a cross-disciplinary field, because "in each of these four areas it is always about the assignment of roles (Data Roles), ensuring compliance with standards and defining processes" (ibid.). In practice, corporate data governance organisations not only have the task of ensuring access to data, identifying and avoiding risks, reducing costs in data storage and

[75] Gola et al. (2017, p. 135) further elaborate on this connection as follows: *"The recitals [Note: of the GDPR] repeatedly remind us that differences in the level of protection of national legal systems not only endanger the fundamental rights of the persons concerned, but also represent an obstacle to the exercise of economic activities throughout the Union (see, for example, recitals 9, 10, 13)."*

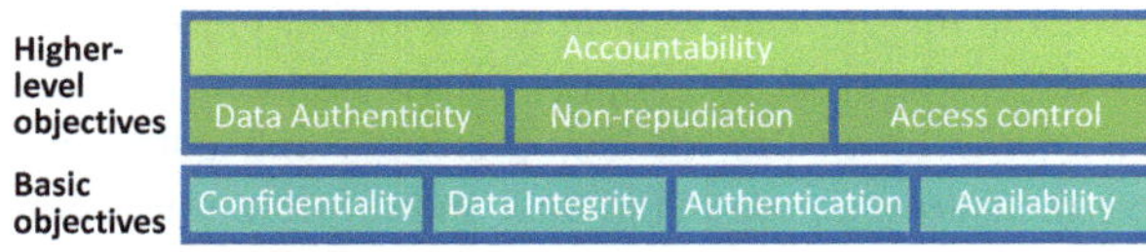

Fig. 14 Scheme for information technology security objectives according to Hansen et al. (2015)

management, but (of course) also the goal of identifying and exploiting economic potentials.

Finally, if we look specifically at the information technology security objectives, according to a scheme by Hansen et al. (2015, p. 374) basic objectives can be distinguished from higher objectives: "The basic objectives include objectives for securing confidentiality, integrity, authentication and availability" (ibid.). According to Hansen et al. (2015), the following higher objectives are based on these basic objectives: "Data authenticity, access control, non-repudiation, accountability and protection of privacy" (ibid. p. 378) (Fig. 14).

The objectives of data and information security form, as above as already mentioned, the foundation of data governance. However, when, ethical guidelines are also developed in the context of data compliance, it is particularly important to ensure that the terminologies do not collide with each other. For example, in the context of orientation directives, three minimal conditions (transparency, authenticity and control) for personal autonomy and digital self-determination were defined, which must not be confused with the information technology security objectives. In the ISO/IEC 27000 series (a series of standards for information security), the term authenticity is explained as "property that an entity is what it claims to be". In contrast to the condition of authenticity in the context of personal autonomy, the term here does not refer to a comparison with the mental states, processes and phenomena of a person (how could it? Only the person concerned could provide this information), but to data authenticity, i.e. to the digital representation of information in an IT system, as Hansen et al. (2015, p. 379) note: *"Data authenticity is understood as the verifiable identification of information (for example messages or files). This includes both the proof of the integrity of the data and the proof of their origin"* (ibid. p. 379). In the context of data quality, it is proclaimed that the concept of Data Governance must be further developed if it wants to go beyond the purely factual level. In addition to the state (macro level) and corporate (micro level) perspective, it is necessary to include the personal (nano level) perspective of those affected more strongly, i.e. beyond data protection, (vgl. Digital Trade & Data Governance Hub 2018).

4.4.2 Privacy by Design

The concerns of people regarding their privacy have been addressed several times in the course of this paper. Most recently, we saw that the protection of privacy or the protection of personal data should not be confused with the information technology security objectives of data-driven companies. In the context of the so-called Privacy Paradox, it was shown that the value of privacy refers to the idea of personal autonomy and is closely linked to the right to digital self-determination. According to Grimm and Krah (2016), a key characteristic of privacy is—and here we can tie in with the initial considerations of Christians (2019) and Silverstone (2008), that a time- and culture-independent definition of what we consider private is not possible.

> *"The culture-dependency of privacy is also articulated in the fact that in different cultures there are not only different conceptions of privacy, but also of their respective cultural performance and their respective importance. This concerns, for example, social spatial demarcation rituals, culturally different weightings of work and private life as well as different acceptance thresholds for camera surveillance"* (Grimm and Krah 2016, p. 178).

According to Nissenbaum (2010), this insight leads to the realisation that the right to privacy is context-dependent. In her analysis, she goes one step further by emphasising not only the cultural, but also the individual contextuality of privacy. Accordingly, we as individuals have always decided situationally (i.e., depending on the function and role we play in a certain social context), whether or which information we share with whom. Since no one has such a privileged access to the definition of their own privacy as the person concerned, privacy can therefore be much better located under the criteria of weighing (see above). *"The right to privacy is rather unspecifically rendered in English as 'right to be left alone' (Warren/Brandeis 1984); more specifically, one can speak of privacy as the control of a person over the access of others to her"* (Seubert 2011, p. 219). Considering the enforcement problem, we have also highlighted the conflict of objectives between the protection of privacy and the capitalisation of our personal interests, and in this context pointed out that this is primarily a system-induced conflict. Therefore, for example, most developers, manufacturers or operators themselves know the feeling of losing control over their privacy in the digital world, from certain situations of personal concern (internal perspective). To bridge the already mentioned gap between theory and practice, it is first necessary to further illuminate the formal and technical dimension (external perspective).

Privacy by design is an example of a value-based IT design, i.e. for the consideration of human values—*here the protection of privacy*—from the beginning, but also throughout the entire development process. In Europe, the concept of "data protection through technology design and through data protection-friendly default settings" is legally anchored in Art. 25 of the GDPR. However, there is still uncertainty today about how "privacy by design" or "privacy by default" is to be implemented in concrete terms, as we have repeatedly explained with regard to the IAB framework TCF 2.0 in the context of consent management. As an example of a technical and organisational measure that should already be considered at the planning stage of a processing system, the GDPR only mentions the pseudonymisation of data. However, as we have shown with reference to the collective dimension of algorithms, neither pseudonymisation nor anonymisation guarantees privacy. And so it is not surprising that in the German version of Wikipedia the lemma "privacy by design" is redirected to the principle of "data avoidance and data economy".

4.4.3 Data Quality

Analogous to the topic of privacy, it is also necessary with regard to data quality to involve the internal perspective of those affected more strongly. This should be a matter of course for the big tech companies. After all, they are almost aggressively advertising to put the wishes of their customers at the centre of their services. For example, David Limp, the device chief of Amazon, makes it clear in an interview: "We are obsessed to satisfy our customers" (Jacoby 2020, 1:13:31). The obsession that Limp displays at this point as a reaction to a journalist's confrontation with the case of a hacked Amazon indoor camera,[76] refers only to the external perspective, which we have outlined in the course of our inventory. However, as shown by the problem of social construction, the danger of discrimination and digital disempowerment, it is not about protecting the 360-degree view of the customer from external views. Privacy and data quality must not only be anchored in the context of data and information security, because no one has such a privileged access to their own goals, interests and wishes as the person concerned.

5 Interim Result: Dimensions of an Algorithm Ethics

The algorithmic search for numbers and values can be viewed from different perspectives. Based on five current fields of action, the i) technical-mathematical, ii) economic and iii) ethical dimension of numbers and values were identified. With regard to the technical-mathematical level, it was shown in reference to Krämer that the outsourcing of algorithmic thinking and action to artificial artefacts leads to a process of flattening. In the context of the control and management of machines, attention was drawn to two opposing centrifugal forces. Thus, the design of human-machine interfaces follows on the one hand the paradigm of complexity reduction, insofar as information for users is increasingly contextualised and optimised for specific target groups. On the other hand, beneath the user interface—in the "artificial special space, whose depth is annulled" (Krämer 2020a, p. 1)—complexity increases at the same time. Transparency and opacity thus form two sides of the same coin. Applied to the so-called layer model of software architecture, Krämer's "inscribed surfaces" can be understood as a demarcation line between media users and media producers. Since the formal languages on the deeper layer each restrict the realm of possibilities on the next higher layer, a target group-specific differentiation of moral actors was proposed based on the layer architecture.

[76]Hackers gained access to a surveillance camera installed in the bedroom of eight-year-old Alyssa Lemay, impersonated Santa Claus, and among other things, urged the girl to destroy her own toys. (available online at https://www.youtube.com/watch?v=ZsJSDX0DfSA).

Furthermore, a procedural perspective on the emergence of algorithmic biases was developed. The starting point was the criticism of the neutrality thesis of technology already presented in the second chapter. Only by admitting that *not only in the use*, but already *in the development* of algorithms (or technologies)—whether consciously or unconsciously—values are inscribed, do we gain a comprehensive view on the process of algorithmic search for numbers and values. The common statement "Technology is neutral—it all depends on its use or application" particularly overlooks the fact that we already enter a normative-desiring relationship regarding the existence or realisation of artificial artefacts with the instantiation of ideas.

Thus, with the desire to develop a "mechanical calculating servant", as we have detailed in the first chapter, the goal of eliminating "human thinking errors" was already associated with Leibniz in the late 17th century. This desire presupposes a certain understanding, i.e. a valuation of what is to be understood as a human thinking error. The pursuit of scientific knowledge based on rational and purposeful thinking, the datafication of reality and the efficiency idea are among the driving forces on the technical-mathematical level. The question to what extent these attributes can be transferred to machines and automated was discussed with reference to the model of synergetics by Hermann Haken. Initially, the conscious or unconscious inscription of values is done by humans (e.g. by the employees of a certain department, the algorithm designers, the media producers, etc.; cf. Demand-Supply model, Fig. 11). Subsequently, it is again humans (media users) who can change the system behaviour through their interaction with the system. Even in the context of technology-based value inscriptions, it is therefore necessary to first carry out reverse engineering to track down the normative sources of self-learning algorithms. Although machines cannot themselves enter a normative-desiring relationship with certain values and goals, the question remains as to whether an inherent dynamic (collective dimension of algorithms) can develop from the interactions between the producers, a certain technology and the users in individual cases, which exceeds the objectives of the individual elements.

The "power of algorithms" is usually discussed in the public in the context of a societal threat situation. This leads to a broad algorithm scepticism among many people. Empirical studies show that trust in AI is still low.[77] The directional tendency of algorithmics outlined in the second chapter underpins the concerns and mistrust towards technological progress, when digitalisation is primarily aimed at optimising and increasing efficiency and thereby undermines the core elements of a free and liberal society; be it with regard to individual ethical concepts such as privacy, personal autonomy and informational self-determination or with regard to

[77] According to the study conducted in five countries by Gillespie et al. (2021, p. 4), only about a quarter (28%) of citizens (in the USA, Canada, Germany, UK, and Australia) trust AI systems. Two out of five citizens are not willing to share their information or data with an AI system, and a third are not willing to trust the output of AI systems (e.g., a recommendation or decision). While many citizens hesitate to trust AI systems, they generally accept (42%) or tolerate (28%) AI, but few advocate (15%) or welcome (6%) it, and some outright reject AI (9%).

socio-ethical aspects such as participation and justice. In this context, the technical-mathematical dimension of algorithmics usually takes a back seat to the economic dimension of numbers and values. Because in practice, it is primarily about maximising the conversion rate and less about the threshold at which synergistic structure formation leads us to an ethics of algorithms in which we understand algorithms as moral actors (*genitivus subjektivus*). However, current observations suggest a shift towards considering generative AI, especially in co-creation processes, as an active element in building trust (Koska et al. 2024). In this context, it remains to be clarified how the active role of generative AI can be distinguished from the quality criteria traditionally associated with passive recipients or mediators of trust.

The driving force on the economic level is data capitalism. The efficiency promise of the algorithmicists meets here the unbridled will for process optimisation and profit increase. Referring to the IAB-Framework TCF 2.0 it was demonstrated that many data-driven companies so far show no serious interest in actively involving media users in the management of their data. The 360-degree view of the customer base thus stands in contrast to the current implementation practice of privacy settings[78] and leads to a dangerous information asymmetry between data donors and data processors.

Referring to Nida-Rümelin (2021), it was further explained that Europe is in a state of tension between two extreme poles, "the commercially driven digitisation (USA) on the one hand and the state-controlled digitisation (China) on the other" (ibid. 10:40).[79] Furthermore, particular attention was paid to the problem of social construction, the danger of discrimination and digital incapacitation, the problem of responsibility gaps and the fear of a disintegration of the public sphere.

With the ethical dimension, based on the European understanding of law or on the basis of the cultural value framework of the European Union, a criteriology was proposed to counter the above mentioned dangers and problems of algorithmisation. This is not a closed set of principles, but an attempt to establish an ethical reference framework that invites further collective consideration regarding its concrete design: *"Values demand affirmation or negation. Even theoretical judgements are based on a valuing, practical behaviour so that in the end all knowledge is related to truth as a 'theoretical value'"* (Wildfeuer 2011, p. 2492). The recognition and implementation of values therefore require a personal identification with the validity of these

---

[78]See for example *"Serious accusations against Google: Court documents have surfaced on the internet indicating that the Android makers have deliberately hidden important privacy options deep in the settings of Android. They also apparently tried to persuade third-party manufacturers to hide these options"* (Feurer 2021).

[79]Thomas Metzinger goes even further in his analysis when he quotes Vladimir Putin as saying that "the nation that wins the AI race in this century will also gain power over this planet" (Jahn 11.06.1021, 4:07). According to Metzinger, we are in "a historically very uncomfortable situation in Europe" (ibid.), as we are already being colonised by the American corporations—which means that we urgently need state-funded AI ethicists and interdisciplinary degree programmes at all faculties—instead, in his view, Germany is currently only training "fake ethicists" financed by Facebook (ibid.).

values. The criteriology primarily intends to provide a categorical structure for the common discourse—but not a complete list of "particularly relevant basic values"—as such a list, as we have shown with reference to Silverstone (2008) and Christians (2019), runs the risk of promoting the form of cultural imperialism that it seeks to prevent. The criteriology was therefore deliberately reduced to a few basic considerations to facilitate entry into the topic and to open the discourse to all those affected. Data and algorithm ethics aim to adequately consider the interests of all involved actors and to make the distinction between right and wrong in dealing with data easier. The present criteriology is intended to merely provide a quick entry into the discourse. Ultimately, this is about jointly adjusting the inner compass to recognise and utilise the scope for a sustainable handling of data.

Starting from the general ethical aspects, the guiding directives, the criteria of consideration as well as the formal and technical criteria (from the above proposed criteriology) a participatory model process can be developed, in which cultural and situational peculiarities are jointly defined and specified. To bridge the gap between theory and practice, it is necessary to capture and further differentiate criteria such as human dignity, autonomy or transparency with the participants. Why is the principle of human dignity non-negotiable for us? *"Human dignity establishes a numerically indeterminable 'value' of the human being, its self-purpose; it therefore must not be the subject of trade-offs. Damage to the dignity of certain individuals cannot be compensated by any increase in the benefits, wealth, advantage or happiness of other people"* (Horn 2011, p. 393). Is the criterion of human dignity therefore a universal basic value that all stakeholders of the guiding principle process recognise? Are there any dissenting voices?[80] If all process participants achknowledge the fundamental validity of human dignity, then the question arises as to which measures specifically ensure that human dignity is respected. Because platitudes like *"we put people at the centre of the development and deployment of technical systems"* (BMJV 2021, p. 5) offer little practical value for algorithm designers.

If the participatory deliberation process in the context of data-driven enterprises leads to a joint formulation and adoption of (self-)binding (company) guiding principles that (analogous to the 10 Commandments) start with *"Thou shalt ... "* or *"Thou shalt not ... "* then it makes sense already during the definition, planning and development phase of algorithms, to work with checklists, to build a data or AI governance, to support the compliance with certain processes with technical aids etc.[81] The commitment to deontological criteria (and especially the machine

[80]For example, the insight into the ability to assist one's own kind, not limited to humans, led Jonas to criticise what he saw as the anthropocentric interpretation of human responsibility, which only serves to preserve his own species. Kant, so Jonas, be the spokesperson for this view and have both in his theory of knowledge as well as in his ethics promoted this speciesist model of responsible action (Jonas 1979)" (Gerhardt 2017, p. 447).

[81]Exemplary tools will be mentioned in the following chapter in connection with the design perspectives.

implementation of rules for compliance with such criteria) however, presupposes that we can already sufficiently specify the scenarios in which these criteria should apply.

In situations where we cannot retreat to an ivory tower and weigh up because the requirements overwhelm us and we have to make a correct decision in a limited time, guidelines which are carved in stone do not help. In fact, it would be completely unrealistic to assume that guidelines could cover all requirements in the everyday work of every employee. Anyone who pursues such a claim must inevitably fail. The know-how is located with the people in the various departments of a company and not in the guideline—whoever seeks it there, usually seeks it in vain. Checkbox guidelines should therefore not be the only instruments of data and algorithm ethics. What is needed is a transition from a rather deontologically oriented, action-restricting ethics, which insists on the universal compliance with principles and rules, to a situation-related ethical approach, which is based on virtues and personality development, knowledge expansion and freedom of action. For this, the gap between ethics and technical discourses must be closed. It is necessary to build bridges between abstract values and the technical implementation.

In this context, recent studies have shown that large language models (LLMs) can be used productively as reflection tools to support ethical decision-making in situations of normative uncertainty or moral conflict. Within the KAIMo research project (Can algorithms calculate morally in situations of conflict? Ethics and digital operationalisation regarding risk assessment in child welfare practice), it was demonstrated that LLMs can help professionals in child welfare practice to simulate ethical dilemmas, surface competing values, and examine alternative courses of action in a non-prescriptive way (see Burghardt et al. 2024; Kraus et al. 2024). Rather than replacing human judgement, LLMs may act as epistemic support systems that foster ethical reflection and dialogue in morally complex contexts.

Against this backdrop, it is essential—especially in the context of digital data profiles—to involve media users more directly and meaningfully, both from an inside and outside perspective. After all, no one has such privileged access to their own goals, needs and interests as the individual themselves. Placing people at the centre of the development and deployment of technical systems (see BMJV 2021, p. 5) must therefore also mean involving them in the journey of responsibility. Only then can they begin to navigate the world of the virtually possible through their own dimensions of meaning (see Chap. 2 on the dimensions of meaning of algorithmics).

Design Perspectives 4

A criteriology has just been developed based on a problem-oriented description, which allows a very general but comprehensive introduction to the theoretical and practical design of algorithm ethics. With the normative dimensions of algorithmics, it was suggested that the ethical dimension cannot be explored independently of the mathematical-technical and the economic dimension of algorithmics. This dependency is shown, among other things, in the tension in which Europe finds itself when foreign value systems are imported to Europe with the technical and economic lead of the United States of America or the People's Republic of China. To counteract colonisation in the virtual world (or of European companies and citizens), the European Union is therefore aiming to strengthen Europe's digital sovereignty and competitiveness with legal regulations (such as the EU GDPR), joint funding initiatives (such as Horizon 2020) and state projects (such as GAIA-X).

Politics and regulation are in the inner circle of those bearing moral responsibility (see Chap. 3, Fig. 12). In the differentiation of the actor groups, we have—from the outer to inner radius—specified science and research as well as the public, then NGOs and journalism, industry associations and auditors as well as in the innermost circle the developers, operators and users (for more details, see Saurwein 2018, pp. 43–48).

In the context of this fourth chapter, design perspectives will finally be presented that build on the previous criteriology[1] and contribute to closing the current gap between theory and practice. The first section deals with the voluntary inclusion of social and ecological concerns in the digitalisation strategy of companies, which has been discussed for some time under the keyword "Corporate Digital

[1]The concept of autonomy was characterised in the criteriology as elementary (possibly even the most central) fix point of the current media-ethical debate with the outsourcing of algorithmic thinking and action (see Chap. 3). Therefore, it will also be in the focus of the following considerations.

C. Koska, *Ethics of Algorithms*,
https://doi.org/10.1007/978-3-662-71518-5_4

Responsibility (CDR)". The second section addresses the need for additional regulations and independent control institutions. The focus of the third and last section is once again on the conditions of the possibility for digital self-determination, which will finally be discussed against the background of a digital educational identity.

1 Corporate Digital Responsibility

The term "CDR" (Corporate Digital Responsibility) is historically linked to the term "CSR" (Corporate Social Responsibility). In general, it is about the responsibility of companies in digital times. The term first appears in 2015 in a brochure by the business consulting firm Accenture and is introduced by the authors with the following words:

> *"As forward-looking companies work out what it means to act responsibly with their customers' personal data, they will also integrate this strategy into their core business as a key lever toward enhanced differentiation and new sources of growth"* Cooper et al. (2015, p. 1).

After a brief inventory of the current CDR discourse (Sect. 1.1) and a recapitulation of the challenges outlined in this book (Sect. 1.2), a design perspective is subsequently presented (Sect. 1.3) that ties in with the understanding intended by Cooper et al. (2015) by anchoring corporate digital responsibility in the digitalisation strategy and data usage practice (i.e. within the value chain in the "core business") of data-driven companies (see Koska 2020).[2]

1.1 A Brief Stocktaking

In the German-speaking discourse, the CDR concept was taken up by Esselmann and Brink (2016) and initially placed in the context of CR management of companies, as "numerous instruments from CR management (sic!) [. . .] also provide valuable blueprints for the implementation of a Corporate Digital Responsibility" (ibid. p. 41). Even if the CSR term does not yet appear in this publication, the measures mentioned[3] already point to numerous interfaces to the (in German-speaking companies) already known topics of Corporate Social Responsibility (CSR) and sustainability. At the core, the two authors are concerned with the development of a new

[2]Individual parts of this analysis—as well as the graphic (Fig. 1)—have already been published in the anthology "Corporate Responsibility in Digital Change" by the Bertelsmann Foundation and the Wittenberg Centre for Global Ethics (Ed.) (see Koska 2020, pp. 239–245).

[3]Explicitly mentioned are: *"Standards and reporting mechanisms for the systematisation of tasks, seals for complexity reduction towards customers, tools for measuring the impact of social effects, remuneration models for minimising risks and including long-term developments, innovation processes for promoting shared value services"* (ibid.).

CDR strategy about "an intelligent moderation between informational self-determination (Digital Autonomy) and real value creation (Shared Value)" (ibid. p. 39). Digital change as an opportunity and challenge for economy and society was, however, primarily still discussed under the terms "CSR and digitalisation", as the title chosen by Hildebrandt and Landhäußer (2017) proves.[4] Breidenbach and Filipović (2017, p. 859) explicitly point out, based on their practical experience at betterplace.org, *"that companies so far mainly take two paths to connect digitality and CSR. On the one hand: digitality becomes the subject of CSR measures, so companies deal with digital topics. On the other hand: CSR works digitally, so companies choose digital formats for their CSR measures."* The latter usually causes a blind spot for the core area of CDR in practice, as I have already elaborated elsewhere (see Koska 2020), as corporate digital responsibility then often only focuses on ecological issues and the climate problem. As important as these topics are, in order not to dilute the CDR discourse in the CSR discourse, it is necessary to first focus on digitality as the subject of corporate responsibility (for more on this see ibid. p. 240).

1.2 Recapitulation of Challenges

As shown in detail in the second chapter of this book, the idea of efficiency plays a superior role in the outsourcing of algorithmic thinking and action to artificial artefacts. The restructuring and further development towards a significantly more efficient handling of data and information also holds great potential for companies. The digital transformation of companies is, however, initially associated with massive investments. The entire organisation needs to rethink, it must question established processes, restructure itself—partly even reinvent itself; it must build fast and agile delivery processes and must not lose sight of the topics of data protection and data security when designing data-driven innovations (see formal and technical criteria). Especially European companies are often already fully engaged with the compliance of law and duty when strategically aligning their data usage practice. For example, the right to freedom and security, the protection of personal data, the freedom of opinion and information, the freedom of art and science, the right to education or also the entrepreneurial freedom is already anchored in the German Constitution. In addition, the European legislator defines rights and duties for companies, especially in the European Data Protection Regulation (GDPR), but also in the ePrivacy Regulation or the currently emerging Regulation for Artificial Intelligence (see next chapter). In this situation, it seems to

[4]In the extensive anthology (approx. 1,200 pages) "CSR and Digitisation" by Hildebrandt and Landhäußer (2017), with a welcoming address from Dr. Wolfgang Schäuble as well as forewords from Julia Klöckner, Jörg Asmussen, the CEOs of Deutsche Telekom AG and Metro AG or the Executive Vice President of Axel Springer SE, neither the terms "CDR" nor "Corporate Digital Responsibility" appear.

many companies to be of little use if they overwhelm their employees with ethical rules of conduct in addition to the legal regulations.

1.3 Design Perspective

Since businesses that want to generate economic added value from data in Europe must comply with legal regulations anyway, if they do not want to incur high fines, it is advisable to anchor data and algorithm ethics for deepening legal understanding directly in the digitalisation strategy of companies (see Fig. 1).

It is important to note that the "ethical self-commitment codes" are not just a translation and condensation of the existing legal framework (see Filipović and Koska 2019). Rather, as Filipović (2023) elaborates, CDR should be understood as a discursive, communication-based concept of responsibility. According to this view, companies act as collective moral agents that must be able to justify their digital practices and related ethical considerations transparently and discursively to their stakeholders.

This discursive understanding does not imply that CDR is reduced to a mere communication or marketing tool, intended only to inform stakeholders about compliance with legal standards (see quadrants "A" and "B" in Fig. 1). Instead, the aim of ethical self-commitments is to recognise, articulate, and integrate industry-specific responsibilities that go beyond legally binding norms into

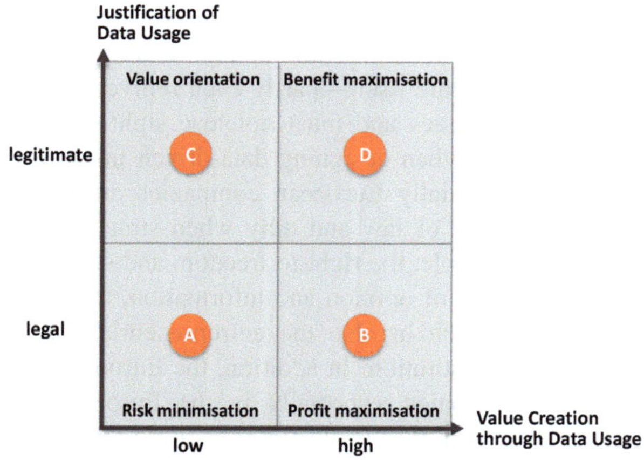

Fig. 1 CDR-quadrant: Model for the strategic orientation of data usage practice: A) Traditional company that only collects data for the immediate business purpose, B) Digitised company that exhausts all legal possibilities of data handling, C) Conservative company that has additional and self-imposed norms and principles for dealing with data, D) Innovative company that ensures economic success with benefits for the customers and the company—taking into account societal values. "Legitimate" in the model is not to be understood as an additional restriction, but as a deepening of the legal motives (Image source: Author's own illustration)

everyday business practices. CDR therefore focuses on the ethically self-designable scope of corporate action—on the legitimation and recognition of entrepreneurial conduct in relation to both internal and external stakeholders (see quadrants "C" and "D" in Fig. 1).

As already outlined in the introductory words of the criteriology, numerous ethical guidelines and corporate self-commitment codes have emerged in recent years, which are intended to provide guidance in the general handling of data and applications from the field of artificial intelligence in particular. Since almost all data ethics and AI guidelines published so far refer essentially to the same terminologies (see above), the responsibility of companies in digital times is no longer about the elaboration of codes, but primarily about implementation.

In Germany, for example, the CDR code of the BMJV (2021) offers an excellent entry point to anchor ethics within the European legal system in the corporate strategy. The code published in June 2021 lists a total of nine principles: 1) Societal basic values, 2) Human-centredness, 3) Creating benefits, 4) Avoiding harm, 5) Autonomy, 6) Fairness, 7) Transparency, 8) Accountability and 9) Sustainability. As already outlined in the interim result of the third chapter, the gap between ethics and technical discourses needs to be closed by mediating between abstract values (such as autonomy, transparency or sustainability) and technical implementation. Companies that recognise this and are aware of their own responsibility are currently in a particularly privileged situation. Through the changed communication and information possibilities (between companies, current and potential customers), they can use the currently (still) existing design space to take the concept of digital self-determination to a new level in a practical way and for their customers, to differentiate themselves from competitors.

2 Legal Regulations and Independent Control Bodies

Starting from the European General Data Protection Regulation (EU-GDPR) (2016) and with a view to the opinion of the Data Ethics Commission of the German Federal Government (2019), specifically the legal regulatory recommendation by Martini (2019), the final report of the Enquete Commission on Artificial Intelligence of the German Bundestag (2020) and the proposal of the European Commission (2021) for a new regulation on Artificial Intelligence, various regulatory proposals are critically examined below in terms of their contribution to ensuring the criteria of transparency, autonomy and digital self-determination (see criteria above).

2.1 A Brief Stocktaking

From the regulations of the European Union on algorithmic decision-making, which came into force throughout the EU with the introduction of the GDPR in 2018, Goodman and Flaxman (2016) have from the outset read out a "right to explanation": "The law will also effectively create a 'right to explanation,' whereby a user can ask for an explanation of an algorithmic decision that was made about them" (ibid. p. 1). Three years after the regulation came into force, we have found that the demand for transparency, which is commonly associated with the right to explanation, is usually reduced to a minimal concept of autonomy in the implementation of the GDPR (see above). Martini (2019, p. 345) also admits that the contribution that the transparency requirement from Art. 12 GDPR has made so far is extremely limited:

> *"Consumers often do not take up well-intentioned consumer information under the time restrictions of everyday life or find it a nuisance that merely follows formalism and in the worst case raises more questions than answers."*

Martini's recommendation in this context is to establish the option to use standardised pictograms, which so far exists on a voluntary basis in Art. 12 para. 7 GDPR, as a "normative duty book" (Martini 2019, p. 345). The combination of written information with pictograms aims to *"provide a meaningful overview of the intended processing in an easily perceptible, understandable and clearly comprehensible form"* (Gola et al. 2017, p. 56). As we have already explained above, this is not only about better orientation in the sense of transparency in terms of data protection, but primarily also about the enforcement of the decision-making and intervention rights of the affected persons, which are fundamental for ensuring informational self-determination (personal rights). Against this background, Martini further explains:

> *"Users should not only act informed, but also in a user cockpit be able to exercise their sovereignty over their data as far as possible in individual cases, in particular grant and revoke disposal rights and be able to trace access to data"* (Martini 2019, p. 345).

The Data Ethics Commission (DEC) of the Federal Government concludes in its report (2019) that the law currently in force, in particular data protection law, but also anti-discrimination and competition law, has so far not adequately met the constitutional mandate. Therefore, it advocates a five-level regulatory system, ranging from no regulation (for AI systems with the lowest risk) to a complete ban (for AI systems with the highest risk), and gives specific advice on the topic "ethically based design" (especially with regard to controlled access to personal data, the topics transparency, explainability and traceability as well as sovereignty of the users).[5] In this context, the DEK recommends, among other things, that the requirements given in the sense of the GDPR should "already become effective at the level of manufacturers as well as service providers" (German Federal Government 2019, p. 20)—for example, through uniform image systems or pictograms that enable consumers to make an informed decision (cf. ibid.).

[5]The report has a total of 240 pages (short version 32 pages). Based on general ethical and legal principles and aspects, guiding principles are developed, technical foundations are discussed, a multi-level governance concept for complex data ecosystems is outlined, requirements regarding the responsible handling of data and algorithmic systems are formulated and the need for a European or global solution is proclaimed.

The final report of the Enquete Commission on Artificial Intelligence of the German Bundestag (2020) also calls for AI systems not to restrict human self-determination. "Autonomy thus emphasises [...] the fundamental right to non-manipulation" (ibid. p. 83). Particular emphasis is placed on the concept of positive freedom and the possibility that "AI systems can be a means to expand human freedom of action" (ibid.). Analogous to the classification of the term in the category of orientation directives, it is also said that "freedom or autonomy is thus a moral guiding principle for AI at a fundamental level" (ibid.). In this context, three approaches are also mentioned through which, in the view of the Enquete Commission on AI, positive freedom can be achieved: i) Human-in-the-Loop ii) Human-on-the-Loop and iii) Human-in-Command. These three approaches are further elaborated as follows:

i. *"Human-in-the-loop": In this approach, humans can directly influence or change the decisions made by an AI product.*
ii. *"Human-on-the-loop": In this approach, for example in the case of an emergency brake assistant, experts set certain parameters during development as the basis for the decision of the AI system; they cannot intervene in the decision itself. Afterwards, the developers check whether the machine has adhered to the guidelines given by humans. If necessary, the parameters can be changed.*
iii. *"Human-in-command": In this approach, the AI product is merely used as a tool. The human decides at all times when and how to use the results presented by the tool. An example is when a machine helps humans with tasks* (see ibid.).[6]

Although the term "transparency (traceability, explainability, openness)" (ibid. p. 86) is associated with different regulatory ideas by the Enquete Commission on AI,[7] the regulatory recommendations in the commission's final report primarily focus on the regulation of information intermediaries in digital discourse spaces (search engines, information platforms, social media etc.) against the backdrop of socially harmful online problems (such as hate, disinformation, terror propaganda etc.).[8] Overall, the impression is created that "autonomy (self-determination of the human as an actor, freedom of decision, non-manipulation)" (ibid. p. 83) is to be brought about more from the outside, e.g. by independent control bodies (experts) and monitoring algorithms, than by empowering those affected themselves.

[6]Especially in the context of so-called upload filters, which are supposed to automatically detect copyright infringements, it is strongly advised against using AI without human control, "in order to preserve freedom of opinion and information on the internet also in the future" (ibid. p. 478).

[7]*"It is about, among other things, transparency regarding the use of AI systems themselves as well as transparency of data origin and their coherence, the system objectives and processing parameters, the responsibilities and levels of autonomous conclusions as well as the control and revision mechanisms"* (ibid. p. 86).

[8]*"As the development of media and intermediaries, especially with increasing use of AI, becomes more internationalised, there is a great need to continue to meet the requirements of Article 5 GG in a regulatory manner"* (ibid. p. 470).

Although "almost all project groups [. . .] have made recommendations for necessary investments for the "Competence building in AI" (ibid. p. 38)—among the "measures that enable society to deal with AI in an informed manner" (ibid. p. 39), there is sometimes a lack of concrete proposals.[9]

Following on from the White Paper on Artificial Intelligence by the European Commission (2020), the proposal for a regulation on a European approach to Artificial Intelligence was published on 21.04.2021, proposing a "legal framework for trustworthy AI" (European Commission 2021, p. 1). Although the concern to create a binding legal framework for trustworthy AI in Europe is generally perceived as positive, many questions remain open regarding the concrete design.[10]

The AI Act (2024) builds upon the GDPR but goes beyond it by imposing premarket transparency and documentation obligations on high-risk AI systems. This includes the mandatory creation of technical documentation, logging capabilities, and user instructions that enable traceability and explainability in line with the system's intended purpose. The Act also explicitly requires that users be informed when they are interacting with an AI system (Article 52), and for certain high-risk applications, it introduces a mandatory 'Fundamental Rights Impact Assessment' prior to deployment. These mechanisms can be interpreted as legal translations of the previously discussed ethical demands for explainability, autonomy and user sovereignty, especially if complemented by participatory instruments such as user cockpits or multi-level information systems.

2.2 Recapitulation of the Challenges

In the above proposed criteriology (see "Criteria for Consideration"), the value "trust" was opposed by the value "transparency (control)". The challenge, therefore, is to find the right balance between trust and transparency (control). It was shown above that neither minimal nor maximum transparency meet the requirements to ensure the digital self-determination rights of those affected in dealing with AI.

The minimal concept of transparency usually only allows for informed consent in practice, as the information regarding the purpose of processing only refers to the point of consent. This form of static consent is extremely inefficient for both the individual and the data-driven industry. The latter already rightly point out that the proactive duty to inform massively slows down the innovation potential of AI in

[9]Instead of strengthening the data sovereignty of those affected, it says, for example: "Concerns from the population should be actively addressed and dispelled through appropriate education as well as through protection mechanisms and obligations" (ibid. p. 42).

[10]See, for example, statements by Dreyer, Heesen, Kersting, Krüger, Matzner, Riechert and Wendehorst from 22.04.2021 in the Science Media Center, available online at https://www.sciencemediacenter.de/alle-angebote/rapid-reaction/details/news/eu-will-kuenstliche-intelligenz-regulieren.

Europe. On the other hand, the information for those affected is usually very vague and general—for example, when it says: "to improve our services" or "for the purpose of data anonymisation." Data anonymisation is not only carried out to protect the privacy of those affected (but usually justified by this), but also because an evaluation of so-called anonymised affinity models no longer falls under the special protection of personal data in the GDPR. What is usually concealed is that the collective character of algorithms can easily override this individual legal logic or what personal disadvantages and long-term societal risks are associated with individual interests or actions being dissolved in the "numerical generality" (Heesen 2018, p. 47) of affinity models (according to the watering can principle). With a maximum concept of transparency, on the other hand, the question arises as to how a scientific treatise on such complex socio-technical details can specifically help the average citizen. Since too much information usually leads to intransparency (cf. Ananny and Crawford 2016), the question of the right measure comes to the fore. From a scientific and legal perspective, it is of course important to mathematically logically penetrate all interpretation methods of black box analyses, to find new models and to explore and investigate in greater detail. However, for most users, a detailed explanation system that represents all factors for a certain prediction or a certain behaviour would usually be counterproductive, because people in their everyday life prefer short and context-related explanations for an event (see Miller 2017; Doshi-Velez and Kim 2017; Molnar 2019). To build sustainable trust in AI applications, the primary focus is therefore on preparing the at times agnostic interpretability of statistical models in a target group-specific manner (cf. Koska and Filipović 2019).

2.3 Design Perspective

Digital self-determination can be located at the level of abstraction where transparency and control can be established for the individual user (cf. Koska 2015b). Since not all users can be assumed to have the same level of knowledge, a tiered information system is suitable for this purpose. For a quick general introduction to the topic, standardised pictograms (as already considered in the GDPR and taken up again by Martini and the Data Ethics Commission) can be used, which ideally are displayed context-sensitively during a specific usage action. Because not all information is helpful in every situation. At this level, complexity reduction is required so that users can make a quick decision based on a uniform visual language. More detailed information should be bundled separately, ideally in an independent self-service portal, so that customers can manage their settings at a central SPOT (Single Point of Truth) across applications. Analogous to the non-digital world, people could then decide situationally (cf. Nissenbaum 2010), when they want to share which data(-segments) with whom, for what purpose. Because in certain situations, e.g. with very specific health issues or for initiating a long-term loan, it may be beneficial for the person or customer to receive tailor-made offers based on personal data, rather than "numerical generality". The introduction of a tiered information system or user

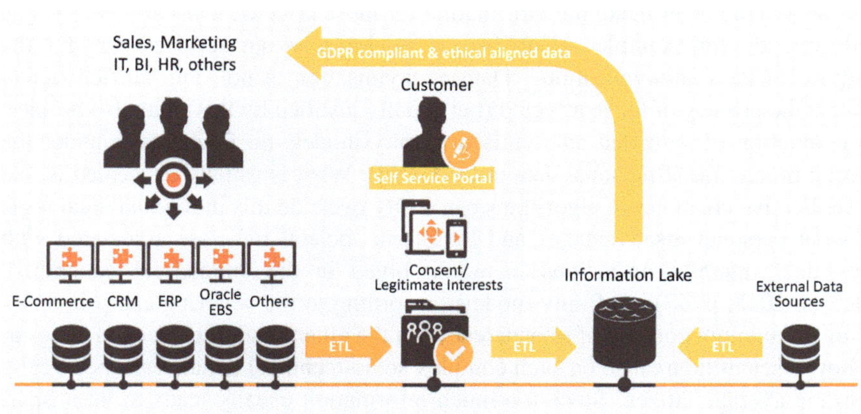

Fig. 2 Model for a target group-oriented consent management (Image source: Author's own illustration)

cockpit could not only improve the information and transparency obligations towards individual citizens. By upgrading the "data lakes" to a central "information lake", departmental and company-wide authorisation concepts can be realised, which strengthen digital sovereignty and competitiveness in Europe, optimise data governance processes, improve data quality and much more (Fig. 2).

The basic values of our society represented in the constitution are the basis of state and political action. The brief inventory and recapitulation of the challenges has shown that the current regulatory debate is no longer about the question of "whether", but "how" a self-determined handling of algorithmic and data-driven business models can be realised. For a detailed justification of why "the law currently in force, in particular data protection law, but also anti-discrimination and competition law [. . .] does not yet accurately reflect the constitutional mandate" (Martini 2019, p. 109), reference is made to the monograph by Martini (2019).

Essentially, the model proposed here differs from the current implementations of privacy settings in that the management of consent no longer lies (solely) with the operator, but also with the consumers. This resolves the thirty-year target conflict between the protection of privacy and the capitalisation of our personal activities that we demonstrated above using the example of the IAB Framework TCF 2.0, and at the same time facilitates access for independent control bodies.

3 Concept of a Digital Educational Identity

Building on the model of a tiered information system or user cockpit proposed above, the following section will outline a design perspective for the topic of digital education and media literacy. The concept of personal autonomy takes, as already mentioned in the introductory words, an important role in the general digitalisation discourse, as it is often synonymous with (informational) self-determination, (digital) sovereignty, freedom, self-control, self-regulation but also self-creation. Other values, such as security or privacy, are often negotiated under the concept of autonomy or ultimately traced back to this concept. In the educational context, the concept of autonomy plays a particularly important role, as it—as shown by the three minimal conditions "transparency, authenticity and control"—is also closely related to the concept of responsibility. The idea of a digital educational identity (cf. Koska 2015b) aims to take this into account.[11]

3.1 A Brief Inventory

The virtual space is overcrowded with "virtual zombies" (Yvonne Hofstetter)[12], i.e. data profiles, to which the users themselves have no access and of whose existence they usually have no knowledge. The concept of digital educational identity as intended here differs from the commercial interests of the advertising internet industry especially in that the "360-degree view" of the consumer's data profile *is made the subject of observation for the users*, in order to initially make abstractly discussed values such as transparency, digital self-determination, (data) sovereignty etc., tangible for the individual. Furthermore, to bring to life the three core areas of computer science education, as already extensively discussed above with reference to Humbert and Losch (2019) (see Chap. 3, Figs. 6 and 7).

Referring to the concepts of Forsythe (1963) and especially Naur (1966), it was shown that the importance and status of computer science education in the context of school and university curriculum has been discussed internationally for more than 50 years. The extent of the "technical and organisational inertia to tackle the necessary changes", criticised by Naur, was finally made clear to everyone by the SARS-CoV-2 pandemic. In Germany, as a result, the focus was mainly on setting up the technical infrastructure for distance learning or homeschooling. The funds provided by the federal and state governments on 17.05.2019 with the DigitalPakt School were therefore primarily used to finance what Naur described in 1966 as "the last point of information of digitalisation".

Building on Humbert and Losch (2019), it was explained that a distinction must be made between the "operation" and the "control" of computer systems and that the core issue is the triad between i) application ii) design and iii) decision-making. Since digital technologies penetrate our personal sphere to create technical identity constructions, it was finally requested that the focus of digital education should be

[11]The idea for the conception of a digital educational identity is based on a prototype that was developed as part of the EU research project EEXCESS (Enhancing Europe's eXchange in Cultural Educational and Scientific reSources, http://eexcess.eu), together with two fellow students (Uwe Stange and Johannes Schukat), at the School of Philosophy in Munich under the name "Sluice Box" (see explanatory video, available online at: https://www.youtube.com/watch?v=veHw6zsNU1Y).

[12]The term "virtual zombies" comes from Yvonne Hofstetter, who used this term during a colloquium on IT ethics at the School of Philosophy.

shifted from personalised content to the administration of the personal learning, education and research profile.

3.2 Recapitulation of Challenges

Transparency can create trust. However, transparency, as also noted by Schneider (2013, Chap. 1, Sect. 5), usually only exists as a futuristic vanishing point: "It shows that 'transparency' can always only be promised. Transparency here and now does not exist." An increase always seems possible. Assuming that data protection transparency, as it has already been made mandatory by the GDPR, is sufficient for the guarantee of digital self-determination, overlooks the actual living conditions of those affected as well as a blind transparency ideology. "It is crucial that a regulation of the media, whether within the legal framework or through voluntary self-control, alone is not sufficient" (Silverstone 2008, p. 253). For Silverstone, the opportunity to participate in the so-called "Mediapolis" (i.e. a form of polis shaped by media) is a condition for the perception of responsibility: "Otherwise, the individual in the Mediapolis would only have the role of the zombie" (Silverstone 2008, p. 169).

> *"Media competence as the ability to receive and produce media should be possessed by all those who participate in the Mediapolis. The forms it must take depend on the power that the respective actor has in the media landscape, and of course what is necessary for real participation will change over time with this environment"* (Silverstone 2008, p. 275 f).

Especially regarding the measures that enable a mature handling of society with AI, we have already criticised in the previous section that there are hardly any concrete proposals for this. On the more than 800 pages of its final report the Enquete Commission AI has addressed the numerous dangers and problems of Artificial Intelligence in breadth much more comprehensively, than is possible within the framework of this paper. In depth, however, the report sometimes lacks precision. For example, in a special vote of the project group "AI and Economy" from correct premises a (at least) misleading conclusion is drawn:

> *"The Free Democrats would like to make it explicitly clear at this point that AI applications are 'only' (digital) technical aids. They are capable, to a certain degree autonomously, of solving complex problems. Technologies have no value system and follow no own goals. They are neutral until people give them a corresponding rating"* (ibid. p. 524).

Even if this supposed clarification[13] of the FDP is made in good intention (probably to not endanger Germany as technology location), such a misleading statement

[13]In the preceding chapters (especially in the section "Conscious and unconscious value inscriptions") it was extensively explained that the mere existence of human artefacts presupposes a human valuation or objective. From the observation that technologies do not have their own value system and their own objectives, it cannot therefore be concluded that technologies *are neutral*. Especially, insofar as they—unlike a 'simple' *technical tool*, for example a hammer—are controlled by anthropogenic algorithms (see above).

does not contribute to responsibly dealing with the opportunities and challenges of AI.[14] On the contrary—it rather shows that the problem is sometimes still misjudged even by selected experts of a party that likes to present itself as understanding digitalisation. That's why it's so important to empower individuals to critically question things: Cui bono—what is the added value of the neutrality thesis—who benefits from it, who has an advantage from it? Without conclusively clarifying this here in individual cases, it remains to be noted that misleading statements in general do not lead to building trust sustainably.

3.3 Design Perspective

In view of the challenge just outlined, the conception of a digital educational identity in a first step is about understanding that the virtual reality is not a value-free sphere—even though science is oriented towards the ideal of value neutrality and objectivity (see media philosophical systematisation as well as ethos of algorithmic thinking and acting in the second chapter). It's about participation, autonomy and digital self-determination, about the perception and visibility of conscious and unconscious value inscriptions, about determining a demarcation line between transparency and trust, and much more.

Intelligent technologies always presuppose a certain degree of loss of control. Because ultimately, the goal of intelligent systems is to take tasks off our hands, to delegate complex computations and monotonous activities to machines, to get to the essentials faster. For a responsible approach by society to AI, expert groups and regulations that publicly discuss or sanction the behaviour of opaque processes are only a necessary, but not a sufficient condition.

If we want to maintain the values and norms rooted in our society, then the administration of digital profiles must not be completely outsourced to third parties. The issue of data and information security is a technical criterion, but not an end in itself. Especially in the context of digital education and media competence, it's not just about "safely surfing through digital everyday life", but about preparing citizens for a self-determined life with intelligent systems.[15] As long as we put people at the centre of the development and deployment of technical systems (see BMJV 2021), we must also enable them to understand the basic workings of algorithmic selection mechanisms by giving them the opportunity to recognise shortcomings that data science professionals cannot avoid, even with the best intentions. For example, that the raw data (the raw material of personal data

[14]The sentence "They are neutral until people give them a corresponding valuation." is roughly identical in content to the sentence "They do not exist (i.e., they do not exist at all—they do not exist), until people inscribe their own objectives and values in them (see "On the outsourcing of algorithmic thinking and action" in the intellectual and historical foundations at the beginning of this book).

[15]The SIMON app introduced by Samsung on 17.06.2021 is just another example of the confusion of the adjective "safe" with "sovereign", see the online press release from 18.06.2021 under https://news.samsung.com/de/digitaltag-simon-app.

profiles), which are recorded from the interaction behaviour with a system, are an abstraction of reality, a digital shadow of reality. The understanding that every digital identity is already a construct of data science (see Koska 2015b, p. 88), is the basis for becoming actively involved in shaping it.

Recent analyses suggest that the widespread framing of bias as a deviation from an objective norm or 'ground truth' tends to obscure the socio-technical and normative dimensions of algorithmic decision-making. Rather than treating bias as a solvable technical problem, a relational, responsibility-centered framework highlights the need to account for situated knowledge, power asymmetries, and the deception of neutrality in data-driven environments (cf. Koska, forthcoming). In line with this, Prinsloo and Slade (2017) argue that the construction of learner profiles through data analytics entails not only technical precision but also ethical responsibility. Educational institutions must ensure that data-driven interventions do not unintentionally reinforce bias or reduce student agency under the guise of optimisation.

Building on the model of a tiered information system or user cockpit presented above, a digital education identity allows, depending on the context and knowledge of the affected person, to look under the bonnet of our technical tools and to individually explore a self-determined handling of intelligent systems.

Analogous to the interest profiles that internet services like Google or Facebook create to display target group-specific advertising on websites, so-called tracking technologies draw an increasingly comprehensive learning and research profile of the users to make their data profile accessible to the data donors (see ibid. p. 81 f). For this purpose, simple tools like "uRank" (see Di Sciascio et al. 2015) can already be used, which combine lightweight text analysis and visual methods for topic-related exploration of learning and education content; but always giving the users the opportunity to reorganise the content (on-the-fly) if the information interest changes. On the next deeper level, media users could understand in which situations and contexts temporary interest profiles are already sufficient to cover a specific information need, and in which situations and contexts only long-term data profiles provide meaningful results.[16] Recent research on Learning Analytics Dashboards shows that learners benefit most when they are not only given access to their data but also actively supported in interpreting it. Dashboards should therefore not merely visualise traces of learning behaviour, but foster reflective engagement and self-regulated learning (see Jivet et al. 2018).

Gradually, the users can be increasingly involved in the search for numbers and values and determine the selection criteria of the selection mechanisms themselves, ideally to increase the data quality (remember: no one has such a privileged access to their own goals, desires and interests as the person concerned themselves).

[16]Short-term user profiles are based on the extracted information from a specific sequence of user activities (e.g. within a "session"). Long-term user profiles extend beyond a single "user session". In principle, usage activities, such as click and search behaviour, can be recorded, the browser history read out, key terms from a read or online self-written text extracted via named entity extractio) and much more (see application scenario in Koska 2015b, pp. 83–84).

If we succeed in taking consumers on the journey of responsibility, then they can sustainably build trust in algorithmic decisions. The journey does not end with self-commitment codes, general transparency declarations and promotionally effective AI guidelines, but rather continues by giving the customers a hand on the steering wheel and making them an integral part of the company's AI responsibility strategy (cf. Ackermann 2017).

5 Summary and Outlook

The design perspectives outlined in the previous chapter represent the result of this study. The yield appears to be the connection between the criteriology and the problem-oriented analysis of algorithmisation, the ethos of algorithmic thinking and action, and the ideological and intellectual-historical foundation. Finally, it is necessary to summarise the line of thought once again and reflect on the conclusion of the investigation.

The research-guiding thesis was developed in the first chapter. The starting point was that the processes of change and transformation, commonly described by the term "Digital Revolution", require an algorithm ethics that places responsible and trustworthy data use at the centre and observes and analyses the transparency and control problem of algorithmic decisions at a normative-principled level.

The central working hypothesis was formulated as follows: *The task of an algorithm ethics essentially consists in comprehending the morality enacted in algorithms and making it accessible to those affected.*

On the one hand, this hypothesis intended to pursue the media-philosophical question of to what extent algorithms exercise their own form of normativity. The context of the control unit of algorithmic processes and the methodological tools for attributing responsibility thus moved into the centre of consideration. It proved crucial, on the other hand, that the transparency and control problem can also be presented as a competence and empowerment problem.

In the second chapter, the ideological and intellectual-historical foundations of algorithmisation were presented, which initially gave us information about various stages of digitalisation and datafication. It could be shown that the concept of the algorithm is of cross-cultural significance for human understanding of the world, self and others. Algorithms have a constitutive and a normative function—from the fundamental structural and ordering principles of reality, through the vision of the digital measurement of the world, to the idea of formalising and outsourcing algorithmic thinking and action to artificial artefacts. Algorithms can be found in

C. Koska, *Ethics of Algorithms*,
https://doi.org/10.1007/978-3-662-71518-5_5

all natural and artificial systems where there are states between which a causal link (A → B) exists. The observation and formalisation of this link was characterised as a specific achievement of the human brain (ability to reflect and abstract). With the media-philosophical systematisation, a distinction was made between natural and anthropogenic algorithms. It was explained that we need media tools to describe the inner logic of natural transformation and reshaping processes, and the media manifestation already marks a pivot towards anthropogenic algorithms. It was further elaborated that algorithmics provides a formal sign system to virtualise reality. Referring to the fundamental motive of humans to overcome mere observation of nature and penetrate the basic structure and normative order of the cosmos with their own dimensions of meaning, we further distinguished between epistemic and moral errors or failures and restricted these two categories to anthropogenic algorithms. In the subject area of an algorithm ethics, it was noted that the difficulties of the basic conceptual system of media also affect the concept of algorithms and the question of the condition of the possibility of algorithmic thinking (the media-aprioristic function of algorithms) seems to run into a dead end *(interim conclusion)*. The geographical location of algorithmic thinking and acting was located in the logos (λόγος) as distinguishing and precising reason. It was pointed out that in the outsourcing or relocation of the geographical location of algorithmic thinking to silicon, especially regarding the condition of the possibility of an ethical consciousness, the importance of embodiment and the significance of human emotionality cannot be ignored. Finally, based on these results, the ethos of algorithmisation and the implicit direction of algorithmics were summarised *(interim result)*.

The third chapter investigated the attribution of actor status, the emergence of conscious and unconscious value inscriptions based on a problem-oriented description of exemplary fields of action and developed a criteriology to normatively counter the dangers and problems of advancing algorithmisation. With the analysis of the five fields of action, not only could the added value of a comprehensive concept of algorithms be demonstrated, but also the previous statements on the ethos and the implicit direction of algorithmics could be confirmed (especially about the increase in efficiency and effectiveness). Using Sybille Krämer's model of flattening, attention was drawn to the two opposing centrifugal forces in connection with the control and regulation of machines. It was explained how transparency and opacity, simplification and complexity, are to be understood as two sides of the same coin. The surface, especially of ontology-based adaptive human-machine interfaces, was identified as the demarcation line between media users and media producers. To illustrate the dynamics of self-learning systems, Hermann Haken's model of synergetics was used and further reference was made to the concept of so-called system images (Norman and Draper, 1986) to reconstruct the "inner reality of the machine" (Krotz 2018, p. 16). Subsequently, the moral actors of algorithmisation were further differentiated. In a next step the dangers and problems were summarised once again (against the background of the inventory of current fields of action) to propose a criteriology based on this. The criteriology considered not only numerous values, norms and principles that have emerged in our cultural circle in recent years (especially in AI and data ethics guidelines, but also in CDR codes, for example), but also arranged and structured these criteria into four groups: 1) general ethical aspects, 2) orientation directives, 3) criteria of balancing and 4) formal and technical criteria. Finally, the results of the third chapter were summarised following the i) technical-mathematical, ii) economic and iii) ethical dimension of numbers and values *(second interim result)*.

With the fourth chapter, a bridge was built between theory and practice, between abstract numbers and values as well as application-related solutions. In the first step, the corporate responsibility concerning the conception and implementation of CDR measures was addressed, which are to be anchored in the *core business* of data-driven enterprises (in the data usage strategy of companies); to build trust in data-driven business models, it is therefore not enough if companies only drive the digitalisation of (peripheral) CSR projects. The CDR code of the BMJV was named as an ideal entry point for companies to further concretise ethics within the European legal system. Starting from the GDPR, the necessity of additional regulations was discussed in a second step. Especially to guarantee criteria such as transparency, autonomy and digital self-determination (see also CDR code of the BMJV) it was found that the regulatory proposals of the various expert groups basically point in the same direction (to improve data sovereignty). Building on the proposal by Mario Martini, the model of a tiered information system was discussed, in which consumers can manage their data usage preferences across applications (SPOT, Single Point of Truth). In the third and final step, the model of a tiered information system or user cockpit was further differentiated in terms of a digital educational identity. It was shown how people—through digital education or targeted measures to increase individual media competence—can be taken on the journey of responsibility.

The three design perspectives stand for themselves, as they can be realised independently of each other. On the other hand, they also build on each other in relation to content, insofar as the transparency and control problem can also be presented as a competence or empowerment problem. Education, participation and justice, autonomy and digital self-determination were identified as central guiding principles for an ethics of algorithms. These guiding principles, it was clarified are not binary terms, but an ideal guiding star, towards which we need to align ourselves step by step. But this alignment must not stop there. The phase of lip service is over. It is necessary to move forward. As long as we put people at the centre of the development and use of technical systems, ethics must again become an integral part of algorithmic thinking and action. "Humans are not machines that process technical data or animals that communicate by signals" (Christians 2019, p. 102). How far can an algorithm ethics go to solve the enforcement problem? In which situations should individual legal aspects (such as data protection) be subordinated to social ethical issues? "The Mediapolis is the scene of the conflict between the search for truth and the disappearance of doubt. Solving it is its most important task" (Silverstone 2008, p. 85). This is precisely why the issue of digital education and media competence is so important. But it is not just about the transmission of technical skills, but especially about the perception of responsibility, as Silverstone also points out with reference to Rüdiger Funiok:[1] "Media competence at a professional level requires a certain state of consciousness or at least begins with it."

[1]"Rüdiger Funiok (2000) has thought about such aspects of media competence by asking what forms of responsibility media users can and should develop." (ibid. p. 274).

Bibliography

Ackermann, Gabriele (2017): CSR in der gesetzlichen Krankenversicherung. In: Alexandra Hildebrandt und Werner Landhäußer (Eds.): CSR und Digitalisierung. Der digitale Wandel als Chance und Herausforderung für Wirtschaft und Gesellschaft. Berlin, Heidelberg: Springer Berlin Heidelberg, pp. 947–960.

Altmeppen, Klaus-Dieter (2015): Automaten kennen keine Moral. Metamorphosen des Journalismus und die Folgen für die Verantwortung. In: Communicatio Socialis 48 (1), 16–33. Available online at https://ejournal.communicatio-socialis.de/index.php/cc/article/view/902/900.

Altmeppen, Klaus-Dieter; Bieber, Christoph; Filipović, Alexander; Heesen, Jessica (2015): Echtzeit-Öffentlichkeiten. Neue digitale Medienordnungen und neue Verantwortungsdimensionen. In: Communicatio Socialis 48 (4), 382–396. Available online at http://ejournal.communicatio-socialis.de/index.php/cc/article/view/1099/1097.

Ambrosetti, Nadia (2016): Algorithmic in the 12th Century: The Carmen de Algorismo by Alexander de Villa Dei. In: Fabio Gadducci und Mirko Tavosanis (Eds.): History and Philosophy of Computing, Vol. 487. Cham: Springer International Publishing (IFIP Advances in Information and Communication Technology), pp. 71–86.

Ananny, Mike; Crawford, Kate (2016): Seeing without knowing. Limitations of the transparency ideal and its application to algorithmic accountability. In: New Media & Society 33 (4), 146144481667664. https://doi.org/10.1177/1461444816676645.

Anderka, Maik (2013): Analyzing and Predicting Quality Flaws in User-generated Content: The Case of Wikipedia. Doctoral Dissertation. Bauhaus-Universität, Weimar.

Anderson, Chris (2008): The End of Theory: The Data Deluge Makes the Scientific Method Obsolete. In: Wired Magazine 16 (7), pp. 108–109.

Andorno, Roberto; Christensen, Birgit (2014): Menschenwürde. In: Christian Lenk, Gunnar Duttge und Heiner Fangerau (Eds.): Handbuch Ethik und Recht der Forschung am Menschen. Berlin, Heidelberg: Springer Berlin Heidelberg, pp. 197–200.

Arndt, Hans W. (1971): Methodo scientifica pertractatum. Mos geometricus und Kalkülbegriff in der philosophischen Theorienbildung des 17. und 18. Jahrhunderts. Berlin: de Gruyter (Quellen und Studien zur Philosophie, 4). Available online at http://www.degruyter.com/doi/book/10.1515/9783110844900.

Asimov, Isaac (1994): Die Gesetze der Robotik. In: Marcel Bieger, Ingrid Hermann und Fredy Köpsell (Eds.): Isaac Asimov. Roboter-Visionen. 1st ed. Bergisch Gladbach: Bastei-Verl. Lübbe (Bastei-Lübbe-Taschenbuch, 21201).

Bächle, Thomas Christian (2015): Mythos Algorithmus. Die Fabrikation des computerisierbaren Menschen. Doctoral Dissertation, 2014. Wiesbaden: Springer VS (Research). Available online at https://doi.org/10.1007/978-3-658-07627-6.

C. Koska, *Ethics of Algorithms*,
https://doi.org/10.1007/978-3-662-71518-5

Bacon, Francis (2013): Große Erneuerung der Wissenschaften: Holzinger. Available online at http://www.zeno.org/Lesesaal/N/9781484030608?page=0.

Baer, Tobias (2019): Understand, Manage, and Prevent Algorithmic Bias. Berkeley, CA: Apress.

Barnes, Susan B. (2006): A privacy paradox: Social networking in the United States. In: FM. https://doi.org/10.5210/fm.v11i9.1394.

Bandy, Diakopoulos (2019): Auditing News Curation Systems: A Case Study Examining Algorithmic and Editorial Logic in Apple News. In: Proceedings of the International AAAI Conference on Web and Social Media, 14(1), pp. 36–47. Available online at https://doi.org/10.1609/icwsm.v14i1.7277.

Barth, Armin P. (2013): Algorithmik für Einsteiger. Für Studierende, Lehrer und Schüler in den Fächern Mathematik und Informatik. 2nd rev. ed. Wiesbaden: Springer Spektrum. Available online at http://dx.doi.org/10.1007/978-3-658-02282-2.

Bartlett, Robert (2019): Solving the AI Accountability Gap. Hold developers responsible for their creations. Available online at https://towardsdatascience.com/solving-the-ai-accountability-gap-dd35698249fe.

Bauberger, Stefan (2003): Was ist die Welt? Zur philosophischen Interpretation der Physik. Stuttgart: Kohlhammer (Kon-Texte, 6).

Becker, Joachim (2016): Bequem chauffiert - oder ferngesteuert ins Verderben? Süddeutsche Zeitung (Eds.). Available online at http://www.sueddeutsche.de/auto/automatisiertes-fahren-bequem-chauffiert-oder-ferngesteuert-ins-verderben-1.3075944.

Bedford-Strohm, Jonas (2019): Verletzliche Öffentlichkeit. Eine Kritik (der Kritik) der Filterblase. In: Jonas Bedford-Strohm, Florian Höhne und Julian Zeyher-Quattlender (Eds.): Digitaler Strukturwandel der Öffentlichkeit: Nomos Verlagsgesellschaft mbH & Co. KG, pp. 201–217.

Beiler, Markus (2013): Nachrichtensuche im Internet. Inhaltsanalyse zur journalistischen Qualität von Nachrichtensuchmaschinen. Doctoral Dissertation, 2012. Konstanz u. a.: UVK.

Berto, Francesco; Tagliabue, Jacopo (2017 Edition): Cellular Automata. Available online at https://plato.stanford.edu/archives/fall2017/entries/cellular-automata.

Betzler, Monika (Eds.) (2013): Autonomie der Person. Münster: mentis (Map - Mentis Anthologien Philosophie).

Bhadani, Yamaya, Flammini, Menczer, Ciampaglia, Nyhan (2022): Political audience diversity and news reliability in algorithmic ranking. In: Nature Human Behaviour (6), pp. 495–505. Available online at https://doi.org/10.1038/s41562-021-01276-5.

Bieber, Christoph (2016): Öffentlichkeit. In: Jessica Heesen (Eds.): Handbuch Medien- und Informationsethik. Stuttgart: J. B. Metzler, pp. 67–73.

Bieber, Christoph (2019): Forschungsfragen der digitalen Öffentlichkeit. Ein Ausblick. In: Jonas Bedford-Strohm, Florian Höhne und Julian Zeyher-Quattlender (Eds.): Digitaler Strukturwandel der Öffentlichkeit: Nomos Verlagsgesellschaft mbH & Co. KG, pp. 151–157.

Bielefeldt, Heiner (2011): Autonomie. In: Marcus Düwell, Christoph Hübenthal und Micha H. Werner (Eds.): Handbuch Ethik. 3rd rev. ed. Ed. Stuttgart: Metzler, pp. 311–314.

Bierhoff, Hans-Werner; Rohmann, Elke (2017): Diffusion von Verantwortung. In: Ludger Heidbrink, Claus Langbehn und Janina Loh (Eds.): Handbuch Verantwortung. Wiesbaden: Springer Fachmedien Wiesbaden, pp. 911–931.

Blömeke, Sigrid (Eds.) (2008): Professionelle Kompetenz angehender Lehrerinnen und Lehrer. Wissen, Überzeugungen und Lerngelegenheiten deutscher Mathematikstudierender und -referendare erste Ergebnisse zur Wirksamkeit der Lehrerausbildung. Münster: Waxmann.

BMJV (Eds.) (2021): Corporate Digital Responsibility-Kodex. Freiwillige Selbstverpflichtung mit Bericht. Corporate Digital Responsibility Initiative. Bundesministerium der Justiz und für Verbraucherschutz. Available online at https://cdr-initiative.de/uploads/files/BMJV_CDR-Initiative_KODEX.pdf.

BMWi (Eds.) (2019a): Das Projekt GAIA-X. Eine vernetzte Dateninfrastruktur als Wiege eines vitalen, europäischen Ökosystems. Bundesministerium für Wirtschaft und Energie. Available online at https://www.bmwi.de/Redaktion/DE/Publikationen/Digitale-Welt/das-projekt-gaia-x.html.

BMWi (Eds.) (2019b): Digitale Souveränität im Kontext plattformbasierter Ökosysteme. Plattform „Innovative Digitalisierung der Wirtschaft“, Fokusgruppe „Digitale Souveränität“ im Rahmen des Digitalgipfels 2019. Bundesministerium für Wirtschaft und Energie.

Boeder, Heribert (2013): Der frühgriechische Wortgebrauch von Logos und Aletheia. In: Lorenzo Perilli (Eds.): Logos. Theorie und Begriffsgeschichte. Darmstadt: WBG - Wissenschaftliche Buchgesellschaft, 207–232.

Boncompagni, Baldassare (1857): Trattati d'Aritmetica. Algoritmi de numero Indorum. Rom: Tipogr. delle Scienze Fisiche e Matematiche.

Boole, George (1847): The mathematical analysis of logic. Beeing an essay towards a calculuc of deductive reasoning. Cambridge.

Borchers, Detlef (2010): Zehn Jahre Dotcom-Bust: Als die Blase platzte. Available online at https://www.heise.de/newsticker/meldung/Zehn-Jahre-Dotcom-Bust-Als-die-Blase-platzte-951796.html.

Bordt, Michael (1999): Platon. Orig. ed. Freiburg: Herder (Herder-Spektrum Meisterdenker, 4761).

Bordt, Michael (2005): Aristoteles' Metaphysik Buch Lambda. Studien-Manuskript. München.

Bostrom, Nick (2005): Transhumanist Values. Ethical Issues for the Twenty-First Century. Available online at https://nickbostrom.com/ethics/values.pdf.

Bostrom, Nick (2015): Was passiert, wenn unsere Computer intelligenter werden als wir? TED, 2015. Available online at https://www.ted.com/talks/nick_bostrom_what_happens_when_our_computers_get_smarter_than_we_are?language=de.

Bostrom, Nick (2018): Die Zukunft der Menschheit. Aufsätze. Originalausgabe, 1st ed. Berlin: Suhrkamp (Suhrkamp Taschenbuch Wissenschaft, 2245).

Bostrom, Nick; Shulman, Carl (2021): "Sharing the World with Digital Minds." In: Rethinking Moral Status, pp.306–326, Available online at https://doi.org/10.1093/oso/9780192894076.003.0018.

Boyd, Danah; Crawford, Kate (2012): Critical Questions for Big Data. Provocations for a cultural, technological, and scholarly phenomenon. In: Information, Communication & Society 15 (5), pp. 662–679. Available online at http://dx.doi.org/10.1080/1369118X.2012.678878.

Bozdag, Engin (2013): Bias in algorithmic filtering and personalization. In: Ethics Inf Technol 15 (3), pp. 209–227. https://doi.org/10.1007/s10676-013-9321-6.

Bratu, Christine (2017): Korporative und kooperative Verantwortung. In: Ludger Heidbrink, Claus Langbehn und Janina Loh (Eds.): Handbuch Verantwortung. Wiesbaden: Springer Fachmedien Wiesbaden, pp. 453–476.

Breidenbach, Joana; Filipović, Theresa (2017): Revolution oder Evolution? Wie die Digitalisierung soziales Engagement von Unternehmen verändert. In: Alexandra Hildebrandt und Werner Landhäußer (Eds.): CSR und Digitalisierung. Der digitale Wandel als Chance und Herausforderung für Wirtschaft und Gesellschaft. Berlin, Heidelberg: Springer Berlin Heidelberg, 859–875.

Brenner, Andreas (2011): Politische Ethik. In: Marcus Düwell, Christoph Hübenthal und Micha H. Werner (Eds.): Handbuch Ethik. 3rd rev. ed. Stuttgart: Metzler, pp. 279–283.

Bringsjord, Selmer; Govindarajulu, Naveen Sundar (2018): Artificial Intelligence. In: Metaphysics Research Lab, Stanford University (Eds.): The Stanford Encyclopedia of Philosophy. Available online at https://plato.stanford.edu/archives/fall2018/entries/artificial-intelligence.

Brockhaus (Eds.) (2019): Singularität (Physik). Available online at https://brockhaus.de/ecs/permalink/5CA9C5606AF6201AE1F4F416AE748AD0.pdf.

Brockhaus Enzyklopädie Online (Eds.) (2019): Gatekeeper-Konzept. (Kommunikationswissenschaft). NE GmbH | Brockhaus. Available online at https://brockhaus.de/ecs/permalink/D48973CED5DB0AD4A713B10B8CC2CEFE.pdf.

Brockhaus Enzyklopädie Online (Eds.) (2021): Entmündigung. NE GmbH | Brockhaus. Available online at https://brockhaus.de/ecs/permalink/C62EC981815C97AEF229975C469462D2.pdf.

Broy, Manfred (1998): Informatik. Eine grundlegende Einführung. Vol. 2: Systemstrukturen und Theoretische Informatik. 2nd rev. ed. Berlin, Heidelberg: Springer (Springer-Lehrbuch). Available online at http://dx.doi.org/10.1007/978-3-642-58911-9.

Bruns, Axel (2006): Towards Produsage: Futures for User-Led Content Production. In: Fay Sudweeks (Eds.): Cultural attitudes towards technology and communication 2006. Proceedings of the Fifth International Conference on Cultural Attitudes towards Technology and Communication; Tartu, Estonia, 28 June - 1 July 2006. Murdoch, Australia: Univ, pp. 275–284. Available online at https://eprints.qut.edu.au/4863/1/4863_1.pdf.

Büchmann, Georg (1898): Geflügelte Worte. Kindle edition: Die Perfekte Bibliothek.

Bundesanstalt für Straßenwesen (Eds.) (2012): Rechtsfolgen zunehmender Fahrzeugautomatisierung (Forschung kompakt, 11/12). Available online at http://www.bast.de/DE/Publikationen/Foko/Downloads/2012-11.pdf.

Bundeskartellamt (Eds.) (2019): B6-22/16. Veröffentlichte Entscheidung zum Facebook Verfahren. Available online at https://www.bundeskartellamt.de/SharedDocs/Meldung/DE/AktuelleMeldungen/2019/29_03_2019_Ver%C3%B6ffentlichung_Entscheidungen_Facebook.html.

Bunz, Mercedes (2012): Die stille Revolution. Wie Algorithmen Wissen, Arbeit, Öffentlichkeit und Politik verändern, ohne dabei viel Lärm zu machen. orig.-ed., 2nd ed. Berlin: Suhrkamp (Edition Unseld, 43).

Burghardt, Jennifer; Kraus, Maximilian; Koska, Christopher; Lehman, Robert; Müller, Nicholas; Reder, Michael (2024): Kann Künstliche Intelligenz sozialarbeiterische Entscheidungsprozesse unterstützen? In: unsere jugend, 76. Jg., S. 300–310. Available online at http://dx.doi.org/10.2378/uj2024.art40d.

Burkhardt, Marcus (2015): Digitale Datenbanken. Eine Medientheorie im Zeitalter von Big Data. Bielefeld, Germany: transcript Verlag. Available online at http://www.oapen.org/search?identifier=595362.

Carpo, Mario (2009): Aufstieg und Fall der identischen Reproduzierbarkeit. Zu Leon Battista Albertis unzeitgemäßer Entdeckung digitaler Technologien in der Frührenaissance. In: Daniel Gethmann und Susanne Hauser (Eds.): Kulturtechnik Entwerfen. Bielefeld: transcript Verlag.

Carpo, Mario (2011): The Alphabet and the Algorithm. Cambridge, Mass: MIT Press.

Case, Amber (2010): We are all cyborgs now. Available online at https://www.ted.com/talks/amber_case_we_are_all_cyborgs_now.

Chi, Ed H. (2013): The Science of Social Interactions on the Web. 13th International Conference on Knowledge Management and Knowledge Technologies. Know Center, TU Graz. Graz, 05.09.2013. Available online at http://i-know.tugraz.at/2013/keynotes/ed-chi.mp3.

Christensen, Clayton M.; Matzler, Kurt (2013): The innovator's dilemma. Warum etablierte Unternehmen den Wettbewerb um bahnbrechende Innovationen verlieren. 1st rev. and exp. ed. München: Vahlen.

Christians, Clifford G. (2019): Media Ethics and Global Justice in the Digital Age: Cambridge University Press (3).

Cooper, Tim; Jade, Siu; Kuangyi, Wei (2015): Corporate Digital Responsibility. Doing Well by Doing Good. Ed. by accenture.

Cortes, Robert (2020): Clifford G. Christians's media ethics theory of global justice. In: Church, Communication and Culture 5 (1), pp. 131–135.

Dachwitz, Ingo (2022): Wichtiger Baustein für Cookie-Banner ist illegal. Available online at https://netzpolitik.org/2022/datenschutzgrundverordnung-wichtiger-baustein-fuer-cookie-banner-ist-illegal/.

Debatin, Bernhard (2012): Soziale Online-Netzwerke aus medienethischer Perspektive. In: Petra Grimm und Oliver Zöllner (Eds.): Schöne neue Kommunikationswelt oder Ende der Privatheit? Die Veröffentlichung des Privaten in Social Media und populären Medienformaten. Stuttgart: Steiner (Medienethik, 11), pp. 83–96.

Deutsche Bundesregierung (Eds.) (2019): Gutachten der Datenethikkommission. Datenethikkommission der Bundesregierung.

Deutscher Bundestag (Eds.) (2020): Bericht der Enquete-Kommission Künstliche Intelligenz – Gesellschaftliche Verantwortung und wirtschaftliche, soziale und ökologische Potenziale. Drucksache 19/23700. Available online at https://dip21.bundestag.de/dip21/btd/19/237/1923700.pdf.

Di Sciascio, Cecilia; Sabol, Vedran; Veas, Eduardo (2015): uRank: Visual analytics approach for search result exploration. In: 2015 IEEE Conference on Visual Analytics Science and Technology (VAST). Chicago, IL, USA, 25.10.2015 - 30.10.2015: IEEE, pp. 217–218.

Dietrich, Eric (2011): Homo Sapiens 2.0. Building the Better Robots of Our Nature. In: Michael Anderson und Susan Leigh Anderson (Eds.): Machine ethics. Cambridge: Cambridge University Press, pp. 531–538. Available online at https://doi.org/10.1017/CBO9780511978036.037.

Digital Trade & Data Governance Hub (Eds.) (2018): Why is it important that Citizens Participate in Data Governance? The George Washington University. Available online at https://datagovhub.elliott.gwu.edu/faq/.

Dirichlet, Peter Gustav Lejeune (1863): Vorlesungen über Zahlentheorie. Edited and supplemented by R. Dedekind. Braunschweig, 1863.

Domingos, Pedro (2015): The Master Algorithm. Google Talks, 2015. Available online at https://www.youtube.com/watch?v=B8J4uefCQMc.

Doshi-Velez, Finale; Kim, Been (2017): Towards A Rigorous Science of Interpretable Machine Learning. Available online at http://arxiv.org/pdf/1702.08608v2.

Drerup, Johannes; Voloj Dessauer, Aaron (2016): Von kleinen Stupsern und großen Schubsern – Politik und Ethik des Libertären Paternalismus auf dem Prüfstand. In: ZfPP 3 (1), pp. 347–436. https://doi.org/10.22613/zfpp/3.1.12.

Eberl, Matthias (2019): Blutspendedienst übermittelte heikle Daten an Facebook. Süddeutsche Zeitung Online (Eds.). Available online at https://www.sueddeutsche.de/digital/blutspende-brk-facebook-patientendaten-1.4576563.

Eickelmann, Birgit; Bos, Wilfried; Gerick, Julia; Goldhammer, Frank; Schaumburg, Heike; Schwippert, Knut et al. (Eds.) (2019): ICILS 2018 #Deutschland. Computer- und informationsbezogene Kompetenzen von Schülerinnen und Schülern im zweiten internationalen Vergleich und Kompetenzen im Bereich Computational Thinking. Münster, New York: Waxmann. Available online at https://kw.uni-pader-born.de/fileadmin/fakultaet/Institute/erziehungswissenschaft/Schulpaedagogik/ICILS_2018__Deutschland_Berichtsband.pdf.

Engisch, Karl (1930): Untersuchungen über Vorsatz und Fahrlässigkeit im Strafrecht. Berlin: O. Liebmann.

Enzensberger, Hans Magnus (2014): Wehrt euch! Ed. by FAZ online. Available online at http://www.faz.net/aktuell/feuilleton/debatten/enzensbergers-regeln-fuer-die-digitale-welt-wehrt-euch-12826195.html.

Esselmann, Frank; Brink, Alexander (2016): Corporate Digital Responsibility. Den digitalen Wandel von Unternehmen und Gesellschaft erfolgreich gestalten. In: Spektrum 12 (1), pp. 38–41. Available online at https://unternehmensethik.org/wp-content/uploads/2016/09/spektrum_2016-1__SONDERDRUCK.pdf.

Euler, Leonhard (1740): Solutio problematis arithmetici de inveniendo numero, qui per datos numeros divisus relinquat data residua. In: Commentarii academiae scientiarum Petropolitanae 7, pp. 46–66. Available online at http://eulerarchive.maa.org/docs/originals/E036.pdf.

Euler, Leonhard (1764): Specimen algorithmi singularis. In: Novi Commentarii academiae scientiarum Petropolitanae 9, pp. 53–69. Available online at http://eulerarchive.maa.org/docs/originals/E281.pdf.

Euler, Leonhard (1767): De usu novi algorithmi in problemate Pelliano solvendo. In: Novi Commentarii academiae scientiarum Petropolitanae 11, pp. 28–66. Available online at http://eulerarchive.maa.org/docs/originals/E323.pdf.

European Commission (2020): Weißbuch zur Künstlichen Intelligenz. Ein europäisches Konzept für Exzellenz und Vertrauen, 19.02.2020. Available online at https://ec.europa.eu/info/sites/info/files/commission-white-paper-artificial-intelligence-feb2020_de.pdf.

European Commission (Eds.) (2021): Proposal for a Regulation on a European approach for Artificial Intelligence. Available online at https://digital-strategy.ec.europa.eu/en/library/proposal-regulation-european-approach-artificial-intelligence.
European Commission (2016): Mobility and transport. Road Safety. Statistics – accidents data. European Commission. Available online at http://ec.europa.eu/transport/road_safety/specialist/statistics_en.
European Commission (Eds.) (2021): Für vertrauenswürdige Künstliche Intelligenz: EU-Kommission legt weltweit ersten Rechtsrahmen vor. Vertretung in Deutschland. Available online at https://ec.europa.eu/germany/news/20210421-kuenstliche-intelligenz-eu_de.
European Commission (2024). Regulation (EU) 2024/1689 of the European Parliament and of the Council of 13 June 2024 laying down harmonised rules on artificial intelligence and amending certain Union legislative acts (Artificial Intelligence Act). Official Journal of the European Union, L 210, 12 July 2024, p. 1–158. Available online at https://eur-lex.europa.eu/eli/reg/2024/1689/oj.
Farmer, Malcolm (1875): Abacus. Encyclopedia Britannica. Available online at https://commons.wikimedia.org/wiki/File:Abacus_6.png.
Feurer, Sebastian (2021): Schwere Vorwürfe gegen Google: Wurden wichtige Android-Datenschutzeinstellungen bewusst versteckt? Ed. by Chip.de. Available online at https://www.chip.de/news/Kritik-an-Google-wegen-versteckter-Einstellungen_183638748.html.
Feynman, Richard P. (1982): Simulating physics with computers. In: Int J Theor Phys 21 (6–7), pp. 467–488. https://doi.org/10.1007/BF02650179.
Filipović, Alexander (2013): Die Enge der weiten Medienwelt. Bedrohen Algorithmen die Freiheit öffentlicher Kommunikation? In: ComSoz 46 (2), pp. 192–208. https://doi.org/10.5771/0010-3497-2013-2-192.
Filipović, Alexander (2015): Die Datafizierung der Welt. Eine ethische Vermessung des digitalen Wandels 48 (1). Available online at http://ejournal.communicatio-socialis.de/index.php/cc/article/view/901/899.
Filipović, Alexander (2019a): Alles Habermas!? Alternative Theorien für eine Ethik öffentlicher Kommunikation in Zeiten der Digitalität. In: Jonas Bedford-Strohm, Florian Höhne und Julian Zeyher-Quattlender (Eds.): Digitaler Strukturwandel der Öffentlichkeit: Nomos Verlagsgesellschaft mbH & Co. KG, 219–232.
Filipović, Alexander (2019b): Auswirkungen von KI auf Verbraucher. 2. Netzwerkkonferenz Verbraucherbelange. ZD.B - Zentrum Digitalisierung Bayern, 14.03.2019.
Filipović, Alexander (2023): Corporate digital responsibility, In: Kiener, Maximilian (ed.): The Routledge Handbook of Philosophy of Responsibility, Routledge, Taylor & Francis, pp. 419–430, Available online at https://doi.org/10.4324/9781003282242-45.
Filipović, Alexander; Koska, Christopher (2019): Corporate Digital Responsibility muss mehr als geltendes Recht abbilden. Zu den „Zehn Regeln für den verantwortungsvollen Einsatz von KI in Human Resources“ des Ethikbeirats HR-Tech. Available online at https://www.future-of-hr.com/2019/10/corporate-digital-responsibility-muss-mehr-als-geltendes-recht-abbilden/.
Filipović, Alexander; Koska, Christopher; Paganini, Claudia; Bertelsmann Stiftung (2018): Ethik für Algorithmiker. Was wir von erfolgreichen Professionsethiken lernen können. Bertelsmann Stiftung. Available online at https://www.bertelsmann-stif-tung.de/fileadmin/files/BSt/Publikationen/GrauePublikationen/Ethik_fuer_Algorithmiker._Was_wir_von_erfolgreichen_Professionsethiken_lernen_koennen._Final.pdf.
Fjeld, Jessica Nele; Achten, Hannah; Hilligoss, Adam Nagy; Madhulika, Srikumar (2020): Principled Artificial Intelligence: Mapping Consensus in Ethical and Rightsbased Approaches to Principles for AI. Available online at https://dash.harvard.edu/bitstream/handle/1/42160420/HLS%20White%20Paper%20Final_v3.pdf?sequence=1&isAllowed=y.
Floridi, Luciano (2009): Against digital ontology. In: Synthese 168 (1), pp. 151–178. https://doi.org/10.1007/s11229-008-9334-6.

Floridi, Luciano; Josh Cowls (2019): "A Unified Framework of Five Principles for AI in Society." Harvard Data Science Review, Available online at https://hdsr.mitpress.mit.edu/pub/l0jsh9d1/release/8.

Forsythe, George Elmer (1963): Educational Implications of the Computer Revolution. In: W. F. Freiberger and William Prager (Eds.): Applications of Digital Computers. Boston (USA), pp. 166–178.

Fortune (2025): Musk says Neuralink implanted third patient with brain device, By Bloomberg, January 11, 2025, Available online at https://fortune.com/2025/01/11/elon-musk-neuralink-third-patient-implanted-brain-device-fda-studies.

Frankfurter Allgemeine Zeitung (Eds.) (2016): Nächstes Jahr fährt das Auto alleine nach New York. Acht Kameras, Ultraschall-Sensoren, mehr Rechenleistung: Tesla rüstet alle neuen Autos dafür aus, komplett eigenständig zu fahren. Chef Elon Musk macht eine große An-kündigung. Available online at http://www.faz.net/aktuell/wirtschaft/tesla-chef-musk-kuendigt-komplett-autonome-autos-fuer-naechstes-jahr-an-14489505.html.

Freeth, Tony; Higgon, David; Dacanalis, Aris; MacDonald, Lindsay; Georgakopoulou, Myrto; Wojcik, Adam (2021): A Model of the Cosmos in the ancient Greek Antikythera Mechanism. In: Scientific reports 11 (1), pp. 5821. https://doi.org/10.1038/s41598-021-84310-w.

Frege, Gottlob (1879): Begriffsschrifft. Eine der arithmethischen nachgebildete Formelsprache des reinen Denkens. Available online at https://gallica.bnf.fr/ark:/12148/bpt6k65658c/f1.item#.

Freitas, Robert A. (1980): A Self-Reproducing Interstellar Probe. In: Journal of the British Interplanetary Society 33, pp. 251–264. Available online at http://www.rfreitas.com/Astro/ReproJBISJuly1980.htm.

Friedman, Batya; Nissenbaum, Helen (1996): Bias in computer systems. In: ACM Trans. Inf. Syst. 14 (3), pp. 330–347. https://doi.org/10.1145/230538.230561.

Fuchs, Thomas (2020): Verteidigung des Menschen. Grundfragen einer verkörperten Anthropologie. 1st ed. (Suhrkamp Taschenbuch Wissenschaft).

Fulde, Verena (2016): Haben Algorithmen Vorurteile? Interview with Ranga Yogeshwar.

Funiok, Rüdiger (2000): Fundamental Questions of Audience Ethics. In: Bart Pattyn (Eds.): Media Ethics. Opening social dialogue. Leuven: Peeters, pp. 403–422.

Funiok, Rüdiger (2016): Verantwortung. In: Jessica Heesen (Eds.): Handbuch Medien- und Informationsethik. Stuttgart: J. B. Metzler, pp. 74–80.

Gadamer, Hans-Georg (Eds.) (2004): Philosophisches Lesebuch. New ed. Frankfurt am Main: Fischer-Taschenbuch-Verl. (Fischer, 16165).

Geldreich, Katharina (2019): Programmieren in der Grundschule – aber wie? In: Schulwelt NRW – Zeitschrift für Lehrerinnen, Lehrer und Schulleitungen in NRW 1 (12), pp. 6–8. Available online at https://www.edu.tum.de/fileadmin/tuedz01/ddi/material/Forschung/Programmierzirkus/Geldreich2019_ProgrammierenGrundschule.pdf.

Gerhardt, Volker (2017): Individuelle Verantwortung. In: Ludger Heidbrink, Claus Langbehn und Janina Loh (Eds.): Handbuch Verantwortung. Wiesbaden: Springer Fachmedien Wiesbaden, pp. 431–452.

Gericke, Helmuth (1984): Mathematik in Antike und Orient. Berlin, Heidelberg: Springer Berlin Heidelberg. Available online at http://dx.doi.org/10.1007/978-3-642-68630-6.

Gillespie, Nicole; Lockey, Steve; Curtis, Caitlin (2021): Trust in Artificial Intelligence. A five country study. Ed. by The University of Queensland und KPMG. Available online at https://doi.org/10.14264/e34bfa3.

Goering, D. Timothy (2017a): Einleitung Ideen- und Geistesgeschichte in Deutschland – eine Standortbestimmung. In: D. Timothy Goering und D. Timothy Goering (Eds.): Ideengeschichte heute. Bielefeld: transcript Verlag, pp. 7–54.

Goering, D. Timothy (2017b): Ideen, Handlungen und Gründe in der Ideengeschichte. In: D. Timothy Goering und D. Timothy Goering (Eds.): Ideengeschichte heute. Bielefeld: transcript Verlag, pp. 95–118.

Goethe, Johann Wolfgang von (1870): Faust. A Tragedy by Goethe. Translated by Bayard Taylor. Boston: Fields, Osgood, & Co. Available online at https://www.gutenberg.org/ebooks/14591.

Gola, Peter; Eichler, Carolyn; Franck, Lorenz; Klug, Christoph; Lepperhoff, Niels (Eds.) (2017): Datenschutz-Grundverordnung. VO (EU) 2016/679: Kommentar. München: C.H. Beck.

Goldberg, Yoav; Levy, Omer (2014): word2vec Explained: deriving Mikolov et al.'s negative-sampling word-embedding method. Available online at http://arxiv.org/pdf/1402.3722v1.

Goodman, Bryce W.; Flaxman, Seth (2016): European Union regulations on algorithmic decision-making and a "right to explanation". Available online at https://arxiv.org/abs/1606.08813.

Grau, Christopher (2006): There Is No "I" in "Robot". Robots and Utilitarianism. In: IEEE Intell. Syst. 21 (4), pp. 52–55. https://doi.org/10.1109/MIS.2006.81.

Graumann, Sigrid (2011): Forschungsethik. In: Marcus Düwell, Christoph Hübenthal und Micha H. Werner (Eds.): Handbuch Ethik. 3rd rev. ed. Stuttgart: Metzler, 253–258.

Greis, Andreas (2003): Konsumentenprofile im e-commerce. Identitätszuschreibungen von außen. In: Peter Fischer, Christoph Hubig und Peter Koslowski (Eds.): Wirtschaftsethische Fragen der E-Economy. Berlin, Heidelberg: Springer-Verlag Berlin Heidelberg GmbH (Ethische Ökonomie, Vol. 8), pp. 135–147.

Grimm, Petra; Krah, Hans (2016): Privatsphäre. In: Jessica Heesen (Eds.): Handbuch Medien- und Informationsethik. Stuttgart: J. B. Metzler, pp. 178–185.

Grzymek, Viktoria; Puntschuh, Michael (2019): Was Europa über Algorithmen weiß und denkt. Bertelsmann Stiftung (Eds.). Available online at https://www.bertelsmann-stif-tung.de/fileadmin/files/BSt/Publikationen/GrauePublikationen/WasEuropaUEberAlgorithmenWeissUndDenkt.pdf.

Hackel-de Latour, Renate (2015): Automaten, Algorithmen, Drohnen. Die Hilfstruppen des Journalismus – Potentiale, Grenzen, Gefahren. In: Communicatio Socialis 48 (1), pp. 4–5. Available online at http://nbn-resolving.de/urn:nbn:de:bvb:824-cs.v48n1.902.g9006.

Haeffner, Gerd (2005): Philosophische Anthropologie. 4th rev. and exp. ed. Stuttgart: Kohlhammer (Kohlhammer-Urban-Taschenbücher, 345).

Hagendorff, Thilo (2020): The Ethics of AI Ethics: An Evaluation of Guidelines. In: Mind Mach 30 (1), pp. 99–120. https://doi.org/10.1007/s11023-020-09517-8.

Haken, Hermann (1990): Synergetik. Nichtgleichgewichts-Phasenübergänge und Selbstorganisation in Physik, Chemie und Biologie. Berlin, Heidelberg: Springer Berlin Heidelberg.

Haken, Hermann (2017): Synergetik: Selbstorganisation in komplexen Systemen. Zürich, 11.05.2017. Available online at https://www.youtube.com/watch?v=l3rnHiweKzM.

Halliwell, James Orchard (1839): Rara Mathematica: Georg Olms Verlag. Available online at https://books.google.de/books?hl=de&lr=&id=z7nQc1esYO4C&oi=fnd&pg=PR9&ots=OPODJdRrDc&sig=1nuaURlJnb1lcMYHj6Bf0d898bA&redir_esc=y#v=onepage&q&f=false.

Han, Byung-Chul (2015): Transparenzgesellschaft. 1st ed. s.l.: Matthes Seitz Berlin Verlag. Available online at http://gbv.eblib.com/patron/FullRecord.aspx?p=4346308.

Handelsverband Deutschland (Eds.) (2019): Wachstumsdifferenz im Handel. HDE. Available online at https://einzelhandel.de/presse/zahlenfaktengrafiken/861-online-handel/11865-wachstumsdifferenz-im-handel.

Hansen, Hans Robert; Mendling, Jan; Neumann, Gustaf (2015): Wirtschaftsinformatik. Grundlagen und Anwendungen. 11th. revised and exp. ed. Berlin, München, Boston: de Gruyter (de Gruyter Studium).

Harari, Yuval Noaḥ (2018): Homo Deus. Eine Geschichte von Morgen. 1st ed. München: C.H. Beck (Beck Paperback).

Harper, Douglas (2010): Algorithm. Online Etymology Dictionary. Available online at http://www.dictionary.com/browse/algorithm.

Hartmann, Frank (2000): Medienphilosophie. Wien: WUV (UTB für Wissenschaft, 2112).

Heesen, Jessica (2018): Wer entscheidet für uns? Big Data, intelligente Systeme und kluges Handeln. In: Petra Grimm und Oliver Zöllner (Eds.): Mensch – Maschine. Ethische Sichtweisen auf ein Spannungsverhältnis. 1st ed. Stuttgart: Franz Steiner Verlag, pp. 47–57.

Heil, Reinhard (2010): Trans- und Posthumanismus. Eine Begriffsbestimmung. In: Annette Hilt, Isabella Jordan und Andreas Frewer (Eds.): Endlichkeit, Medizin und Unsterblichkeit.

Geschichte - Theorie - Ethik. Stuttgart: Franz Steiner Verlag (Medizin-Philosophie, Vol. 1), pp. 127–150.

Heise, Nele (2016): Algorithmen. In: Jessica Heesen (Eds.): Handbuch Medien- und Informationsethik. Stuttgart: J. B. Metzler, pp. 202–209.

Heller, Siegfried (2013): Theaetets Bedeutung als Mathematiker. In: Lorenzo Perilli (Eds.): Logos. Theorie und Begriffsgeschichte. Darmstadt: WBG - Wissenschaftliche Buchgesellschaft, 115–134.

Hermann, Martina (2011): Diskriminierung. In: Ralf Stoecker, Christian Neuhäuser und Marie-Louise Raters (Eds.): Handbuch Angewandte Ethik. Unter Mitarbeit von Fabian Koberling. Stuttgart: Carl Ernst Poeschel Verlag, 290–292.

Hermann, Ursula; Matschiner, Arno (2003): Herkunftswörterbuch. Das informative Nachschlagewerk zur Bedeutungsgeschichte interessanter Wörter der deutschen Gegenwartssprache über 10.000 Stichwörter unter Berücksichtigung vieler neu entstandener Begriffe und Ausdrücke. 4th rev. and exp. ed. 1998. Gütersloh: Wissen Media Verl. (Wahrig, 6).

Hilbert, David (1930): Radioansprache von David Hilbert. Available online at http://math.sfsu.edu/smith/Documents/HilbertRadio/HilbertRadio.mp3.

Hildebrandt, Alexandra; Landhäußer, Werner (Eds.) (2017): CSR und Digitalisierung. Der digitale Wandel als Chance und Herausforderung für Wirtschaft und Gesellschaft. Berlin, Heidelberg: Springer Berlin Heidelberg.

Hill, Kashmir (2019): I Cut the 'Big Five' Tech Giants From My Life. It Was Hell. Available online at https://gizmodo.com/i-cut-the-big-five-tech-giants-from-my-life-it-was-hel-1831304194.

Hilt, Annette (2010): Überleben - Weiterleben: Suche nach einem menschlichen Ethos zwischen Endlichkeit und Unsterblichkeit. In: Annette Hilt, Isabella Jordan und Andreas Frewer (Eds.): Endlichkeit, Medizin und Unsterblichkeit. Geschichte - Theorie - Ethik. Stuttgart: Franz Steiner Verlag (Medizin-Philosophie, Vol. 1), pp. 229–248.

Hoeres, Peter (2017): Zum Programm einer Ideengeschichte des Digitalzeitalters. In: D. Timothy Goering und D. Timothy Goering (Eds.): Ideengeschichte heute. Bielefeld: transcript Verlag, pp. 215–234.

Höfer, Thomas (1990): Was macht die Giraffe im Fluß? Interview mit Dr. Ernst-Michael Kranich. In: Naturwissenschaft und Ethik. [1. - 7. Tsd.]. Flensburg: Flensburger-Hefte-Verl. (Flensburger Hefte, H. 28), pp. 5–29.

Höffe, Otfried (Eds.) (2008): Lexikon der Ethik. Unter Mitarbeit von Maximilian Forschner, Christoph Horn und Wilhelm Vossenkuhl. Originalausgabe, 7th rev. and exp. ed. München: Verlag C.H. Beck (Beck'sche Reihe, 152).

Höffe, Otfried (2018): Ethik. Eine Einführung. 2nd ed. München: Verlag C.H. Beck (C.H. Beck Wissen, 2800).

Hoffmann, Dirk W. (2013): Grenzen der Mathematik. Eine Reise durch die Kerngebiete der mathematischen Logik. 2nd ed. Berlin, Heidelberg: Springer. Available online at http://dx.doi.org/10.1007/978-3-642-34720-7.

Hofmann-Riedinger, Monika (2011): gut/das Gute/das Böse. In: Marcus Düwell, Christoph Hübenthal und Micha H. Werner (Eds.): Handbuch Ethik. 3rd rev. ed. Stuttgart: Metzler, pp. 387–391.

Hofstetter, Yvonne (2014): Sie wissen alles. Wie intelligente Maschinen in unser Leben eindringen und warum wir für unsere Freiheit kämpfen müssen. München: C. Bertelsmann.

Honnefelder, Ludger (2011): Sittlichkeit/Ethos. In: Marcus Düwell, Christoph Hübenthal und Micha H. Werner (Eds.): Handbuch Ethik. 3rd rev. ed. Stuttgart: Metzler, pp. 508–513.

Horn, Christoph (2011): Güterabwägung. In: Marcus Düwell, Christoph Hübenthal und Micha H. Werner (Eds.): Handbuch Ethik. 3rd rev. ed. Stuttgart: Metzler, pp. 391–396.

Hoyningen-Huene, Paul (1998): Formale Logik. Eine philosophische Einführung. Stuttgart: Reclam (Universal-Bibliothek, 9692).

Hull, Dana (2016): Musk Says Tesla's New Autopilot Could Have Saved Driver. Ed. by Bloomberg. Available online at https://www.bloomberg.com/news/articles/2016-09-11/tesla-alters-autopilot-to-emphasize-radar-images-over-cameras.

Hülswitt, Tobias (2018): Werden wir ewig leben, Mister Kurzweil? Interview mit Ray Kurz-weil. Boston. Frankfurter Allgemeine.

Humbert, Ludger; Losch, Daniel (2019): Informatische Bildung für alle von Beginn an. 2. Symposium Informatisches Lernen zum Verstehen der digitalen Medienwelt. Bergische Universität Wuppertal. Wuppertal, 01.02.2019. Available online at https://www.digitalisierung.education/informatische-bildung-fuer-alle-von-beginn-an.

Humbert, Ludger; Müller, Dorothee; Fricke, Martin; Haselmeier, Kathrin; Siebrecht, Daniel (2018): Because the music is not inside the piano. In: LOG IN Verlag GmbH (Eds.): LOG IN. Informatische Bildung und Computer in der Schule (189/190), 67–72. Available online at https://ddi.uni-wuppertal.de/website/repoLinks/v116_LOG_IN_189-190_2018_Seiten_067-072_Humbert-andere.pdf.

Ḫwārizmī, Muḥammad Ibn-Mūsā al; Folkerts, Menso; Kunitzsch, Paul (1997): Die älteste lateinische Schrift über das indische Rechnen nach al-Ḫwārizmī. München: Verlag der Bayerischen Akademie der Wissenschaften (Abhandlungen/Bayerische Akademie der Wissenschaften, Philosophisch-Historische Klasse, N.F., 113).

IAB Europe (Eds.) (2022): APD Ruling Clears Way For Work on Developing TCF into a For-mal GDPR Code of Conduct: IAB Europe Statement on the APD Decision Announced To-day. Available online at https://iabeurope.eu/all-news/apd-ruling-clears-way-for-work-on-developing-tcf-into-a-formal-gdpr-code-of-conduct-iab-europe-statement-on-the-apd-decision-announced-today/.

Imseng, David; Motlicek, Petr; Garner, Philip N.; Bourlard, Herve (2013): Impact of deep MLP architecture on different acoustic modeling techniques for under-resourced speech recognition. In: 2013 IEEE Workshop on Automatic Speech Recognition and Understanding. 2013 IEEE Workshop on Automatic Speech Recognition & Understanding (ASRU). Olomouc, Czech Republic, 08.12.2013 - 12.12.2013: IEEE, pp. 332–337.

Isaacs, Tracy (2017): Kollektive Verantwortung. In: Ludger Heidbrink, Claus Langbehn und Janina Loh (Eds.): Handbuch Verantwortung. Wiesbaden: Springer Fachmedien Wiesbaden, pp. 453–476.

James Jacoby (Regie) (2020): Amazon Empire: The Rise and Reign of Jeff Bezos. Deu. Weltmacht Amazon - Das Reich des Jeff Bezos. Weitere Beteiligte: Anya Bourg und James Jacoby. Available online at https://www.zdf.de/dokumentation/zdfinfo-doku/weltmacht-amazon—das-reich-des-jeff-bezos-100.html.

Jaume-Palasí, Lorena; Spielkamp, Matthias (2017): Ethik und algorithmische Prozesse zur Entscheidungsfindung oder -vorbereitung. Arbeitspapier 4. Ed. by Algorithm Watch. Available online at https://algorithmwatch.org/wp-content/uploads/2017/06/AlgorithmWatch_Arbeitspapier_4_Ethik_und_Algorithmen.pdf.

Jivet, I.; Scheffel, M.; Specht, M.; Drachsler, H. (2018): License to evaluate: Preparing learning analytics dashboards for educational practice. In: Proceedings of the 8th International Conference on Learning Analytics & Knowledge (LAK18), pp. 31–40. Available online at https://doi.org/10.1145/3170358.3170421

Jobin, Anna; Ienca, Marcello; Vayena, Effy (2019): The global landscape of AI ethics guidelines. In: Nature Machine Intelligence 1 (9), pp. 389–399. https://doi.org/10.1038/s42256-019-0088-2.

Jonas, Hans (1984): Das Prinzip Verantwortung. Frankfurt am Main: Suhrkamp.

Kahneman, Daniel (2012): Thinking, fast and slow. London: Penguin Books.

Kahneman, Daniel; Tversky, Amos (1984): Choices, values, and frames. In: American Psychologist 39 (4), pp. 341–350. https://doi.org/10.1037/0003-066X.39.4.341.

Kak, Subhash (2007): Quantum Mechanics and Artificial Intelligence. In: Alfons J. Schuster (Eds.): Intelligent Computing Everywhere, Vol. 5. London: Springer London, pp. 81–101.

Kammerer, Dietmar (2016): Überwachung. In: Jessica Heesen (Eds.): Handbuch Medien- und Informationsethik. Stuttgart: J. B. Metzler, pp. 188–194.

Kay, Alan (1972): A Personal Computer for Children of All Ages. Available online at https://dl.acm.org/doi/10.1145/800193.1971922.

Kleeman, Jenny (2025): Elon Musk put a chip in this paralysed man's brain. Now he can move things with his mind. Should we be amazed - or terrified?, In: The Guardian, February 8, 2025, Available online at https://www.theguardian.com/science/2025/feb/08/elon-musk-chip-paralysed-man-noland-arbaugh-chip-brain-neuralink.

Koska, Christopher (2014): Markus Beiler. Nachrichtensuche im Internet. Inhaltsanalyse zur journalistischen Qualität von Nachrichtensuchmaschinen. In: Communicatio Socialis 47 (2), pp. 254–256. Available online at http://ejournal.communicatio-socialis.de/index.php/cc/article/download/665/664.

Koska, Christopher (2015a): User- and Usagemining | Privacy Preservation. Schritte zur Integration beider Welten. In: Petra Grimm, Tobias O. Keber und Oliver Zöllner (Eds.): Anonymität und Transparenz in der digitalen Gesellschaft. Stuttgart: Franz Steiner Verlag (Medienethik, Vol. 15).

Koska, Christopher (2015b): Zur Idee einer digitalen Bildungsidentität. In: Harald Gapski (Eds.): Big Data und Medienbildung. Zwischen Kontrollverlust, Selbstverteidigung und Souveränität in der digitalen Welt. Düsseldorf, München: kopaed (Schriftenreihe zur digitalen Gesellschaft NRW, 3), pp. 81–93. Available online at http://www.grimme-institut.de/schriftenreihe/downloads/srdg-nrw_band03_big-data-und-medienbildung.pdf.

Koska, Christopher (2018): Autonomes Fahren vor dem Durchbruch: Künstliche Intelligenz und Big Data als Antwort auf ethische Dilemma-Situationen. In: Petra Grimm und Oliver Zöllner (Eds.): Mensch – Maschine. Ethische Sichtweisen auf ein Spannungsverhältnis. 1st ed. Stuttgart: Franz Steiner Verlag, pp. 73–92.

Koska, Christopher (2020): Von der Digitalisierungsstrategie zur Datennutzungspraxis. In: Bertelsmann Stiftung und Wittenberg-Zentrum für Globale Ethik (Eds.): Unternehmensverantwortung im digitalen Wandel. Ein Debattenbeitrag zu Corporate Digital Responsibility, pp. 239–245.

Koska, Christopher; Filipović, Alexander (2017): Gestaltungsfragen der Digitalität. Zu den sozialethischen Herausforderungen von künstlicher Intelligenz, Big Data und Virtualität. In: Ralph Bergold, Jochen Sautermeister und André Schröder (Eds.): Dem Wandel eine menschliche Gestalt geben. Sozialethische Perspektiven für die Gesellschaft von morgen. Freiburg: Herder Verlag.

Koska, Christopher; Filipović, Alexander (2019): Blackbox AI - State Regulation or Corporate Responsibility? In: Claudia Linnhoff-Popien (Eds.): Artificial Intelligence. Wie Algorithmen Maschinen zum Leben erwecken. Digitale Welt. Das Wirtschaftsmagazin zur Digitalisierung. (4), pp. 28–31. Available online at https://link.springer.com/article/10.1007/s42354-019-0208-5.

Koska, Christopher; Prugger, Julian; Jörg, Sophie; Reder, Michael (2024): Die Verlagerung von Vertrauen vom Menschen zur Maschine: Eine Erweiterung des zwischenmenschlichen Vertrauensparadigmas im Kontext Künstlicher Intelligenz. *The Shift of Trust from Human to Machine: An Expansion of the Interpersonal Trust Paradigm in the Context of Artificial Intelligence*, In: Beck, Birgit; Reinhardt, Karoline; Schweiger, Gottfried; Zichy, Michael (Hg.): Zeitschrift für Praktische Philosophie, Band 11, Heft 1, S. 343–366. Available online at https://doi.org/10.22613/zfpp/11.1.14

Koska, Christopher; Breuer, Svenja; Reder, Michael; Schlögl-Flierl, Kerstin; Ziethman, Paula; Rathgeber, Benjamin (forthcoming): Beyond Bias: Shifting from the Deception of Neutrality to a Concept of Responsible AI (under review).

Kraus, Maximilian; Burghardt, Jennifer; Koska, Christopher (2024): AI-assisted reflection in child welfare, In: Reder, Michael; Koska, Christopher (Eds.): Künstliche Intelligenz und ethische Verantwortung, Transcript, S. 63-83. Available online at https://doi.org/10.14361/9783839469057

Krämer, Sybille (1988): Symbolische Maschinen. Die Idee der Formalisierung in geschichtlichem Abriß. Darmstadt: Wissenschaftliche Buchgesellschaft.

Krämer, Sybille (1992): Symbolische Maschinen. Computer und der Verlust des Ethischen im geistigen Tun. In: Wolfgang Coy, Frieder Nake, Jörg-Martin Pflüger, Arno Rolf, Jürgen

Seetzen, Dirk Siefkes und Reinhard Stransfeld (Eds.): Sichtweisen der Informatik. Wiesbaden: Vieweg+Teubner Verlag (Theorie der Informatik), pp. 335–341.
Krämer, Sybille (2008): Medium, Bote, Übertragung. Kleine Metaphysik der Medialität. 1st ed. Frankfurt: Suhrkamp.
Krämer, Sybille (2020a): Kulturgeschichte der Digitalisierung. (Handout zum Vortrag vom 13.02.2020). Available online at https://www.hiig.de/wp-content/uploads/2020/01/Kulturgeschichte-der-Digitalisierung_Sybille-Kra%CC%88mer_Februar-2020.pdf.
Krämer, Sybille (2020b): Kulturgeschichte der Digitalisierung, 13.02.2020. Available online at https://youtu.be/S8Mtjqil5_s.
Krotz, Friedrich (2018): Die Begegnung von Mensch und Roboter. Überlegungen zu ethischen Fragen aus der Perspektive des Mediatisierungsansatzes. In: Matthias Rath, Friedrich Krotz und Matthias Karmasin (Eds.): Maschinenethik. Normative Grenzen autonomer Systeme. Wiesbaden: Springer Fachmedien Wiesbaden (Ethik in mediatisierten Welten), pp. 13–34.
Küchlin, Wolfgang; Weber, Andreas (2003): Einführung in die Informatik. Objektorientiert mit Java. 2nd rev. and exp. ed.. Berlin, Heidelberg, s.l.: Springer Berlin Heidelberg (Springer-Lehrbuch). Available online at http://dx.doi.org/10.1007/978-3-662-21841-9.
Kucklick, Christoph (2016): Soziologische Aspekte von Big Data. Audioprotokoll. Deutscher Ethikrat. Berlin. Available online at http://www.ethikrat.org/sitzungen/2016/big-data.
Kühl, Christiane (2017): Willkommen in E-Land. Available online at https://www.zeit.de/kultur/2017-10/estland-einwohner-e-residency-10nach8.
Lanier, Jaron (2013): Who owns the future? First Simon & Schuster hardcover edition. New York: Simon & Schuster.
Lanier, Jaron (2014): Wem gehört die Zukunft? "Du bist nicht der Kunde der Internetkonzerne. Du bist ihr Produkt". Hamburg: Hoffmann und Campe.
Laube, Johannes (1984): Dialektik der absoluten Vermittlung. Hajime Tanabes Religionsphilosophie als Beitrag zum "Wettstreit der Liebe" zwischen Buddhismus und Christentum. Marburg, 1984. Freiburg: Herder.
Lautebach, Urs (2018): Informatik für alle. Der Koalitionsvertrag verspricht Computer und WLAN für die Schulen. Aber ohne ein Pflichtfach Informatik bleiben die Schüler digital unmündig. Ed. by Zeit online. Available online at https://www.zeit.de/gesellschaft/schule/2018-02/digitalisierung-informatikunterricht-schulen-bildung/komplettansicht.
Lei, Dian; Chen, Xiaoxiao; Zhao, Jianfei (2018): Opening the black box of deep learning. Available online at unter http://arxiv.org/pdf/1805.08355v1.
Leibniz, Gottfried Wilhelm (1960): Fragmente zur Logik. Unter Mitarbeit von Franz Schmidt. Berlin: Akademie Verlag. Available online at https://archive.org/details/fragmentezurlogi0000leib/page/90/mode/2up.
Leibniz, Gottfried Wilhelm; Schneider, Ulrich Johannes (2002): Monadologie und andere metaphysische Schriften. Französisch - deutsch. Hamburg: Meiner (Philosophische Bibliothek, 537).
Lem, Stanisław (1964): Summa technologiae. Kraków: Wydwo literackie.
Lesch, Harald (2008): Quantenmechanik. Eine Einführung. Vorlesung. Uni-Auditorium Physik. Grünwald: Komplett-Media. Available online at https://youtu.be/FwNV_e-Xz68.
Lesch, Harald (2015): Quantenmechanik für die Westentasche. München: Piper.
Lessig, Lawrence (1999): Code and other laws of cyberspace. New York, NY: Basic Books. Available online at http://www.loc.gov/catdir/enhancements/fy0831/00271772-d.html.
Leupold, Jakob (1727): Theatrum arithmetico-geometricum, das ist: Schau-Platz der Rechen- und Mess-Kunst: darinnen enthalten dieser beyden Wissenschafften nöthige Grund-Regeln und Handgriffe so wohl, als auch die unterschiedene Instrumente und Machinen: den annoch beygefüget: Die Theilung aller Linien, insonderheit wie durch Transversal-Linien die Grade in Minuten weit correcter als nach der alten und sonst gewöhnlichen Art abzutheilen und aufzureisen: gedruckt bey Christoph Zunkel; zufinden bey dem Autore und Joh. Friedr. Gleditschens seel. Sohn.

Lewanczik, Niklas (2019): LinkedIn kauft Drawbridge, um Marketing-Lösungen auszubauen. Available online at https://onlinemarketing.de/unternehmensnews/linkedin-kauft-drawbridge-marketing-loesungen-ausbau.

Li, Wenchao (1999): Buddhistisch philosophieren. Eine Einführung. Münster: Waxmann.

Lichtenstein, Ernst (2017): Bildung. In: Joachim Ritter, Karlfried Gründer, Gottfried Gabriel, Jann Holl, Hans Lenk und Matthias Maring (Eds.): Historisches Wörterbuch der Philosophie online. Basel: Schwabe Verlag. Available online at https://doi.org/10.24894/HWPh.491.

Lin, Patrick (2015): Why Ethics Matters for Autonomous Cars. In: Markus Maurer, J. Christi-an Gerdes, Barbara Lenz und Hermann Winner (Eds.): Autonomes Fahren. Technische, rechtliche und gesellschaftliche Aspekte. Berlin, Heidelberg: Springer Vieweg, pp. 69–85. Available online at https://link.springer.com/content/pdf/10.1007%2F978-3-662-45854-9_4.pdf.

Lobo, Sascha (2018): Wer macht mir die geileren Vorschriften? Available online at https://www.spiegel.de/netzwelt/web/datenschutzgrundverordnung-dsgvo-wer-macht-mir-die-geileren-vorschriften-a-1206979.html.

Lösch, Holger (2015): Nudging als politisches Instrument - legitimer Eingriff oder staatlicher Übergriff? In: Zentralverband der deutschen Werbewirtschaft ZAW e. V. (Eds.): Werbung 2015. Berlin: edition ZAW, pp. 30–31.

Lück, Anne-Kathrin (2013): Der gläserne Mensch im Internet. Ethische Reflexionen zur Sichtbarkeit, Leiblichkeit und Personalität in der Online-Kommunikation. Zugl.: Zürich, Univ., Doctoral Dissertation, 2012 u.d.T.: Lück, Anne-Kathrin: Zwischen Sichtbarkeit und Gläsernheit: ethische Überlegungen zur Kommunikation in sozialen Netzwerken und Online-Bewertungsportalen. Stuttgart: Kohlhammer (Forum Systematik, 45). Available online at http://d-nb.info/1034216120/04.

Ludlow, Peter; Nagasawa, Yujin; Stoljar, Daniel (Eds.) (2004): There's something about Mary. Essays on phenomenal consciousness and Frank Jackson's knowledge argument. Reprint. Cambridge, London: The MIT Press.

Luhmann, Niklas (1965): Grundrechte als Institution. Ein Beitrag zur politischen Soziologie. Berlin: Duncker & Humblot.

Luna-Benoso, B.; Martinez-Perales, J. C.; Flores-Carapia, R. (2013): Modeling traffic flow for two and three lanes through cellular automata. In: imf 8, pp. 1091–1101. https://doi.org/10.12988/imf.2013.3486.

Lüneburg, Heinz (2008): Von Zahlen und Größen Vol. 1. Dritthalbtausend Jahre Theorie und Praxis. Basel: Birkhäuser Verlag.

Madary, Michael; Metzinger, Thomas K. (2016): Real Virtuality: A Code of Ethical Conduct. Recommendations for Good Scientific Practice and the Consumers of VR-Technology. In: Front. Robot. AI 3 (Suppl. 3), pp. 235. https://doi.org/10.3389/frobt.2016.00003.

Mainzer, Klaus (2014): Die Berechnung der Welt. Von der Weltformel zu Big Data. München: C. H.Beck. Available online at http://lib.myilibrary.com/detail.asp?id=625600.

Mainzer, Klaus (2020): Selbstorganisation – Von der nichtlinearen Dynamik komplexer Systeme zur Künstlichen Intelligenz. In: Kathrin Viol, Helmut Schöller und Wolfgang Aich-horn (Eds.): Selbstorganisation – ein Paradigma für die Humanwissenschaften. Wiesbaden: Springer Fachmedien Wiesbaden, pp. 31–47.

Mandry, Christof (2011): Bildung und Erziehung. In: Ralf Stoecker, Christian Neuhäuser und Marie-Louise Raters (Eds.): Handbuch Angewandte Ethik. Unter Mitarbeit von Fabian Koberling. Stuttgart: Carl Ernst Poeschel Verlag, pp. 248–251.

Marcus, Gary; Ernest Davis (2019): Rebooting AI: Building Artificial Intelligence We Can Trust. New York: Pantheon Books.

Marcus, Gary (2023): „Senate Testimony." 16. Mai 2023. Available online at https://www.judiciary.senate.gov/imo/media/doc/2023-05-16%20-%20Testimony%20-%20Marcus.pdf.

Martini, Mario (2019): Blackbox Algorithmus – Grundfragen einer Regulierung Künstlicher Intelligenz. Unter Mitarbeit von Michael Kolain und Jan Mysegades: Springer.

Matthias, Andreas (2004): The responsibility gap. Ascribing responsibility for the actions of learning automata. In: Ethics Inf Technol 6 (3), pp. 175–183. https://doi.org/10.1007/s10676-004-3422-1.
Mayer-Schönberger, Viktor; Cukier, Kenneth (2013): Big Data. Die Revolution, die unser Leben verändern wird. 2nd ed. München: Redline.
McGoogan, Cara (2016): 'You're killing people': Elon Musk attacks critics of self-driving cars. Ed. by The Telegraph. Available online at http://www.telegraph.co.uk/technology/2016/10/20/youre-killing-people-elon-musk-attacks-critics-of-self-driving-c/.
McLuhan, Marshall (1962): The Gutenberg galaxy. The making of typographic man. Toronto: University of Toronto Press. Available online at http://search.ebscohost.com/login.aspx?direct=true&scope=site&db=nlebk&db=nlabk&AN=468925.
Meixner, Werner (2016): Die Ausbeutung des geistigen Rohstoffes. Zur Veröffentlichung in der Süddeutschen Zeitung. Available online at http://wwwmayr.in.tum.de/personen/meixner/AusbeutungGeistigenRohstoffes_Okt2016.pdf.
Menninger, Karl (1958): Zahlwort und Ziffer. Eine Kulturgeschichte der Zahl. 2 volumes in 1. 2nd rev. and exp. ed. Göttingen: Vandenhoeck & Ruprecht.
Miller, Tim (2017): Explanation in Artificial Intelligence: Insights from the Social Sciences. Available online at http://arxiv.org/pdf/1706.07269v3.
Minsky, Marvin (1967): Why programming is a good medium for expressing poorly under-stood and sloppily formulated ideas. In: Martin Krampen und Peter Seitz (Eds.): Design and Planning II. Computers in Design and Communication. New York.
Misselhorn, Catrin (2018): Grundfragen der Maschinenethik. Ditzingen: Reclam (Reclams Universal-Bibliothek, 19583).
Mitchell, Melanie (2021): Why AI Is Harder Than We Think. Communications of the ACM. Available online at https://arxiv.org/abs/2104.12871.
Mitchell, Tom M. (1997): Machine learning. New York, NY: McGraw-Hill.
Mittelstadt, B. D.; Allo, P.; Taddeo, M.; Wachter, pp.; Floridi, L. (2016): The ethics of algorithms. Mapping the debate. In: Big Data & Society 3 (2). https://doi.org/10.1177/2053951716679679.
Molnar, Christoph (2019): Interpretable Machine Learning. A Guide for Making Black Box Models Explainable. Available online at https://christophm.github.io/interpretable-ml-book.
Morozov, Evgeny (2013): Smarte neue Welt. Digitale Technik und die Freiheit des Menschen. Unter Mitarbeit von Henning Dedekind und Ursel Schäfer. München: Blessing.
Mühlhoff, Rainer (2019): Big Data Is Watching You. Digitale Entmündigung am Beispiel von Facebook und Google. In: Rainer Mühlhoff, Anja Breljak und Jan Slaby (Eds.): Affekt Macht Netz. Auf dem Weg zu einer Sozialtheorie der Digitalen Gesellschaft. 1st ed. Bielefeld: Transcript (Digitale Gesellschaft, 22), 81–106.
Mullin, Emily (2025): Synchron's Brain-Computer Interface Now Has Nvidia's AI, In: Wired, March 19, 2025, Available online at https://www.wired.com/story/synchrons-brain-computer-interface-now-has-nvidias-ai.
Münker, Stefan (2003): After the medial turn. Sieben Thesen zur Medienphilosophie. In: Stefan Münker, Alexander Roesler und Mike Sandbothe (Eds.): Medienphilosophie. Beiträge zur Klärung eines Begriffs. Orig. ed. Frankfurt am Main: Fischer-Taschenbuch-Verlag (Fischer, 15757), pp. 16–25.
Münker, Stefan; Roesler, Alexander; Sandbothe, Mike (Eds.) (2003): Medienphilosophie. Beiträge zur Klärung eines Begriffs. Orig.-ed. Frankfurt am Main: Fischer-Taschenbuch-Verlag (Fischer, 15757).
Musk, Elon (2016): Master Plan, Part Deux. Available online at https://www.tesla.com/de_DE/blog/master-plan-part-deux?redirect=no.
Nagel, Thomas (1986): The view from nowhere. New York: Oxford Univ. Press. Available online at http://www.loc.gov/catdir/enhancements/fy0638/85031002-d.html.
Nagel, Thomas (2016): What is it like to be a Bat? Wie ist es, eine Fledermaus zu sein? English/German. [Was bedeutet das alles?]. Ditzingen: Reclam Verlag (Was bedeutet das alles?).

Naghibi, Fereydoun; Delavar, Mahmoud Reza; Pijanowski, Bryan (2016): Urban Growth Modeling Using Cellular Automata with Multi-Temporal Remote Sensing Images Calibrated by the Artificial Bee Colony Optimization Algorithm. In: Sensors (Basel, Switzerland) 16 (12). https://doi.org/10.3390/s16122122.

Napoli, Philip M. (2014): Automated Media. An Institutional Theory Perspective on Algorithmic Media Production and Consumption. In: Commun Theor 24 (3), pp. 340–360. https://doi.org/10.1111/comt.12039.

Nassehi, Armin (2019): Muster. Theorie der digitalen Gesellschaft. 1st ed. München: Verlag C.H. BECK Literatur - Sachbuch - Wissenschaft.

Naur, Peter (1966): The science of datalogy. In: Commun. ACM 9 (7), p. 485. https://doi.org/10.1145/365719.366510.

Neumann, John von (1951): The General and Logical Theory of Automata. In: Lloyd A. Jef-fress (Eds.): Cerebral Mechanisms in Behavior: The Hixon Symposium. New York: John Wiley & Sons, pp. 1–31.

Neumann, John von (1967): Theory of Self-reproducing Automata: University of Illinois Press.

Nida-Rümelin, Julian (2021): Engineering Responsibility. Zur Verantwortung. In: bidt (Eds.): Ethisches Design von Software und Künstlicher Intelligenz. Bayerisches Forschungsinstitut für Digitale Transformation.

Niederbacher, Bruno (2013): Emotion und Entscheidung: Erkenntnistheoretische Bemerkungen zur kognitiven Funktion affektiver Zustände in den Geistlichen Übungen des Ignatius von Loyola. In: Zeitschrift für katholische Theologie 135 (2/3), pp. 212–229. Available online at unter http://www.jstor.org/stable/24171504.

Nissenbaum, Helen Fay (2010): Privacy in context. Technology, policy, and the integrity of social life. Stanford, California: Stanford Law Books an imprit of Standford University Press. Available online at http://site.ebrary.com/lib/academiccompletetitles/home.action.

Noller, Stephan (2012): Plädoyer für eine Algorithmen-Ethik. Relevanz ist alles. Frankfurter Allgemeine Zeitung. Available online at http://www.faz.net/aktuell/feuilleton/debatten/plaedoyer-fuer-eine-algorithmen-ethik-relevanz-ist-alles-11934495.html.

Norman, Donald A.; Draper, Stephen W. (1986): User centered system design. New perspectives on human-computer interaction. Hillsdale, N.J.: Erlbaum.

OLG Düsseldorf (2019): Beschluss. Oberlandesgericht (Eds.). Available online at http://www.olg-duesseldorf.nrw.de/behoerde/presse/Presse_aktuell/20190826_PM_Facebook/20190826-Beschluss-VI-Kart-1-19-_V_.pdf.

Opal (1804): Della pittura e della statua di Leonbatista Alberti. Ed. by Università degli Studi di Torino. Available online at https://commons.wikimedia.org/wiki/File:Alberti_-_Della_pittura_e_della_statua,_Milano,_1804_(page_155_crop).jpg.

Ott, Konrad (2011): Prinzip/Maxime/Norm/Regel. In: Marcus Düwell, Christoph Hübenthal und Micha H. Werner (Eds.): Handbuch Ethik. 3rd rev. ed. Stuttgart: Metzler, pp. 474–480.

Pariser, Eli (2011): The filter bubble. What the Internet is hiding from you. New York, NY: Penguin Press.

Parisi, Luciana (2018): Das Lernen lernen oder die algorithmische Entdeckung von Informationen. In: Christoph Engemann und Andreas Sudmann (Eds.): Machine Learning - Medien, Infrastrukturen und Technologien der Künstlichen Intelligenz. Bielefeld: Transcript (Digitale Gesellschaft, Vol. 14), pp. 93–116.

Paslack, Rainer (1991): Urgeschichte der Selbstorganisation. Wiesbaden: Vieweg+Teubner Verlag.

Passig, Kathrin (2017): Fünfzig Jahre Black Box. Merkur. Available online at https://www.merkur-zeitschrift.de/2017/11/23/fuenfzig-jahre-black-box.

Pauen, Michael; Welzer, Harald (2015): Autonomie. Eine Verteidigung. Frankfurt am Main: Fischer.

Peitsmeier, Henning (2015): Der Autopilot will endlich ans Steuer. Weniger Unfälle, weniger Staus: Autonomes Fahren ist technisch machbar, Kunden gäbe es auch bereits. Noch kämpft die neue Technik aber mit alten Verkehrsregeln. Frankfurter Allgemeine Zeitung (Eds.).

Available online at http://www.faz.net/aktuell/wirtschaft/neue-mobilitaet/selbstfahrende-wagen-der-autopilot-will-endlich-ans-steuer-13624203.html

Perilli, Lorenzo (Eds.) (2013a): Logos. Theorie und Begriffsgeschichte. Darmstadt: WBG - Wissenschaftliche Buchgesellschaft. Available online at http://gbv.eblib.com/patron/FullRecord.aspx?p=1273441.

Perilli, Lorenzo (2013b): Logos. Das Bauzeug der Welt. In: Lorenzo Perilli (Eds.): Logos. Theorie und Begriffsgeschichte. Darmstadt: WBG - Wissenschaftliche Buchgesellschaft, pp. 1–18.

Piperal, Anna (2016): Keynote: Digital Society "e-Estonia". Code Blue Conference. Tokyo, 2016. Available online at https://www.youtube.com/watch?v=kE8D8X5b8m0.

Preskill, John (2018): "Quantum Computing in the NISQ Era and Beyond." Quantum, vol. 2, 2018, p. 79. Available online at https://doi.org/10.22331/q-2018-08-06-79.

Prinsloo, P.; Slade, S. (2017): An elephant in the learning analytics room: The obligation to act. In: British Journal of Educational Technology, 48(6), pp. 1168–1179. Available online at https://doi.org/10.1111/bjet.12592

Rath, Matthias (2016): Publikums- und Nutzungsethik. In: Jessica Heesen (Eds.): Handbuch Medien- und Informationsethik. Stuttgart: J. B. Metzler, pp. 298–305.

Reineck, Dennis (2014): Markus Beiler (2013): Nachrichtensuche im Internet. Inhaltsanalyse zur journalistischen Qualität von Nachrichtensuchmaschinen. Konstanz: UVK. In: M&K 62 (1), pp. 102–103. https://doi.org/10.5771/1615-634x-2014-1-102.

Reisch, Gregor (1503): Margarita Philosophica. Typus arithmeticae. Available online at https://commons.wikimedia.org/wiki/File:Margarita_Philosophica_1503_-_Typus_arithmeticae.jpg.

Reisch, Gregor (1504): Margarita philosophica. Straßburg. Available online at http://dl.ub.uni-freiburg.de/diglit/reisch1504.

Richter, Philipp (2016): Big Data. In: Jessica Heesen (Eds.): Handbuch Medien- und Informationsethik. Stuttgart: J. B. Metzler, pp. 210–216.

Ricken, Friedo (2000): Philosophie der Antike. 3rd rev. and exp. ed. Stuttgart: Kohl-hammer (Urban-Taschenbücher, 350).

Rickmann, Hagen (2019): Wir übernehmen digitale Verantwortung. In: Wirtschaftskurier 3, 2019, pp. 15–16.

Rössler, Beate (2011): Autonomie. In: Ralf Stoecker, Christian Neuhäuser und Marie-Louise Raters (Eds.): Handbuch Angewandte Ethik. Unter Mitarbeit von Fabian Koberling. Stuttgart: Carl Ernst Poeschel Verlag, pp. 93–99.

SAE international (Eds.): Automated Driving. Levels of driving automation are defined in new SAE international standard J3016

Samuel, A. L. (1959): Some Studies in Machine Learning Using the Game of Checkers. In: IBM J. Res. & Dev. 3 (3), pp. 210–229. https://doi.org/10.1147/rd.33.0210.

Sandbothe, Mike (2003): Der Vorrang der Medien vor der Philosophie. In: Stefan Münker, Alexander Roesler und Mike Sandbothe (Eds.): Medienphilosophie. Beiträge zur Klärung eines Begriffs. Orig. ed. Frankfurt am Main: Fischer-Taschenbuch-Verlag (Fischer, 15757), pp. 185–197.

Sandstein (2009): Tally sticks. Ed. by Wikipedia. Available online at https://commons.wikimedia.org/wiki/File:SAM_PC_1_-_Tally_sticks_1_-_Overview.jpg.

Saurwein, Florian (2018): Automatisierung, Algorithmen, Accountability. Eine Governance Perspektive. In: Matthias Rath, Friedrich Krotz und Matthias Karmasin (Eds.): Maschinenethik. Normative Grenzen autonomer Systeme. Wiesbaden: Springer Fachmedien Wiesbaden (Ethik in mediatisierten Welten), pp. 35–56.

Scantamburlo, Teresa; Cortés, Atia; Foffano, Francesca; Barrué, Cristian; Distefano, Veronica; Pham, Long; Fabris, Alessandro (2023): Artificial Intelligence across Europe: A Study on Awareness, Attitude and Trust, Available online at https://doi.org/10.48550/arXiv.2308.09979

Scarano, Nico (2011): Metaethik - ein systematischer Überblick. In: Marcus Düwell, Christoph Hübenthal und Micha H. Werner (Eds.): Handbuch Ethik. 3rd. rev. ed. Stuttgart: Metzler, pp. 25–35.

Schicha, Christian (2019): Medienethik. Grundlagen - Anwendungen - Ressourcen (utb Medien- und Kommunikationswissenschaft).

Schirrmacher, Frank (2011): Payback. Warum wir im Informationszeitalter gezwungen sind zu tun, was wir nicht tun wollen, und wie wir die Kontrolle über unser Denken zurückgewinnen. 1st ed. München: Pantheon.

Schirrmacher, Frank (2013): Ego. Das Spiel des Lebens. 5th ed. München: Blessing. Available online at http://www.socialnet.de/rezensionen/isbn.php?isbn=978-3-89667-427-2.

Schneider, Manfred (2013): Transparenztraum (ebook). Literatur, Politik, Medien und das Unmögliche. 1st ed. Berlin: Matthes & Seitz. Available online at http://sub-hh.ciando.com/book/?bok_id=1016191.

Schramme, Thomas (2016): Die politische Quacksalberei des libertären Paternalismus. In: ZfPP 3 (1), pp. 531–558. https://doi.org/10.22613/zfpp/3.1.15.

Schuldt, Christian (2019): Der Sinn der Digitalisierung. Available online at https://www.zukunftsinstitut.de/artikel/digitalisierung/der-sinn-der-digitalisierung/.

Searle, John (1980): Minds, Brains and Programs. Pre-Print. Available online at http://cogprints.org/7150/1/10.1.1.83.5248.pdf.

Seck, Friedrich (1978a): Philosophus amphdexios. In: Friedrich Seck (Eds.): Wilhelm Schickard 1592-1635. Astronom, Geograph, Orientalist, Erfinder der Rechenmaschine. Tübingen: Mohr (Contubernium, 25), pp. 391–394.

Seck, Friedrich (Eds.) (1978b): Wilhelm Schickard 1592-1635. Astronom, Geograph, Orientalist, Erfinder der Rechenmaschine. Available online at https://commons.wikimedia.org/wiki/File:Rechenmaschine_wilhelm_schickard.png.

Seemann, Michael (2014): Das neue Spiel. Strategien für die Welt nach dem digitalen Kontrollverlust. Freiburg i. Br.: orange-press. Available online at http://ctrl-verlust.net/DasNeueSpiel.pdf.

Seubert, Harald (2011): Privatsphäre. In: Ralf Stoecker, Christian Neuhäuser und Marie-Louise Raters (Eds.): Handbuch Angewandte Ethik. Unter Mitarbeit von Fabian Koberling. Stuttgart: Carl Ernst Poeschel Verlag, pp. 219–222.

Shilton, Katie (2013): Values Levers. Building Ethics into Design. In: Science, Technology, & Human Values 38 (3), pp. 374–397. https://doi.org/10.1177/0162243912436985.

Siegfried, Tom (2014): If the world is a computer, life is an algorithm. Cellular automata could describe quantum physics, the universe and biological evolution. Available online at https://www.sciencenews.org/blog/context/if-world-computer-life-algorithm.

Silverstone, Roger (2008): Mediapolis. Die Moral der Massenmedien. 1st ed. Frankfurt am Main: Suhrkamp (Edition Zweite Moderne).

Simmel, Georg (1908): Soziologie. Untersuchungen über die Formen der Vergesellschaftung. Duncker & Humblot. Berlin. Available online at http://socio.ch/sim/soziologie/index.htm.

Simonyi, Károly (2001): Kulturgeschichte der Physik. Von den Anfängen bis heute. 3rd rev. and exp. ed. Frankfurt am Main: H. Deutsch.

Sivaramakrishnan, Kamakshi (2014): System and Method for Determining Related Digital Identities. United States Patent Application Publication. Available online at https://patentimages.storage.googleapis.com/68/a4/d7/c75fe51b8ec1fc/US20140095320A1.pdf.

Smith, Barry (2000): Ontological Imperialism. Savannah, Georgia (First International Conference on Geographic Information Science), pp. 11. Available online at https://philarchive.org/archive/SMIOI.

Sobe, Peter (2014): Grundlagen der Informatik. Algorithmen. Available online at https://www2.htw-dresden.de/~sobe/Info1_Jg14/Vo/1d_Grundlagen_Algorithmen_Teil1.pdf.

Sorgner, Stefan Lorenz (2018): Schöner neuer Mensch. Berlin: Nicolai Publishing & Intelligence GmbH.

Spiekermann, Sarah (2015): Ethical IT Innovation. A Value-Based System Design Approach. s.l.: CRC Press. Available online at http://gbv.eblib.com/patron/FullRecord.aspx?p=4096994.

Statistisches Bundesamt (Eds.) (2016): Unfallursachen. Fehlverhalten der Fahrzeugführer bei Unfällen mit Personenschaden. Available online at https://www.destatis.de/DE/ZahlenFakten/Wirtschaftsbereiche/TransportVerkehr/Verkehrsunfaelle/Tabellen/FehlverhaltenFahrzeugfuehrer.html.

Stegemann, Jana (2019): Eine Göttin soll Europas Daten schützen. Süddeutsche Zeitung Online (Eds.). Available online at https://www.sueddeutsche.de/digital/gaiax-altmaier-cloud-eu-digitalgipfel-1.4660662.

Stiller, Sebastian (2015): Planet der Algorithmen. Ein Reiseführer. 1st ed. München: Knaus.

Stoecker, Ralf; Neuhäuser, Christian; Raters, Marie-Louise (Eds.) (2011): Handbuch Angewandte Ethik. Unter Mitarbeit von Fabian Koberling. Stuttgart: Carl Ernst Poeschel Verlag.

Sudmann, Andreas (2018): Zur Einführung. Medien, Infrastrukturen und Technologien des maschinellen Lernens. In: Christoph Engemann und Andreas Sudmann (Eds.): Machine Learning - Medien, Infrastrukturen und Technologien der Künstlichen Intelligenz. Bielefeld: Transcript (Digitale Gesellschaft, Vol. 14), pp. 9–23.

Suh, Bongwon; Convertino, Gregorio; Chi, Ed H.; Pirolli, Peter (2009): The singularity is not near. Slowing Growth of Wikipedia. In: Dirk Riehle und Amy Bruckman (Eds.): Proceedings of the 5th International Symposium on Wikis and Open Collaboration - WikiSym '09. the 5th International Symposium. Orlando, Florida, 25.10.2009 - 27.10.2009. New York, New York, USA: ACM Press, pp. 1.

Sun, Yi; Wang, Xiaogang; Tang, Xiaoou (2014): Deep Learning Face Representation from Predicting 10,000 Classes. In: 2014 IEEE Conference on Computer Vision and Pattern Recognition. 2014 IEEE Conference on Computer Vision and Pattern Recognition (CVPR). Columbus, OH, USA, 23.06.2014 - 28.06.2014: IEEE, pp. 1891–1898.

Sveinsdottir, Edda; Frøkjær, Erik (1988): Datalogy — The copenhagen tradition of computer science. In: BIT 28 (3), pp. 450–472. https://doi.org/10.1007/BF01941128.

Thaler, Richard H.; Sunstein, Cass R. (2009): Nudge. Improving decisions about health, wealth, and happiness. Rev. and expanded ed., with a new afterword and a new chapter. New York, NY: Penguin.

Thiel, Rainer; Deimel, Lucas; Schmidtmann, Daniel; Piesche, Klaus; Hüsing, Tobias; Rennoch, Jonas et al. (2018): #SmartHealthSystems. Digitalisierungsstrategien im internationalen Vergleich. Bertelsmann Stiftung. Available online at https://www.bertelsmann-stiftung.de/de/publikationen/publikation/did/smarthealthsystems-auszug-estland.

Thiess, Christian (2011): Wille/Entscheidung. In: Marcus Düwell, Christoph Hübenthal und Micha H. Werner (Eds.): Handbuch Ethik. 3rd rev. ed. Stuttgart: Metzler, pp. 553–558.

Thom, René (Eds.) (1999): Structural stability and morphogenesis. An outline of a general theory of models. Cambridge, Mass.: Perseus Books (Advanced book programm).

Thorhauer, Yvonne (2003): Menschenbild und Verdinglichung im E-Business. In: Peter Fischer, Christoph Hubig und Peter Koslowski (Eds.): Wirtschaftsethische Fragen der E-Economy. Berlin, Heidelberg: Springer-Verlag Berlin Heidelberg GmbH (Ethische Ökonomie, Vol. 8), pp. 159.

Tiedemann, Michaela (2020): Data Governance: Grundlagen, Herausforderungen und Lösungen im Bereich Data Management. Available online at https://www.alexanderthamm.com/de/blog/data-governance-grundlagen-herausforderungen-und-loesungen-im-bereich-data-management/.

Toffoli, Tommaso (1982): Physics and computation. In: Int J Theor Phys 21 (3-4), pp. 165–175. https://doi.org/10.1007/BF01857724.

Trogemann, Georg (2005): Der Computer als Artefakt. In: Georg Trogemann und Jochen Viehoff (Eds.): CodeArt. Eine elementare Einführung in die Programmierung als künstlerische Praktik: Springer Vienna (Ästhetik und Naturwissenschaften), pp. 21–46.

Trogemann, Georg; Viehoff, Jochen (Eds.) (2005): CodeArt. Eine elementare Einführung in die Programmierung als künstlerische Praktik: Springer Vienna (Ästhetik und Naturwissenschaften).

Turing, Alan Mathison; Cooper, Stuart B.; van Leeuwen, Jan (2013): Alan Turing. His work and impact. Amsterdam: Elsevier. Available online at http://site.ebrary.com/lib/alltitles/docDetail.action?docID=10685819.

Tuygunkhujaev, Yunuskhuja (2016): Khiva. Available online at https://commons.wikimedia.org/wiki/File:Khiva.jpg.
Tversky, A.; Kahneman, D. (1974): Judgment under Uncertainty: Heuristics and Biases. In: Science (New York, N.Y.) 185 (4157), pp. 1124–1131. https://doi.org/10.1126/science.185.4157.1124.
Ulrich, Peter (2011): Wirtschaftsethik. In: Marcus Düwell, Christoph Hübenthal und Micha H. Werner (Eds.): Handbuch Ethik. 3rd rev. ed. Stuttgart: Metzler, pp. 297–302.
Urban, Tim (2017): Neuralink and the Brain's Magical Future. Available online at https://waitbutwhy.com/2017/04/neuralink.html.
Vanhoucke, Vincent (2014): Interpretability and Post-Rationalization. What neuroscience teaches us about making machines accountable. Available online at https://becominghuman.ai/interpretability-and-post-rationalization-b812eda13783.
Verisign (Eds.) (2021): The Domain Name Industry Brief (1). Available online at https://www.verisign.com/assets/domain-name-report-Q42020.pdf.
Vitzthum, Kathrin (2020): Androhung von Bußgeld wegen Datenschutzproblemen beim Distanzunterricht ist ein Schlag ins Gesicht der engagierten Lehrkräfte. Gewerkschaft Erziehung und Wissenschaft Thüringen. Available online at https://www.gew-thueringen.de/presse/detailseite/neuigkeiten/androhung-von-bussgeld-wegen-datenschutzproblemen-beim-distanzunterricht-ist-ein-schlag-ins-gesicht-d/.
Vogel, Kurt (1968): Chiu Chang Suan Shu. Neun Bücher Arithmetischer Technik. Wiesbaden: Vieweg+Teubner Verlag.
Vogel, Matthias (2001): Medien der Vernunft. Eine Theorie des Geistes und der Rationalität auf Grundlage einer Theorie der Medien. Frankfurt (Main), Univ., Doctoral Dissertation, 1994–1995. 1st ed. Frankfurt am Main: Suhrkamp (Suhrkamp-Taschenbuch Wissenschaft, 1556).
Vogel, Matthias (2003): Medien als Voraussetzungen für Gedanken. In: Stefan Münker, Alexander Roesler und Mike Sandbothe (Eds.): Medienphilosophie. Beiträge zur Klärung eines Begriffs. Orig. ed. Frankfurt am Main: Fischer-Taschenbuch-Verlag (Fischer, 15757), pp. 107–134.
Voss, Catalin (2016): Autism Glass Project. Kann uns künstliche Intelligenz emphatischer machen? DENK:Raum Gesellschaftliche Verantwortung & Digitalisierung 2025. Eberhard von Kuenheim Stiftung. München, 28.11.2016.
Wagner, Peppo (2018): Über:Digitalisierung – Die SMARTE Versuchung. Available online at http://www.pwfilm.at/dokumentation/digitalisierung.
Wahyudi, Agung; Liu, Yan (2016): Cellular Automata for Urban Growth Modelling. In: IRSPSD International 4 (2), pp. 60–75. https://doi.org/10.14246/irspsd.4.2_60.
Waldrop, Mitchell (1987): A question of responsibility. In: The AI Magazine (8).
Wallach, Wendell; Allen, Colin (2009): Moral machines. Teaching robots right from wrong. Oxford: Oxford University Press. Available online at http://dx.doi.org/10.1093/acprof:oso/9780195374049.001.0001.
Walter, Guido (2016): Dieser Gürtel kann für Blinde sehen. Ed. by Welt. Available online at https://www.welt.de/sponsored/barrierenueberwinden/article156904455/Dieser-Guertel-kann-fuer-Blinde-sehen.html.
Weber, Karsten (2018): Autonomie und Moralität als Zuschreibung. Über die begriffliche und inhaltliche Sinnlosigkeit einer Maschinenethik. In: Matthias Rath, Friedrich Krotz und Matthias Karmasin (Eds.): Maschinenethik. Normative Grenzen autonomer Systeme. Wiesbaden: Springer Fachmedien Wiesbaden (Ethik in mediatisierten Welten), pp. 193–210.
Weigert, Martin (2018): Algorithmenethik Erlesenes #44. Bertelsmann Stiftung. Available online at https://algorithmenethik.de/2018/11/02/algorithmenethik-erlesenes-44.
Weizenbaum, Joseph (1976a): Computer Power and Human Reason. New York, San Francisco: W.H. Freeman and company.
Weizenbaum, Joseph (1976b): Die Macht der Computer und die Ohnmacht der Vernunft.
Werner, Micha H. (2011): Verantwortung. In: Marcus Düwell, Christoph Hübenthal und Mi-cha H. Werner (Eds.): Handbuch Ethik. 3rd. rev. ed.. Stuttgart: Metzler, pp. 541–548.

Wheeler, John Archibald (1982): The computer and the universe. In: Int J Theor Phys 21 (6–7), pp. 557–572. https://doi.org/10.1007/BF02650185.
White, David Manning (1950): The "Gate Keeper": A Case Study in the Selection of News. In: Journalism Bulletin 27 (4), pp. 383–390. https://doi.org/10.1177/107769905002700403.
Wiegerling, Klaus (2013): Ubiquitous Computing. In: Armin Grunwald und Melanie Simonidis-Puschmann (Eds.): Handbuch Technikethik. Stuttgart: J.B. Metzler, pp. 374–378.
Wiegerling, Klaus (2016): Umfassende IT-Systeme. In: Jessica Heesen (Eds.): Handbuch Medien- und Informationsethik. Stuttgart: J. B. Metzler, pp. 217–226.
Wiener, Norbert (1960): Some Moral and Technical Consequences of Automation. In: Science, New Series 131 (3410), pp. 1355–1358.
Wikimedia Foundation (Eds.) (2011): Wikimedia Strategic Plan. A collaborative vision for the movement through 2015. Available online at https://upload.wikimedia.org/wikipedia/commons/c/c0/WMF_StrategicPlan2011_spreads.pdf.
Wikipedia (Eds.) (2019): Gatekeeper. Nachrichtenforschung. Available online at https://de.wikipedia.org/wiki/Gatekeeper_(Nachrichtenforschung).
Wildfeuer, Armin G. (2011): Wert. In: Petra Kolmer, Armin G. Wildfeuer, Hermann Krings und Wolfram Hogrebe (Eds.): Neues Handbuch philosophischer Grundbegriffe. Orig. ed. Freiburg im Breisgau: Alber, pp. 2484–2504.
Wilhelms, Günter (2017): Systemverantwortung. In: Ludger Heidbrink, Claus Langbehn und Janina Loh (Eds.): Handbuch Verantwortung. Wiesbaden: Springer Fachmedien Wiesbaden, 501–524.
Wils, Jean-Pierre (2011): Würde. In: Marcus Düwell, Christoph Hübenthal und Micha H. Werner (Eds.): Handbuch Ethik. 3rd. Rev. ed. Stuttgart: Metzler, pp. 558–563.
Wirth, Karl-August (1986): Fingerzahlen. RDK Labor. Available online at http://www.rdklabor.de/wiki/Fingerzahlen.
Wolfram, Stephen (2002): A new kind of science. 1. ed., 4. print. Champaign, Ill.: Wolfram Media.
Wolfram, Stephen (2017): A New Kind of Science: A 15-Year View. In: ComplexSystems 26 (3), pp. 197–223. https://doi.org/10.25088/ComplexSystems.26.3.197.
World Health Organization (Eds.) (2015): Global Status Report on Road Safety 2015. WHO. Genf. Available online at http://docs.dpaq.de/9791-2015_who_sicherheit_stra_enverkehr_.pdf.
Wulff, Matthias (2013): Presseinfo zur schrittweisen Einstellung der inmediaONE] GmbH von Matthias Wulff, Leiter Unternehmenskommunikation Club- und Direktmarketinggeschäfte. Ed. by Bertelsmann.
Young, Tom; Hazarika, Devamanyu; Poria, Soujanya; Cambria, Erik (2017): Recent Trends in Deep Learning Based Natural Language Processing. Available online at http://arxiv.org/pdf/1708.02709v7.
Zeidler, Eberhard (2013): Springer-Handbuch der Mathematik II. Wiesbaden: Springer Fachmedien Wiesbaden.
Zellini, Paolo (2013): Logos und Zahl. In: Lorenzo Perilli (Eds.): Logos. Theorie und Begriffsgeschichte. Darmstadt: WBG - Wissenschaftliche Buchgesellschaft, 171–191.
Zeng, Yi; Lu, Enmeng; Huangfu, Cunqing (2018): Linking Artificial Intelligence Principles. Available online at http://arxiv.org/pdf/1812.04814v1.
Ziegenbalg, Jochen; Ziegenbalg, Oliver; Ziegenbalg, Bernd (2016): Algorithmen von Hammurapi bis Gödel. Mit Beispielen aus den Computeralgebrasystemen Mathematica und Maxima. 4th rev. and exp. ed. 2016. Wiesbaden: Springer Fachmedien Wiesbaden GmbH; Springer Spektrum.
Zimmer, Dieter E. (1997): Die Elektrifizierung der Sprache. Über Sprechen, Schreiben, Computer, Gehirne und Geist. Revised paperback edition. München: Heyne (Heyne-Bücher 19, Heyne-Sachbuch, 483).
Zitzler, Eckart (2017): Dem Computer ins Hirn geschaut. Informatik entdecken, verstehen und querdenken. In collaboration with Susanne Staubli. Berlin: Springer.

Zurstiege, Guido (2016): Propaganda. In: Jessica Heesen (Eds.): Handbuch Medien- und Informationsethik. Stuttgart: J. B. Metzler, 146–153.

Zuse, Konrad (1982): The computing universe. In: Int J Theor Phys 21 (6–7), pp. 589–600. https://doi.org/10.1007/BF02650187.

Zuse, Konrad (2012): Konrad Zuse's Rechnender Raum. (Calculating Space). 1st. re-edition written in LATEX by A. German and H. Zenil. Available online at http://www.mathrix.org/zenil/ZuseCalculatingSpace-GermanZenil.pdf.

MIX
Papier aus verantwortungsvollen Quellen
Paper from responsible sources
FSC® C105338

If you have any concerns about our products,
you can contact us on
ProductSafety@springernature.com

In case Publisher is established outside the EU,
the EU authorized representative is:
Springer Nature Customer Service Center GmbH
Europaplatz 3, 69115 Heidelberg, Germany

Printed by Libri Plureos GmbH
in Hamburg, Germany